BUCKSKIN AND BLANKET DAYS

Buckskin and Blanket Days

MEMOIRS OF A FRIEND OF THE INDIANS

Written in 1905 by

Thomas Henry Tibbles

UNIVERSITY OF NEBRASKA PRESS

Lincoln

Library of Congress Catalog Card Number 57–7289
Copyright © 1957 by Vivien K. Barris
All Rights Reserved
Manufactured in the United States of America

First Bison Book printing: October, 1969
Second Bison Book printing: May, 1971

Bison Book edition reprinted from the first (1957) edition
by arrangement with the publisher.

TO THE MEMORY OF THE
FREE MEN
WHO MADE THIS NATION

"It is more than ten years since we went on our last hunt. The poles of the holy tent remain. There is no one who remembers the sacred words which were said at the feast preparatory to the start. We camp no more in the great circle. The habitations of the bands are mixed in inextricable confusion. Soon we can no more tell to which band we belong than can a Jew of today tell whether he is of the tribe of Judah or the tribe of Benjamin. A few of the old men only remember our laws and customs and try to keep them. The young are passing into another life."

BRIGHT EYES

Publisher's Preface

Thomas Henry Tibbles, the son of William and Martha (Cooley) Tibbles, was born near Athens, Washington County, Ohio, on May 22, 1840. He died in Omaha, Nebraska, on May 14, 1928. He wrote these memoirs, *Buckskin and Blanket Days*, in 1905, when he was sixty-five years old. Although they are, in many respects, his autobiography, they contain by no means all of the facts of his life. He makes, for example, only passing mention of the "painful initiation ordeal" that made him a member of the Soldier Lodge during the winter he spent with the Indians. It was, however, an extraordinary honor, and, to earn it, he had to dance with a thong tied to a sliver of wood that had been thrust through a slit in his flesh until it tore out.

He entered Bleeding Kansas with Lane's troop in the summer of 1856, serving until this troop was disbanded in mid-September. From 1858 to 1861 he studied at Mount Union College, Alliance, Ohio. On October 1, 1861, he married in Freedom, Pennsylvania, Amelia Owen, born in England, daughter of William Owen and Sarah Hall, who was herself the granddaughter of a leading English glass manufacturer, John Hall of Bedminster, England.

From 1861 on he did free-lance writing and newspaper work. Although he does not mention his services in the Civil War, he did serve as a scout and newspaper correspondent. In newspaper interviews later on he alluded to having served on General Curtis's staff as scout and guide in Missouri and Kansas, and to have only narrowly escaped being hanged by Quantrill's raiders. At least one newspaper account says that he took part in the "engagements at Pea Ridge and in the battles near Memphis," and that he emerged with the rank of major.

From 1871 to 1873 he became a circuit preacher in western Missouri, and in 1873–74 in the Republican Valley, Nebraska. In 1874 he was active in bringing from the East relief for the grasshopper-famine sufferers. From 1874 to 1879 he worked on the staffs of various Omaha papers, finally reaching the post of assistant editor of the Omaha *Herald* in 1879. Meanwhile he had assembled a congregation there and had built a church and a parsonage. In 1877 he retired from the ministry.

On March 29, 1879, he pledged himself to the cause of the unhappy Ponca tribe. He then took the lead in obtaining Judge Dundy's famous decision that an Indian is a person. From 1879 to 1883 he lectured every winter throughout the East in behalf of the Poncas and all other Indians, and presented their claims at numerous Congressional hearings.

His wife, Amelia Owen Tibbles, died of peritonitis in Omaha, and was buried there on October 29, 1879. She left two daughters, Eda and May.

On June 29, 1882, Mr. Tibbles married at the Omaha Reservation his fellow-worker in the Indian relief campaigns, Susette La Flesche (Bright Eyes), born 1854, daughter of Iron Eye, former head chief of the Omahas. For a year beginning with May 1886, Mr. and Mrs. Tibbles carried out a successful lecture tour in England and Scotland.

In 1883 Mr. Tibbles had located a homestead claim near Bancroft, Nebraska, built a sod house, and started farming. To this he and his wife returned from their English trip, but in 1888 they leased the farm. Rejoining the *World-Herald* editorial staff, he worked in Omaha until 1893, when both he and his wife went to Washington as correspondents for an Indiana weekly, *The Nonconformist,* and for a syndicate of weekly newspapers, mostly published by the Farmers' Alliance. For these Bright Eyes reported the Senate and he the House.

In 1895 he founded *The Independent* at Lincoln, Nebraska— a weekly that, as the national organ of the People's (Populist) Party, throve well and enjoyed a wide circulation.

In 1898 Bright Eyes, who had become increasingly interested in painting, illustrated *Oo-Mah-Ha Ta-Wa-Tha,* a book about the Omaha tribe, written by Fanny Reed Giffen, and supposed to be the first book ever illustrated by an American Indian. Bright Eyes died on May 26, 1903. On her stone is the inscription: "She did all that she could to make the world happier and better."

At the People's-party national convention held at Springfield, Illinois, July 4, 1904, Mr. Tibbles was nominated for Vice-President of the United States, with Thomas E. Watson of Georgia nominated for President. In November they polled over 100,000 votes under difficult political conditions.

While Mr. Tibbles was touring several states as a candidate, the ownership of *The Independent* changed hands. Lacking Mr. Tibbles' individual touch, it soon lost its prestige and petered out. From 1905 to 1910 Mr. Tibbles edited a weekly, *The Investigator,* and from 1910 to his retirement, not long before his death, he was again editorial and feature writer for the Omaha *World-Herald.*

On February 24, 1907, he married at Ute, Iowa, Ida Belle Riddle, who survived him, and who gave him the devoted care he especially needed in his final years of extreme old age. Mr. Tibbles died in Omaha on May 14, 1928.

His writings in book form consisted of *Ponca Chiefs,* published in 1880 over the pen name of Zylyff; *Hidden Power,* June 1881; *The American Peasant,* 1892. This last book dealt with the problems of the Western farmers.

In the years following 1890, Mr. Tibbles had advocated an income tax, the Australian ballot, an inheritance tax, and government regulation of the railroads. All of these then-radical ideas have become today's commonplaces, but in the beginning of every movement, as Mr. Tibbles himself wrote:

"The reformer must always travel a lonesome trail."

Theodora Bates Cogswell edited the whole manuscript, checked all its facts and made the additions that have been provided in brackets. Mrs. Cogswell, a writer herself, had known Mr. Tibbles in 1894, in Lincoln, Nebraska, when she was eleven years old, and her brother had just married Mr. Tibbles' daughter Eda. As a child she had listened to the accounts of his adventures, and as an adult she made a great contribution to these memoirs. She said:

"In the whole Kansas section I carefully checked Mr. Tibbles' report with both contemporary and later ones. Wherever first-hand knowledge was lacking, I found that all the existing accounts varied bewilderingly; but often I could see that Mr. Tibbles' matter-of-fact statements supplied the hitherto-missing logical solution. I also found that wherever proven facts existed, Mr. Tibbles' account practically always endorsed them."

It is possible that one or two of the author's very earliest memories, such as his story of being chased by wolves when he was five years old, may be questioned for their accuracy. Certainly his recollection could have been distorted by the passage of sixty intervening years, but there is no way to make an independent check now of the events of his extreme youth. He later became famous for his integrity, and wherever recent confirmation of his facts has been made, his account has proved correct. In the light of present verification he appears to have been a consistently fair and honest reporter.

Mr. Tibbles' manuscript did not include two chapters that

are included here by Mrs. Cogswell. His "Guest of the Indians" chapter was one of his early manuscripts which she added to this book. Also, the account of his courtship is not exactly in his own words. He wrote that account for his daughter, May Tibbles Barris, and it became lost when he once borrowed it from her. Mrs. Barris, knowing it from loving memory, wrote it out as she remembered it for Mrs. Cogswell, and that chapter is here included.

The "Highflyer" of the Dakota trip was the famous ethnologist Alice Cunningham Fletcher. She helped put through the act of August 7, 1882, to secure the Omahas their land in severalty, thus repaying their hospitality. The successful Indian woman doctor mentioned in the final chapter was Bright Eyes' sister, Dr. Susan La Flesche (Mrs. Picotte).

Mrs. Cogswell's own acknowledgments for help in preparing the manuscript follow:

"My earnest thanks are hereby expressed to Dr. Addison E. Sheldon of the Nebraska State Historical Society for his kindly letters of information, advice, and encouragement; to Mr. Floyd C. Shoemaker, Secretary of the State Historical Society of Missouri, for his extended and careful search through his Society's records along various lines in which I had asked for his help; to Mr. A. B. Banfield, Borough Secretary of Freedom, Pa., and to Reverend Charles D. Beatty, Pastor of the Methodist Episcopal Church of Freedom, for their efficient help in tracing the marriage record of Reverend Thomas H. Tibbles and Amelia Owen; to Mrs. M. Diddock (Marguerite La Flesche) of Walthill, Nebraska, for the date of her sister Bright Eyes' marriage to Mr. Tibbles; to Mrs. Lucy Tibbles Davis for much valuable information about the Tibbles and Owen families; to my dear daughter, Dorothea Barton Cogswell, for her competent and cheerful help in all the research, and in preparing this manuscript for the press; to Chester Barris, Mr. Tibbles' grandson, for his unfailing advice, encouragement, and cooperation; and most of all, to Mr. Tibbles' late daughters, Eda Tibbles Bates and May Tibbles Barris, for the patience and exactitude with which they answered my incessant questions."

Contents

Contents

BUCKSKIN AND BLANKET DAYS

1.

Son of the Wilderness

In 1840 this nation was in embryo, and every man who has since lived in it has had his part in making it. Though the deeds of some have been recorded, those of the thousands of others who laid out the trails, bridged the streams, turned deserts into fertile fields, started a flow of gold and silver from the mountains, fought and were victorious over the bravest of primitive peoples, and opened a new path to the Orient are known to only a few. Those few will soon pass over the Great Divide. It is for us who survive to tell some of the deeds while yet we may.

I was born in Washington County, on the southeastern border of Ohio, in 1840, but already that region was too thickly settled to content a family of father, mother, and nine children, whose forefathers had been pioneers for generations. We soon migrated to Hancock County, on the extreme western border of Illinois, where my father built his three-room log cabin on the western edge of a great shellbark-hickory forest. His choicest personal possessions were his trusty rifle and his faithful hunting dog. Through the forest meandered a stream full of swimming holes. Westward and southward ran a "neck of prairie." Game was everywhere. From our own doorstep one early autumn morning we children counted fifty-five deer grazing calmly. When our pioneer mother wanted meat, she gave my father or my eldest brother a specific order for a half-dozen prairie chickens or a saddle of venison, and the order was promptly filled. It was a point of honor to shoot every chicken through the head.

In a year or so another family "located on a claim" two miles from us. Wildly excited, we children, who had never before had other children to play with, talked of nothing but a visit to the new settler's household. At last four of us were allowed to go, with our loyal deer dog Trip for escort, on the strict agreement that we would surely reach home before dusk. My father knew that timber wolves lived in the great hickory forest to the east; he had often caught glimpses of them in the woods to the west, as well. But we, happy children on our very first visit, played and played—and forgot. The shadows lengthened and deepened—and suddenly we remembered. I, five years old, was the only boy in the group.

Halfway home on our prairie route we had to pass through a grove. As we bunched together in its green dimness and scurried along with closed ranks, old Trip tried to push in between those in the rear line. We struck him roughly to drive him away, but he stuck to his post. As we came clear of the grove, a pack of timber wolves rushed out behind us. Old Trip gave a queer warning cry and dashed at them.

We flew out onto the prairie, the little girls first, I next and, last of all, the officer in command of our retreat, the wise old scout Trip. On came the wolves, close at our heels. We could almost feel their great teeth. Then Trip wheeled and dashed. They halted, ready for defense. We children, desperate, breathless, silent, with every muscle frantically strained in flight, pelted a little farther; then Trip overtook us; then up came the wolves again; again Trip wheeled and dashed at them. So on and on across that strip of prairie for nearly a mile.

Mother, from inside the house, heard the howling of the pack and the dog's fierce barking. She ran out—and took in the scene at a glance. Rushing in, she snatched the rifle from the hooks where it hung by the bed, then sped out to our log fence and climbed it. There, trained pioneer markswoman that she was, she fired past her children into the outposts of the pack. Still the wolves came on, racing toward the house. But now the children were inside the fence. The house door, which opened outward, stood ready. Children, mother, dog, and all piled in through it together and pulled it shut, just as the wolves came hurtling against it like an avalanche.

Then with a war whoop five Indians dashed out of the brush. With one gun and bows and arrows they disposed of some of the wolves and drove away the rest—for a time.

Meanwhile my father and my eldest brother had been out in the "hoop pole patch" cutting poles which they planned soon to haul twenty-five miles to the nearest town on the Mississippi River, for shipment by boat to St. Louis. They had heard the distant howling of the wolves without anxiety, knowing that the family's precious cattle—three or four cows and two calves —were safely housed in a high, wolf-tight pen. Now they came home and heard the story from the tired household.

Trip lay stretched as usual before the wide fireplace. Suddenly he grew uneasy, and prowled from the closed door to the oiled-paper window, back and forth, refusing to lie down again. From door to window and window to door, again and again, he went until at last Father let him out. In a moment there was a terrible, snarling fight outside and Trip came thump against the door. Father partly opened it to let him in, but saw that the wolves would be right in on top of him.

Father loved Trip and loved a fight, so he and my brother snatched up an ax and a hatchet and dashed out. For a few minutes they fought furiously; then it was over. The pack vanished. A few wolves lay dead; my brother was unharmed; Trip was badly wounded; and my father's clothes had been nearly torn off him.

Trip's wounds healed and he lived to a ripe old age. His

fate was sad. He had taken an old blind mare under his especial care. When she died and was hauled away about a mile, he traced her, and was badly crippled warding off a pack of dogs from his friend's body. Very soon afterward, when all of us were away, a visiting uncle decided to do us the favor of disposing of Trip.

Never did any family mourn more sincerely over the death of one of its members. We children laid Trip in a leaf-lined grave, and next day we took the yoke of oxen and went ten miles to a place where we knew there were big stones. We hauled one of these to the grave, and with our only tools—a small strip of steel broken from a plow, and a hammer—we worked for days until we had carved on it: "Old Trip."

As more settlers came into the region, a few common interests occasionally drew them together—athletic sports, shooting at a mark, and before long, once a year, a Methodist camp meeting which lasted for days. This was the talk among the housewives and families for weeks beforehand—and afterwards; great preparations were made for it. Peter Cartwright, the presiding elder of that district, always came to it with the most eloquent of his preachers. I remember one meeting close to the bank of the Mississippi, not many miles beyond our home. At Peter Cartwright's glowing metaphors describing the beauties of heaven and terrors of hell, waves of excitement swept over the vast audience. There were tears and shouts and screams. Some of his hearers fell to the ground helpless; pandemonium reigned for hours.

Right at the start of one session there came drifting past, down the river, a crew of the raftsmen who used to go to the great forest at the headwaters of the Mississippi to cut long trunks of white pine, bind them into rafts, and float them down the current. These rough rivermen were noted for breaking up religious meetings wherever they could find a chance. Now their leader, "Mike Fink," named from the leader of twenty-five years ago who had whipped every man he had fought in St. Louis and Cincinnati, tied his raft to the bank and led his whole crew up to a front seat. Like all the camp-meeting folk, I held my breath, but then I saw old Peter Cartwright calmly mount his split-log platform and read, in his usual fashion, the first two lines of a hymn for the people to sing. Mike Fink and his crowd groaned hideously to drown out the words. Peter merely tried again. So did they. The fourth time I saw old Peter quietly turn around, take off his coat and his vest, and tie his suspenders around him. Then he stepped forward, smiling, and offered to whip the best man they had. I decided that camp meetings were very interesting places.

Old Peter then told the assembly, "Brothers and sisters, you stay here and pray, while I make this man pray."

But as he led away that gang of raftsmen, I ran after them till they stopped on a bit of clear ground; there I climbed a tree to make sure of a good view.

Mike Fink faced the preacher. Then Cartwright said, "All I ask is these gentlemen's word of honor that there shall be a fair fight." They gave it.

Soon Cartwright sent home a telling blow that laid Mike Fink on his back; then, as formal rules didn't exist in those days, he jumped astride the bully, grabbed him by the throat, and choked the breath out of him. But of course that was perfectly fair, as the crew agreed.

Then Peter Cartwright, loosing his hold, announced:

"I promised the brothers and sisters that I was going to teach you to pray. You've got to pray."

Mike refused—vehemently. Peter repeated the dose, and then Mike gasped, "I'd pray but I don't know how!"

So, word by word, Peter dictated a long and highly personal prayer for him to repeat meekly. When at last Mike rose, weak-kneed and trembling, Peter asked the crew to come back to the meeting and behave themselves like gentlemen. "I want to get some of you converted," he wound up.

They shook hands with him—and I trotted back after them to the campground.

There in the front seat we found a lot of brothers and sisters praying with all their might, but old Peter made all of them move back to make room for Mike and his crew. That night I watched two of those men join the church—on probation.

Originally my father's domain had stretched for miles in every direction. He—a dollarless millionaire—was lord of it all. Unlike the Wall Street capitalists, he did not have his wealth in pieces of paper, but in the rich, inexhaustible soil, the noble forest to the east, the pure running brook, the endless supply of game. Though money was a rare thing to him, his parks, lawns, and hunting privileges extended beyond the limit of his vision. He stood erect, looking every man in the eye, a type of the men who have built this nation.

He and his like neither put up nor needed "No Trespassing" signs. In winter they smoked their pipes by glowing hickory fires; in summer they rested in the shade of mighty trees; in the autumn they slept by sparkling campfires and hunted bear, elk, and deer as the impulse moved them. No board of directors controlled them; no government officials interfered with their business or pleasure. They were free men. From their number have come many of the great minds that have largely shaped the affairs of the nation and of the world. Men of their kind will never appear on this earth again. Their lives will form the groundwork of the poetry and tragedy to be written in the future.

Five years after our coming, however, a change threatened. More settlers had taken up claims, until there were several families within two or three miles of us. The game began to disappear. My father, descendant of six generations of pioneers, soon felt that the country was "too thick with people." As a last straw the title to his land, which he had supposed secure, was declared void under some military grant. Therefore we held a family council and decided that it was time to seek a new frontier.

In midwinter we packed our things into a prairie schooner, crossed the Mississippi, and again started on toward the setting sun. There in Iowa we found on a stream a place which was heavily wooded with great black walnut trees. When we had been there only a few days, however, and had laid the foundation for a cabin, United States soldiers came to tell us that, though a treaty with the Indians for this region was pending, their title had not become extinct. We must go back to Illinois and wait. We obeyed, chose fresh ground there, and built another log house, but I believe that the order to return eastward to the "thick" settlements broke my father's heart. Something went from him which never returned.

He had always been an athlete, and was able even then at fifty to jump twenty feet on the level, and lightly to clear a pole set six feet six inches from the ground—exactly his own height. The autumn after our return he chanced to ride up just as my eldest brother, who had inherited Father's build, and another strong young pioneer were out cutting hay from the prairie grass—which rose high above their heads—and were bragging about their skill in mowing.

Father laughed and remarked, "Now you boys would feel bad if I got off and mowed around you."

They dared him to try it. He did—and won his boast, but at a cost. Overheated, he remounted to ride home, and caught cold in a cool breeze that sprang up. Eighteen months later he died.

In the meantime the California fever had swept across the country, and that eldest brother, who already was resenting our return to civilization, had caught it and had run away to California with one of the first emigrant trains to cross the Great Plains. The other children older than I was had married and had scattered over the West. I, Thomas Henry, was now the man of the household, the main support of my mother, whose youth was over, and of two younger brothers—and I was ten years old.

I picked out and rented a farm of forty acres with a house to shelter us, and undertook to maintain my family. I proudly planted corn, wheat, and potatoes. Then came the first over- whelming disaster that overtook me; the memory of it makes me shudder now whenever I think of it. One day the sheriff appeared. He told us that the county authorities had taken charge of the family and that I had been "bound out" under the laws of the state. Thus our family was broken up, and I was led away to hard labor.

I am thankful that the cruel and inhuman laws of those days for apprenticing children have now been discarded. As a chap- ter of history I will record here my own experience of them.

The terms of the contract under which I was "bound out" were read to me three times by the sheriff. Perhaps the law required him to do this, but the document was replete with legal terms I did not understand. However, when I asked ques- tions, the sheriff explained the meaning to me in simple words. In effect, I must stay with the man to whom I was bound until I was twenty-one years old. He must send me to school for three months each year, and at the end of my time must give me a horse, a saddle, and a bridle, and a new suit of clothes before he sent me out into the world. If I ran away during my apprenticeship, the sheriff must find me and bring me back.

I went with the sheriff as a prisoner would go, planning all the way how, when I was grown up, I would give every man concerned, especially the man who had secured my indenture, the best thrashing he had ever got in all his life.

My lot proved no exception to the general hard experience of apprentice boys. The man to whom I was bound had six girls and no boys. From the first day he put me to the hardest kind of labor. I rose at four, made the fires, fed the horses, cattle, and hogs, and milked the cows before breakfast. Then my day's toil of a man's work began.

Until now I had never been away from home a night. In a month I was torturingly homesick for my mother, who was twenty miles away. I asked for leave to go to see her. My employer refused. More months passed; I asked again and again, and was always refused. An entire year had gone by. Finally one Friday morning the man told me:

"If you will cultivate that whole piece of corn tomorrow, you can go home Sunday."

The rows of corn were eighty rods long. I counted them and found that they covered a little over six acres. The man had thought that the task would be impossible. In those days corn was cultivated with a "single shovel" plow and single horse; and it took two furrows to each row. When I began, the sun was half an hour high, and it promised to be a fearfully warm day, but I said to myself, "I can do it!"

The man and his family, who were going away for the whole day on a visit, soon disappeared over the prairie. There were four horses in the stable, and I harnessed them all. The corn rows ran right up to the stable. It grew deadly hot. I took out a horse and drove him so hard that he soon was exhausted. Then I stabled him and brought out another. I drove them all in turn in the same furious fashion, changing them as they showed signs of being overheated. Just as the sun sank below the western horizon that Saturday night, I finished the last row.

Next morning I woke at four, as usual, and without rousing anyone, took a horse and rode away to see my mother. I had with me a dollar and a half, which I had kept carefully hidden in a knothole in a log all the time I had been in that place. Now in this moment of freedom, after a lot of thinking, I resolved to remain free. I would go so far away the sheriff could never find me.

Ten miles from the farm I met a boy whom I knew. I gave him two bits (twenty-five cents) to take the horse back. Then I fled on afoot with all the energy I had. I reached my mother and told her how the man had been overworking me, and what I planned to do. She raised no objection. Indeed, I remember well how she went into the house, got four or five pieces of bread, which she spread very thick with butter, gave them to me, and kissed me good-by.

Then I hurried on to Warsaw, the nearest town on the Mississippi River. There I sat down on the cobblestoned wharf. Toward evening a woman came along and asked:

"Little boy, what are you doing here?"

I answered that I was waiting to go on the steamboat.

"Why, the boat won't come till midnight!" she exclaimed.

"I know it," I told her, "but I've nowhere to go and I'm staying here so as to be sure to get it."

"Come with me to my house for some supper," she urged.

She lived on top of a hill, apparently alone. After supper she told me to lie down on a couch, while she read to me. She read from the Bible.

"Go out and be a man, my son," she told me then, "and make your way in the world—but promise me now that you will never touch any whiskey."

Gratefully I gave her a very solemn promise. When the boat came in at midnight, she went down to the landing with me and watched me run on board. Thirty years later I made a long journey on purpose to visit her town. I recognized the spot where the house once stood, but it had been torn down. I never could learn who the woman was who gave me those words of advice and encouragement.

The steamboat which traveled on that great artery of transportation, the Mississippi River, was crowded with passengers. With my dollar and a quarter in hand I went up to an officer and asked, "Where do you pay for a passage?"

After a few questions he told me, "Look here, they don't charge little boys on this boat."

The next morning he provided me with a good breakfast. About nine o'clock we stopped at Quincy, Illinois. Sure that now I really had carried out my dream and come so far that the sheriff could never find me, I went ashore; as a matter of fact, though I had not actually traveled far, I had succeeded in reaching the next county.

While I stood there alone and longing for company, I saw with inexpressible delight a young man I had once seen at a shooting match. He shook hands with me and took me up the wharf and along at the foot of a hill that was lined with saloons. Then he said:

"Come in and have something to drink."

He ordered "peach brandy." To my ears that sounded like something made of peaches, which would be pretty good; so I asked the barkeeper for the same. He handed me a bottle and I poured out nearly a glassful. To this day I remember the look of that barkeeper. It seemed to say:

"You're a tough."

I began to drink the brandy and found it quite different from what I had expected, but I kept at it till I had downed it all. Then I walked out of the saloon and started up the hill toward the town. I remember clearly how that road kept coming up and striking me in the face. After a while I got off to one side of it and lay down on the grass.

As the sun went down, I woke, to realize that I had been drunk. I remembered the kind woman's words. In spite of that day's record they were not lost on me, for I have never been drunk since.

Though I still had my dollar and a quarter, I was afraid to spend it. As I was passing the Quincy House, I looked into the kitchen. A girl glanced out and saw me.

"Little boy," she asked gently, "are you hungry?"

"Yes!" I answered.

"Then come in here."

The kitchen was full of eatables and she piled up a great plate for me. I just turned to and ate all I could. Then she asked:

"Have you got a place to sleep?"

"No," I told her.

"You stay right here," she ordered. "I'll get you a place."

As soon as the dishes were washed, she took me up to a little corner off the room for the help. I crept in there and slept. The next morning she gave me breakfast and sent me forth rested and well filled.

I saw a man shingling a house and asked him for work, saying that I could nail on shingles. After denying that I could he looked up and saw some threatening clouds. The roof must go on at once, so he growled to me, "Get up there and go at it." So I nailed on shingles as my first job.

From that day I never lacked work while I stayed in Quincy. For a time I was employed in a candy-manufacturing shop under an Irish foreman who, after having been educated for the Catholic priesthood, had felt that he lacked the true vocation for that life and had come to America. When I told him that I was determined to get an education, he advised me to study Latin. I went at once and bought a Latin grammar. Then I committed the whole book to memory from beginning to end —to my great benefit later. I have never regretted those long nights in the back shop when by the light of a tallow candle I learned to decline all the nouns and conjugate all the verbs without the slightest idea as to why such things should be done.

2.

Pursuing the Frontier

After three years of town life in Quincy the pioneer longing, inborn and irresistible, for the woods, the prairies, and the Indians came over me. I dreamed of them by night and thought of them all day. At last, obedient to instinct, I turned my face again toward the setting sun and did not stop until I reached the westernmost settlement in Iowa.

The building of a frontier town follows a recognized course. First a land speculator selects a townsite. He must have a lawyer to assist him. Then a trader turns up. Next a Methodist preacher puts in an appearance, and three or four families who have "claims" nearby build cabins on the "townsite." The town is started.

Thus far had Winterset progressed in 1854, when I arrived there and went into a lawyer's office to serve as office helper and to "read law," after the fashion of the times; that is, I read Blackstone, Pufendorf, and Chitty's *Pleadings*. After fifty years I am still of the opinion that Chitty's *Pleadings* is the most infernal book that ever was printed. At the same time I eagerly galloped through several classes of a neighboring school, but my finest classroom was the growing region about me, and behind it the growing nation in which I bore a part.

Nearly all the people who had settled in that section had been Whigs. Now that the Republican party was taking form, they joined it, but I remember that in a vote taken to strike

the word "white" out of the suffrage clause of the state constitution there was only one affirmative vote in the whole county.
My own people had all been Whigs, opposed to slavery, and
slavery was now almost the sole topic of conversation everywhere.

One day in the spring of 1856 a great caravan came through
Winterset. The emigrant wagons and the men on horseback
stretched back over the prairie for more than a mile. Boy-
fashion, I went out to find what it was all about. I learned that
these emigrants, armed with the still-novel Sharp's rifles, the
most efficient breech-loading guns yet invented, and called by
the men who carried them "Beecher Bibles," formed a band or
colony which Henry Ward Beecher and other anti-slavery sympathizers were sending to settle in Kansas to reinforce the Free
State group there.

When the travelers told me that they were going to Kansas
to help to free the Negroes, I was so fired with enthusiasm and
the love of liberty that I asked leave to join them. The commander, General James H. Lane,* afterward United States senator from Kansas, eager to gain young recruits, gave me a hearty
welcome. We journeyed across Iowa to the Missouri River,
where, with only one little flatboat available as transport, it
took three days to ferry our train across.

On the other bank some Indians stood watching us, and
Indian women were waiting in a line near the landing place
with baskets of Indian corn, all roasted ready for eating. Each
woman held a small wooden bowl, but none of them could
count the newcomers' money. They let each customer take all
the ears of corn he desired and toss a piece of money into the
bowl. I saw one man take a dozen ears, throw twenty-five cents
into the impromptu till, and take out fifty cents. There and

* Formerly a colonel in the Mexican War, he was appointed to the rank
of brigadier general actually in 1861.

then began my lifelong fight to secure justice for the Indians. I knocked that man down and hammered him until he agreed to put a dollar into the wooden bowl and to go away without any corn.

The caravan moved slowly across Nebraska Territory to its southern boundary. There, just short of the Kansas border, we camped.

That evening, a little to one side, I noticed another camp of twenty-five to thirty men who did not belong to our train. I strolled toward it and saw a tall, gaunt man with piercing gray eyes, which looked almost black, and very thick, slightly gray hair, cut rather close. He walked along to a large log and sat down astride it. From his belt he took two large Colt revolvers, removed the cylinders, and began to clean them. After a little while I went over and sat on the log, facing him. He had one cylinder in his hand, cleaning it. The other cylinder he had laid farther away in front of him; I picked it up. Though he had filled its chambers with powder, he had not yet put in the bullets. As I turned it a little to one side, some of the powder fell out. Instantly he issued a sharp command to me to put down that cylinder.

"See there!" he told me. "You have spilled enough powder for one good shot, and that shot might kill a Border Ruffian. It might help to free some black man."

He went on at some length telling me the disastrous consequences that might "come to the cause of freedom from spilling even that much powder." I rose, walked away a little distance, and asked some of his campmates who that man was. They told me it was Old John Brown.

Our cavalcade journeyed on to Topeka, Kansas. I settled down in camp there and was drilled in military tactics. The company's drill sergeant was a mystery to everyone. Though he said his name was John C. Frémont, we all knew that it was not. Assumed names were common in Kansas then. He was not only a perfect drill master, but also an expert swordsman. He must have had many years of training in some military institution. After a few days he suddenly told me:

"This thing's all a humbug. It's only a political row; there isn't going to be any fighting. It's just something that a lot of politicians have cooked up. Come along over to Lecompton with me and have a look at the Border Ruffians' headquarters."

In those days I was always ready to look at anything new. We took our muskets and tramped the nearly twenty miles on foot. Late in the afternoon [of August 15] we reached Lecompton, very tired. I went to a hotel, stood my old gun up in a corner of the front room, and hunted up a small washroom where I began to wash my face and hands. A man stepped up behind me and laid a rough hand on my shoulder, saying:

"You're my prisoner."

When I asked him why, he answered that these were wartimes and that I was accused of being an abolitionist. He took me outside and put me under guard of two armed men. After I had sat with them about an hour, another man came to tell me that I was to be tried by court-martial. I was only sixteen years old. Perhaps the last frontier of all lay just ahead.

3.

Sentenced to Be Hanged

Soon I was taken before a drumhead court-martial. Its members were Colonel Titus, I. B. Donelson, the United States marshal appointed by President Pierce, and Sheriff Jones. The sheriff had been elected by the Border Ruffians, who, crossing over by the thousand from Missouri to pack the Kansas polls, had voted in a whole set of pro-slavery officers. Governor Shannon also was present at my trial. My accusers had drawn up charges and specifications in regular military form, claiming that I was an abolitionist. They proceeded to try me on that ground. Before long they retired, but quickly brought in a verdict of "Guilty." I was sentenced to be hanged the next morning at eight o'clock.

They marched me down the street to a big frame building where several Free State men already were held as prisoners. Each of these had a log chain locked around his leg. I had been starting over toward them when the sight of those chains brought me to a halt.

"You're not going to put any log chain on me," I told my guards.

Four or five men near me lowered their bayonets threateningly, but I backed away into a corner where I had noticed some stacked muskets. I grabbed up one of these, brought it to "charge," and said again:

"You're not going to put a log chain on me. I die right here fighting. That's all there is to this business."

The officer in command hesitated and then ordered me:

"Young man, lay that gun down! We can run you through forty times in a minute."

"All right," I answered. "Go ahead! There'll be somebody else run through—one of you, at least. I am not going to have a log chain put on my leg."

The officer ordered his men to stand back a little, and sent for another officer. I stood there, musket in hand. The other officer came in and looked me over.

"Well, I like your grit," he decided. "You're nothing but a boy. You don't know the seriousness of this thing you're doing. On account of your being a boy, I'm inclined to overlook it."

"Boy or no boy," I insisted, "I'm not going to have a log chain put on my leg."

At that the officer laughed. He stood there thinking a minute. Then he told me:

"All right, my boy. You go over there and sit down. We won't put a log chain on your leg."

So I sat down with the other prisoners. Soon another officer came in and beckoned me to follow him. When I had gone out with him, he remarked:

"Evidently you're a fighter, and I want you in my company."

"What is your company?" I asked.

"We're here to enforce the laws and run the government in Kansas; and these Free State fellows are interlopers. We are the legal government. You come into my company, and you'll be all right."

"I'm not going to fight for slavery," I answered. "That's all there is about that. If you're fighting on that side, I'm not going to fight in your company. But how about this thing? I'm sentenced to be hanged tomorrow at eight o'clock."

"I'm trying to get you out of that. You enlist in my company and it will be all right with you."

"No!" I asserted. "I won't do it."

He walked along, leading me to where his company was drilling, and put me into the ranks. They did a good deal of wheeling by platoons, and I understood that drill. As I was on the tail end of the company, I had a tremendous amount of marching to do. After a while the platoon halted near a big rock. I broke ranks and sat down on that rock. When they ordered me back to the ranks, I refused to go. Then they sent a guard of four men to take me back to where the other prisoners were.

Soon after dusk I was marched out of Lecompton to a place called Fort Titus, at that time a military headquarters of the pro-slavery forces in the territory. I was put into a tent, with two guards set over me. At nine o'clock the officer of the guard came to give these men their orders, which he was very particular to read loud enough for me to hear.

"You are to guard this prisoner," he directed them. "If he makes an attempt to escape, shoot him on the spot. If the place is attacked during the night, at the first sound of musketry you will shoot him. He has been sentenced to die and will be hanged tomorrow at eight o'clock."

I remember pulling a blanket over me as I lay down to sleep on the bare ground. Because I was young, hearty, and healthy it was not two minutes before I was fast asleep; but I dreamed all night long of being hanged.

I was wakened next morning [August 16] by the rattle of musketry. Looking up, I saw a dozen bullet holes in the tent. Only one guard was there, and he stood at my feet with his musket at "ground arms" by his side. He at once brought it to his shoulder and pointed it at my breast. Instinctively I threw out my left hand and struck the bayonet just as he pulled the trigger. The bayonet scar is still on my hand; the musket shot tore away the whole sleeve of my shirt. But while the guard's finger pulled that trigger, a bullet from outside the tent had struck him under the left eye. He fell dead at my feet.

I ran out of the tent full of fight, but at the instant thought "I have no gun" I ran back to the dead guard and took his. Then I started toward the Free State force who lay on the brow of a hill a little to the west. Behind me was the small log house they called Fort Titus. When I was halfway between the fort and the Free State men, they saw me coming with the musket in my hand. Certain that I was a Border Ruffian, they fired a volley at me. The Border Ruffians, back in the fort, saw me going. Knowing exactly who I was, they also fired a volley at me. I ran on, and came within shouting distance of the Free State line. "Don't shoot!" I called. "I'm the man you're after!" For, boylike, I took it for granted that they had attacked the place to release me. Then I ran on through the Free State line. Later I found that from those two volleys I had acquired three slight wounds and fourteen bullet holes in my clothes.

The Free State men were lying flat on the ground just at the brow of the hill. As I passed through them, I saw Captain Shombre (or Chambrée) mortally wounded by a shot through the groin. In the rear I found one or two other wounded men.

Bound to take a hand in the fight, I still carried my musket, but I had no ammunition. I went along the line begging for cartridges. All the men had Sharp's rifles. These used a bullet with a ring around its butt which made it just that degree too large to fit my musket. So when the men had given me a dozen cartridges, I sat down to whittle off the rims. Meanwhile desultory firing went on. When I had my musket loaded, I went to the extreme edge of the right flank and took my stand under a tree.

By this time the Free State men had taken a small brass cannon around to the east of the log fort, which thus was in direct line between us and them. I had no idea that they would miss the fort, but the ball of their first shot struck a limb over my head and fell beside me. It must have been aimed a hundred feet too high. At the third try they got the range and began to pour the shots into the house. In a few minutes I saw a white flag run up.

Away I dashed down the hill, hard as I could pelt, and was the first to reach the fort. On the way I had made up my mind to kill old Colonel Titus because he was the fellow who had sentenced me to be hanged. As the door was thrown open, I ran in. There were wounded men inside, and blood stained the floor. As this was my first fight, the sight of that blood cooled me down a little. I looked around but failed to see Colonel Titus. A man pointed to a shed saying:

"He's in there."

I passed in with my gun. Colonel Titus was sitting in the far corner. Holding up both hands, he called to me:

"I surrender! I surrender!"

He had been shot through his right hand and his right shoulder; the blood was streaming down from his hand. He repeated:

"Don't shoot! Don't shoot! I surrender!"

I replied, "I ought to shoot you. You're the man who sentenced me to be hanged!"

I ordered him to march out. He rose and started to go, but before we reached the middle of the outer room, the place was full of Free State men, who came pouring down upon the fort from both sides. There was great excitement and uproar.

The next few minutes are indistinct in my mind. I remember going to a springhouse where the Border Ruffian officers had kept their supplies. I saw one fellow making off with a jar of pickles into which he had rammed his hand; now he could not get it free. Ever afterward he was known as Pickles.

I went back to the fort where the men had gathered in mobfashion. Since Captain Shombre had been wounded, Captain Walker had been in command. Colonel Titus was seated on a horse. The incident which follows has been misrepresented in each history of Kansas that I have seen which mentioned it. Here are the facts.

Captain Walker came to me and asked if I had a revolver. I said I had not. He took a Colt revolver out of his belt and handed it to me, saying, "There are six good shots in there, and that is old Colonel Titus," pointing to that officer. The evident meaning of his remark was an invitation to shoot the colonel. I took the revolver, stuck it into my belt and walked to Colonel Titus's side. A few moments later Walker came up and demanded the revolver and I gave it to him. In every report of this happening that has come under my notice Captain Walker is described as knocking me down with the butt end of a revolver because I wanted to shoot Colonel Titus while he was a prisoner.

4.

I Join Lane's Staff

It was evident to me that there was something wrong down in that part of the country. I was certain of two irreconcilable things: that slavery was wrong; and that the result of an election should be accepted by all the people. That was as far as my statesmanship went, and in the Kansas of that era it naturally did not settle things at all. Here apparently were six governments, all trying to rule the people at the same time.

First, there was the United States Government in Washington under President Pierce, with its own ideas of governing Kansas. Then there were the United States troops, commanded by Colonel Sumner, who marched all over the territory and ruled wherever they happened to be. The Free State governor was in control in and around Lawrence. The pro-slavery governor wielded authority around Lecompton and over on the Missouri River. General Jim Lane and Old John Brown governed wherever they were located. Colonel Titus and the Border Ruffians were supreme wherever they camped. A boy could not serve six governments at once; and the only way for him to do was to find out which one was the nearest right.

On a hill a little way out of Lawrence stands a picturesque windmill. Artists have painted it, sketched it, and etched it times without number. The afternoon [August 16] after I reached the town, I went out to this hilltop to try to settle in my own mind that major question of statesmanship. It was a big undertaking for a boy. To the east were the Delaware Indians. In all other directions the prairies rolled away—practically un-inhabited—to the British possessions on the north, the Rocky Mountains on the west, and the borders of Texas on the south. In the entire tract the only white men were the Border Ruffians and Henry Ward Beecher's immigrants.

While I sat on the hill, I came to one clear conclusion, namely: six governments were too many. Furthermore I was convinced it would be better to make all that space a free country than to add it to the existing slave territory of the United States. Just as I was about to settle the whole matter and decide how that vast region was to be made free soil, a man rode up to tell me that General Lane wanted to see me.

Lane had his headquarters in a little shack on the main street of the town. Taking me into the rear room, he gave me the following account of affairs as they stood. As a result of the Fort Titus fight we had captured several prisoners, including three officers of high rank. On the other hand, over in Lecompton the Border Ruffians were holding nine Free State men in custody. They had sent down a flag of truce, offering to exchange prisoners. However, on the night before the Fort Titus attack two Free State men near there had been killed and their families murdered. There was some evidence that this had been the work of men under Titus. Now many of the Lawrence men were demanding that Colonel Titus, Marshal Donelson, and Sheriff Jones should be court-martialed and shot for those murders. A committee had been appointed to decide the question. Those in favor of executing these officials had chosen me for a member of that committee because they thought that, as Colonel Titus had ordered me to be hanged, I should probably be anxious to return the compliment.

"I wish to explain matters fully to you," Lane went on.

Then he told me how the Missourians had captured supplies sent up the Missouri River on steamboats to the Free State men, and how there were not enough provisions in Lawrence to keep the people from starvation for even one month. More than that, the Missourians had captured a lot of arms sent out by Beecher. Lane believed, however, that he could work out a scheme to induce the pro-slavery men to exchange those arms and also a lot of provisions in return for the extra prisoners we held. He wanted to know what I thought of this plan.

I told him that Colonel Titus ought to be hanged, both for favoring slavery and for sentencing me to be hanged for not favoring it; however, if we were likely to starve as the result of hanging Titus, I thought I should vote to exchange him for sacks of flour or Sharp's rifles.

Our committee met. Two members favored hanging Titus; two were against it. I cast my vote to exchange him, and the matter was settled in that way. Who appointed that committee I never knew. War was carried on in a strange way in Kansas in 1856.

[On August 18] a large party of armed men, who guarded the prisoners, followed not far behind, though under cover, by practically the whole Free State force, met in a valley a similar party of pro-slavery men to make the exchange as agreed upon by the plenipotentiaries. A company of United States cavalry was just visible on the hills to the west. The two groups halted some distance apart. As long as the pro-slavery party had any Free State men to hand over, the prisoners were exchanged man for man. Then we exchanged the officers in our custody for sacks of our own captured flour. Then, as we still had several prisoners left, a good deal of parleying followed. At last the pro-slavery men brought over several cases of "Beecher Bibles," in order to receive prisoners for them.

We opened the cases and found that the rifles had no breech-blocks and therefore were useless. For a few minutes our men raised a great row and refused to release those prisoners for imperfect rifles. Though we were under a flag of truce, one

Free State man actually fired at the band of pro-slavery men, who stood about four hundred yards away from us.

At that shot Lane rushed hatless down our line, shouting at the top of his voice, and ordering every man to ground arms. His fury of action and word so awed the crowd that they allowed the prisoners to march away as agreed. Just then Lane ordered up about fifty unarmed men whom he had placed at some distance to the rear. Each man's hand was in his pocket. When he was given one of the Sharp's rifles just turned over to us by the pro-slavery men, he pulled out of his pocket a breech-block, which he promptly inserted in the rifle. Though the stocks and barrels had been shipped up the Missouri River, Lane had brought the breechblocks clear across Iowa with him on our march into Kansas. But the pro-slavery men who had delivered the rifles to us had considered them useless and had rejoiced at driving a sharp bargain.

When the exchange of prisoners was completed, the two parties marched off in opposite directions, and the United States troops vanished from sight. It would be hard to find in all history a parallel to that scene. In sight on that plain were three organized military forces: the Free State men, the pro-slavery men, and the United States troops, with each group claiming full authority over the region. In which force resided the moral and legal right to govern?

When we reached Lawrence, I was given a Sharp's rifle and joined in several little raids. Finally Lane asked me to stay there as a member of his staff and carry orders. When I mentioned that I had no horse, he told me:

"Go to the corral and pick one out."

There I found five wretched specimens of horseflesh. After looking the lot over several times, I chose a flea-bitten gray, a former United States cavalry horse. He had been condemned and sold, and the marks of many brands showed plainly on him. Just below his left ear he had a small running sore from a gunshot wound, but otherwise he seemed sound. I drew a saddle and bridle for him and named him Colonel Titus.

Next day [August 19] I was ordered to take six men on a reconnaissance twenty miles to the southwest, where Border Ruffians were said to be raiding. Lane explained his order to me over and over again, and asked if I understood that a military order must be obeyed without any deviation whatever. Its substance was that our party should keep under cover whenever possible and should make a thorough search of the country, but should not get into a fight under any circumstances whatsoever. If attacked, we must run away and return to Lawrence by the shortest route.

When I had assembled my squad, I noticed that every man had a better horse than mine. When I protested to General Lane, he said there was no better horse to be had at present. Perhaps one could be found in a few days.

At that time there were no roads or bridges in Kansas. We rode out of Lawrence about ten o'clock that night, forced to trust to an inborn sense of direction to find our way. For some miles we examined both banks of a stream and found plenty of evidence that a party of at least seventy or eighty men had been raiding in that section. Just at sunrise [of August 20] we passed the mouth of a little valley; half a mile up the creek which flowed through it the pro-slavery men were encamped. Their sentry saw us before we saw them.

Before I could order a retreat fifteen or twenty of them had mounted. We wheeled and fled, but just as we got under good headway, I saw another hostile party straight ahead. We were trapped—and we were under strict orders not to fight. At the moment we were close to the point of a ridge that ran up from the main stream. I suddenly realized that, until they came to the spot where we now were, our two parties of enemies could not see each other. So I ordered my men to dash right up the ridge—and there we were, out and away on the open prairie with a lead of nearly a mile before the two parties met and fell in behind us together.

Fifteen long miles to Lawrence and reinforcements! We ran in a bunch, while I kept urging the men not to press their horses too hard. Unluckily for us these raiders who were chasing us came from Platte County, Missouri, where they raised a splendid breed of horses. After a mile or so we could have no doubt that they were gaining on us. After another mile they began to fire an occasional shot, but the utmost effective reach of such firearms as they carried was six hundred yards. I threw my men out at least ten yards apart and called to them to sit steady in the saddles and give their horses a chance. Now we could hear at intervals not only the crack of a gun but the whizzing of a bullet. The second man to my right suddenly clapped his hand to his thigh, saying, "I'm hit!" But it proved to be a spent bullet that made only a bruise.

As I glanced along our irregular line, I could see that some of the riders were still holding in their horses. I called out, "Every man for himself! Get away while you can!"

Our enemies had given up wasting ammunition on chance firing and were trying their best to get within effective range. At my command "Every man for himself!" my companions plunged ahead and began to draw away from me. Soon I was nearly a hundred yards in the rear. The firing began again, and for a while I was occupied in imagining that I could feel bullets going through me. Suddenly I realized that Old Titus was running splendidly in long, steady leaps, and with each leap was giving a sort of grunt. Presently I saw that I was making up the lost ground between my squad and me. I thought, "The boys have made up their minds to wait for me, and all die together."

Soon I came abreast of one of them. "Don't wait for me!" I called.

"Wait?" he shouted back. "If I've been doing any waiting, I'd like to know how to stop it!"

44

Old Titus stuck out his long neck, with his nose turned a little to one side as if he were watching our pursuers. His leaps were even longer and quicker now; his grunting had stopped. I could hear the other horses panting furiously; not a sound came from Old Titus's nostrils. Gradually he drew away from the rest and took the lead. Riding him was easy as sitting in a rocking chair.

For a time the raiders had made no gain on us. We were running along a narrow divide. Across this, here and there, streams that ran off at right angles on either side, reaching almost to the top of the ridge, made depressions. In one of these gullies I called a halt. Then I bade my men dismount, leave the panting horses, and crawl back; for I knew that three miles more of that furious gait would have meant the death of every horse and, orders or no orders, I was going to put up a fight to save them. But before we had come up out of the depression to a spot where we could see the enemy, we were startled and amazed at hearing heavy firing back along the divide. Rushing up the final slope, we found that our pursuers were being pursued. Old John Brown, who was camping on one of those side streams, had come out on the flank of the twenty or thirty men who followed us.

There were many occurrences in that Kansas war about which historians have said nothing. No history of Kansas I have seen contains a line about the fate of those pursuers of ours. A few days later, when I visited Brown's company at his request, not one of his men would answer a question on that subject.

Three of the horses belonging to my squad had to be left on the prairie; the other three were got back to camp with much difficulty; but when I had returned to the horses from the hilltop, I had found Old Titus quietly grazing. I mounted him and rode to General Lane's headquarters to make my report.

5.

Lent to Old John Brown

As I have said, a few days afterward [on August 22] a man came to tell me that Old John Brown wanted to see me. When I told Lane, he urged me to go and meet Brown, because he himself wanted to know "what that old lunatic intended to do next." It took me several hours to ride from Lawrence to the queer rendezvous Brown had appointed—the spot where he was encamped on the bank of a creek. The men in the group with him were queer too. Some of them were as high-minded and brave a lot of fanatics as ever fought for a cause, but I had then, as now, a suspicion that some were cutthroats and murderers who followed him for the prey and booty they could get in those disturbed times.

Brown had in his camp a fine-looking Negro, who said that he had run away from his master in Platte County, Missouri, because the man was going to sell him and his wife to a dealer who would take them south to the Louisiana sugar plantations. The average Missouri Negro looked upon being sold south as one or two degrees worse than being sent straight to hell. This viewpoint was fostered by the masters, who always threatened, when things went wrong, to sell them down the river. John Brown had planned a raid into Platte County to rescue this Negro's wife and as many more slaves as possible.

He asked me, "Do you want a part in this holy crusade to free some of God's black children?"

"I do," I answered, "but I must report first to General Lane and get permission."

"That is proper and right," he agreed. Then he directed me, if Lane allowed me, to meet him at a certain place on a certain day.

When I reported to Lane, he laughed at me.

"Why, my boy," he argued, "if you go across the Missouri River stealing niggers, those Missourians will hang you sure! And this time they won't take the trouble to assemble a drumhead court-martial. They'll swing you up to the first tree they come to."

"They'd have to catch me first," I insisted.

"Catch you! The whole county over there would be after you, and every man in it is a Border Ruffian."

Though I pressed my request further, it was no use. Lane positively refused to let me go, but that evening he sent for me again.

He questioned me for a long time about Brown and his company, urging me to describe each man personally as nearly as I could. He inquired exactly what the old man had said to me, at what point he expected to cross the river, what types of arms they had, the condition of their horses, and many other matters of that nature. Then he asked abruptly:

"Do you still want to go?"

"I do," I answered.

"You may go; but you must file a request in writing with me so that I could prove, if there was any trouble, that I never ordered you to go. I would not order any man to go over into Platte County, much less a boy. I hope that someone of that crowd may get back, but I very much doubt if even one will escape. You go and see Brown, and after you get orders from him report to me before you make the trip."

When I reached Brown again, he told me that each man of

his party would try to cross the river alone, keep hidden in the brush and the woods during the daytime, and meet at a designated place on a certain night at nine o'clock to receive further orders.

I reported again to Lane, who gave me a lot of written orders which I was to study until I knew them by heart. Then I was to burn them. Their substance was that I was to ride out of Lawrence after ten o'clock at night. After the first day I was to travel only by night. I was given the names of two Free State men who furnished Lane with information. I was also given a description of their houses and a rough map of the two little towns in which they lived on the west bank of the Missouri River. These men were of vast importance to the Free State cause, and I must do nothing that would bring suspicion on them in the slightest degree. I was to call upon them only after midnight, obtain what information and assistance I could, and get away without letting anyone else learn that I had been there. Before I had read that document half through, I saw the importance of burning it. I committed it to memory, and then put it into my first campfire.

That first night out I spent in an Indian camp, and traded for "jerked meat" some of the tobacco with which our New England friends, who had the sense to know that a man out of tobacco "wouldn't fight worth a cent," kept us well supplied. I got from the Indians enough meat, which could be eaten cooked or uncooked, wet or dry, to last me about ten days. All the next day Old Titus and I stayed in the camp and then stole away at nightfall.

I tried for two days to get to the house of one of those two Free State men. He lived in a tiny town of only two or three log houses and a shanty or two, but a guard was always posted there. Failing in my effort, I went to the other town, which was farther up the river. With its map indelibly printed on my brain, I easily found the house and the man.

He gave me a great deal of information which he advised me to carry straight back to Lane.

"Let Old John Brown do his 'nigger stealing' himself," he urged me. "It's vitally important for Lane to know some of these facts I'm telling you immediately."

The most important fact of all was that a lot of Border Ruffians were congregating at Westport and Independence in Missouri, preparing to make a raid into Kansas. When I refused to go back, he advised me to ride up along the river for some distance to where there was a flatboat ferry. I had not a cent of money—in fact had had none for a long time. The man gave me ten dollars—did Beecher send it out there?—all in silver, as there would be no way for me to get change to pay small charges in that country.

Just before daylight [of August 27] I started on my way up the river; just before sundown that afternoon I appeared at the ferry and was carried across. On the Missouri side I "took to the brush" until it grew quite dark. During the night I made my way toward the appointed meeting place.

Once that night I was fired at by one of the "nigger patrols" which the slaveholders had organized to protect their property by riding around nightly in turn to see that none of their "niggers" ran away or were stolen. Finally I found a safe waiting spot in a mass of willows on low ground by the river, not more than two miles from the place where we were to meet. At dawn I left my horse, made my way to the nearest high ground, climbed a tree, and verified my location. I could plainly see on a hill the landmark house, which stood one mile east of our assembling point. Near me was a corncrib from which I carried away enough corn to give Old Titus three good feeds. As I went toward him, I all but stumbled over a "nigger" who very evidently had been out chicken stealing. He dropped his loot and ran for his life. I pretended I had not seen him.

This Platte County, into which John Brown had invited me, was thickly settled. Though most of the houses were built of logs, there were a few fine frame residences. Also, behind these residences, there were always "nigger quarters," ramshackle stables, and loom-houses where Negro women wove the jeans and linsey-woolsey which formed the outer clothing of the whole population. The planters' wealth was made up of fine horses, "likely niggers," and a rich soil which produced immense crops of corn and hemp. Though many of the owners of this countryside could neither read nor write, they were proud and rich. How long John Brown had been secretly lingering there near his chosen rendezvous, or how many men he had with him, I never knew.

Night settled down dark and moonless. Clouds hung low in the west. I had difficulty in making my way to the appointed place, but there I found Brown and the Negro whom I had seen in his camp. There were eight or ten dismounted men there also, who had left their horses across the Missouri. I learned from conversation I overheard that there were other men, farther down the river, who were mounted. These had crossed the river on a captured flatboat, and expected to recross by the same means before daylight. I noticed that Brown seemed to know the name of every slaveholder in that region, the number of his slaves, and the exact location of the road that led from his plantation to the river.

Brown directed our group to go to a certain cabin belonging to a certain house and get the slaves who were expecting us. We all were to take them to the river by a road he described. Then the rest of our group were to take these Negroes over the river in skiffs that would be found at a designated place, but I was to make my way back to the same ferry by which I had come and to cross by it as soon after daybreak as the man in charge turned up to navigate it.

Brown said there was a regular road in front of the house where we were to get the Negroes, but that, as it was guarded by the planters' patrol, our party was to enter the farm from the rear and approach the slave quarters through a cornfield. He bade me go alone a mile up the direct front road to watch for the patrol and keep our main party informed of any danger from that source. Just where a dim side road led off down to the river where the skiffs were waiting, he said, there was a certain sharp bend in the road. My orders were to tie my horse in a patch of pawpaw bushes nearby and take my station there in the turn itself, so that I could see in both directions.

When I objected to dismounting and separating myself from my horse, Brown told me with a metallic ring in his voice: "You will obey orders."

Doubtless if there had been more light, I should have seen a peculiar gleam in his eye. Anyone who had anything to do with Brown in Kansas learned that it was death, after one joined his band, to disobey any order he issued.

I went with his men as he had ordered. Because the night was so very dark, we had difficulty in finding the right place. I took my post in the bend, while the other men crept up through the cornfield. Just then the wind blew furiously and the rain poured down. I could see nothing except when lightning flashed now and then. I stood in the road barely outside the bushes, impatiently waiting for our men and the Negroes to climb over the fence and follow with me that vague side road to the river. Without warning someone threw his arms around me from behind, pinioning my elbows to my sides. Instantly two more men leaped upon me, but before they could clap a hand over my mouth, I uttered the loudest yell that had ever come out of me. It was the only warning I could give my associates.

My captors tied my hands and feet; they put a rope around my neck and dragged me along the ground by it for some distance. Then they lifted me to my feet, threw the rope end over the limb of a tree, and demanded:

"Tell us where the rest of this low-down gang of nigger stealers are, or up you go."

Without waiting for a reply they pulled away on the rope. When they let me down, I was "pretty tolerable mad." I gave them my opinion as to what sort of scoundrels they were. They cut that discourse short by swinging me up again. When next they let me down, they spent a few minutes in giving me their opinion of "nigger stealers." They wound up by declaring most solemnly that if I would tell them where the rest of the gang was, they would let me go and would hang the others.

I was not in condition to make a very good speech in reply. Still, I started—but before I had forced out a dozen words, they pulled away on the rope. One of them chuckled:

"We'll give him enough this time to make him reasonable."

Just at that moment pistols flashed. Two of the men who had been holding the rope dropped to the ground; the other ran away. My "gang," who had succeeded in creeping up through the cornfield and bringing away two Negro men and one woman, had then overheard the rather loud talk of the patrol at my "hanging bee." Thanks to the black night and the rain, they had stolen up to us unnoticed.

They soon had me on my feet and helped me to find Old Titus and mount him—for in fact there was little energy left in me. They said they would take the Negroes over the river, and they urged me to strike for the woods and reach my ferry by daybreak if possible. I noticed then that both my revolvers were gone, though I still had my Sharp's rifle, which I had left strapped to Titus's saddle. Two of my companions went back to the tree where the Platte County slaveholders had been giving me their "necktie reception," and soon brought me two revolvers, but only one of them was mine.

One of the Negroes pulled down the fence for me and told me to follow the corn rows to the other side of the field. If I tore down the fence there and went straight on, I would soon come to a road that led up the river. I rode away feeling rather uncomfortable.

Long before daylight it became obvious that the entire district was out on the warpath. I heard shots in several directions; I caught the baying of hounds; I saw signal fires both ahead of me and behind me. Twice I hid in the brush until bodies of armed men had passed. Certainly John Brown's "nigger stealing" raid into Platte County had started a tremendous uproar. By now, however, probably all the rest of Brown's men were safely back across the river, and here was I, at sixteen, left alone to fight the whole county.

Traveling through an unknown region in the night, with the population of an entire countryside, bloodhounds and all, on your trail and every man of the lot bent on swinging you up on a tree, as soon as caught, may make interesting reading when transferred to the printed page; it produces quite different sensations in the person chased, especially if his neck already is a bit sore from a recent hanging. I realized plainly before daylight that every approach to the river, as well as every road which ran north and south, was being guarded. Once I decided to strike out into the district to the east, but I had hardly made up my mind to that when I caught from that very direction such a racket of hounds and horns that I gave up the plan.

Just as day broke, I reached a dim lane that led toward the river. From sounds behind me I knew that not much over a mile away a large party was on my trail. After following that lane for a mile or so, I saw that a fence had been built across it, though there was not a human being in sight. I could hear the mob behind me drawing closer. In a moment I made my decision. I put my bridle reins in my teeth, took a revolver in each hand, and dashed toward the fence, trusting Old Titus to get over it somehow. I heard two shots fired at me from ambush, and I banged away right and left with my revolvers—and dug my spurs into Old Titus's sides. He went over the obstruction without touching a rail of it.

We forded quite a large stream and pressed on. Just as I was beginning to think that I had got well to the north of that whole raging section, with an open approach to my ferry, I saw ahead of me, to my disgust, a large group on horseback, gathered near a house which had just come into view. Hoping to escape notice, I leaped a fence into a cornfield—but they had seen me. I have never heard a more fiendish yell than they loosed then and there. I think that afterward, toned down several degrees, it became the famous "rebel yell," the battle cry of the Confederate troops. As that gang gave tongue to it, it fully convinced me that there was blood on the moon.

I plunged across the cornfield and finally reached the bottom lands of the river, which were covered in some places with grass as high as a man on horseback and in others with a dense growth of willows. My pursuers evidently had wholly lost my trail. At various times during the day I could see a patrol on the road that ran by the foot of the hills a mile or two away, but no one searched the bottom land where I was hiding. I stole out once during the day, crossed the road, and brought Old Titus an armful of corn from a field. The "jerked meat" I had bought from the Indians now did me good service.

Toward night I held a one-man council of war. It was clear that every road up or down the river was now patrolled both night and day. If I left the shelter of these willows and got back into the inhabited country, I must expect another night like the last. My only way of escape was to swim the Missouri River with its rapid current, its rushing, mud-colored water, and its treacherous quicksands. After much thought I decided to take the risk.

When evening closed down, I stripped. After tying all my clothing and accouterments to the top of my saddle, I led Old Titus down to the bank. I had expected to have a hard time to get him under way, but he went down the slope into the water without trouble and struck out for the far shore. I took hold of his tail and swam behind him; thus I not only relieved him of my weight, but was able to steer him wherever I wished. We landed in a wild and desolate spot.

I dressed and mounted. By riding all night I reached my Indian friends again at ten o'clock the next day. They all noticed my swollen neck and were very inquisitive about it. I concocted a story of how a lariat had got tangled around it. This satisfied them—and was not so very far from the truth, either.

I rested in their village for two days while the medicine man doctored up my wounds. The Indians had a certain amount of rivalry as to who should have the honor of entertaining me. Johnny Cake, one of the chiefs, could talk some English, and I had learned a little of the sign language, so we got along very well. Johnny Cake was a great joker, poking fun at both the white people and the Indians. To keep even with him, I commented mischievously on some of the latter's dirty habits. A couple of months later Johnny Cake got more than even with me on that score.

[It is necessary to explain here that the sign language which was used in common by all the Indian tribes on the Great Plains was not any crude series of casual gestures to suggest actions with pointings to indicate objects. Instead, it was a highly elaborated system of signs, somewhat akin to the deaf-

and-dumb language. It was based on standardized movements and positions of the arms, hands, and fingers. Entire conversations were carried on in it between tribes who had no interpreter available.

Whole stories could be told in it. For instance, it would be simple indeed for one Indian to tell another: "A white man came down the river in his canoe to visit our tribe. Our chief went out to meet him. He stayed here three days. He exchanged his canoe with the chief for a horse. He was very much pleased. He rode away toward the west. After he had gone, the chief found that he had stolen the canoe during a rainstorm from a boy in the next tribe up the river."

Every word of that little tale could be conveyed by one Indian to another by the use of signs almost as definite as those of shorthand.]

6.

The Final Skirmishes

My reappearance at Lane's headquarters took everyone there by surprise. Brown's men, when I had failed to join them after their return, had notified General Lane that I surely had been killed. How many Negroes Brown had brought away in all from that raid I never knew, but current rumor stated that he had come back with seventeen.

I reported in full to General Lane the information I had received in my call on his agent—especially the assembling of the pro-slavery men at Westport and Independence. When, the next day, he sent out scouts in that direction, I was eager to go with them, but he told me that I had better stay around headquarters until my neck did not look so disgraceful. A day or two later, however, our whole force marched off southward. After passing a place called Prairie City, where there were two or three shanties, we engaged in a small fight at Bull Creek. When the pro-slavery men there hurriedly retreated toward Missouri, our force started back to Lawrence. Besides the men in the wagons and on foot we had about a hundred mounted fighters. I was ordered off with these on some sort of an expedition. I had never before seen the man who commanded this venture; and where he was trying to go or what he was trying to do I could not find out either then or later.

We wandered around for three days without any commissary stores. For the first day most of the men had some food of their own along, but after that we had nothing. Because a Border Ruffian force came in between us and Lawrence, we could not get back there. At last we reached a very high hill from which we were able to make signals. Reinforcements were sent to us, and the enemy decamped.

We were all ravenously hungry. I, for one, had not eaten for the whole three days. As we neared the town, a doctor, who had been one of the troop, rode down our line to warn us not to eat too much at first. If we did, death might be the result. Meanwhile the women of Lawrence had turned out to build a row of small campfires and bake slapjacks for us. They piled these up on tin plates. Then they poured bacon grease over them. From three miles away we smelled those slapjacks. As soon as our men came in sight of them, they leaped from their horses and ran to grab them. After a while, as I passed down the line, I saw the doctor again. He had run his sword through a pile of slapjacks, tin plate and all, and was eating faster than any private in the ranks.

For those three days we had badly lacked not only food but sleep. As each man of us finished eating, he dropped to the ground and went to sleep right where he had stood. Bystanders lariated our horses for us.

After dark I was roused by someone's kicking me most vigorously. When I was wide enough awake to understand who he was and what he was saying, I got to my feet. He was one of Lane's most trusted lieutenants, and we called him Colonel. He told me that Border Ruffians were marching from Lecompton to Topeka and that we must march there at once to save the place.

Through the dark night I could dimly see a column moving past us and hear the tramp of marchers. These men had hurried miles to our rescue already that day, and were now half dead on their feet—but they were starting away. The Colonel told me to help to get our men awake and mounted. If Topeka should be taken, the Free State cause would be lost. More than that, every man of us would be captured, convicted, and hanged for high treason. Marshal Donelson, he said, had summoned a United States grand jury under the orders of Judge Lecompte, and each one of us already had been indicted. All that remained to be done was to capture us and hang us.

It took a lot of hard pounding to get those sleepers awake, but I did my full share of it. Finally our troop staggered to their feet; we all mounted and started. Before we had gone far, someone brought me an order from Lane to select three good helpers and one of the wagons and follow in the rear. If anyone gave out from exhaustion, I was to pick up his arms and ammunition, load them into the wagon, and bring them along.

Soon we rear guards began to find men so tired that even the fear of death could not keep them awake. Some of them marched right out of the ranks while asleep and started off at a tangent. A few officers tried to keep themselves and their troops awake by swearing the most fearful oaths—and among these officers were two or three who were noted for being especially religious.

We seemed to be marching along a ridge with a valley on our right. Right then a thing occurred which no man who saw it will ever forget. In that black night the road could be seen for only a few feet ahead. Suddenly a brilliant radiance shed itself over the whole countryside so that for a few seconds everything for miles away could be seen distinctly. Down in the valley on our right we saw the Border Ruffian forces—and we knew that at that moment we were already ahead of them on the road to Topeka.

I have heard many opinions about that light. The religiously disposed thought it a special act of Providence; but I myself think that it came from some great meteor which happened to fall just then. At all events, brief though the strange radiance was, it seemed to put heart into our troops.

Soon afterward, however, I found two more men lying exhausted by the road. I stopped my wagon to gather up their arms and ammunition. Although I had ordered that, before guns were put into the wagon, their loads must be withdrawn, a helper put one of these two latest guns in hastily while I was not looking. When I asked him if it was still loaded, he told me that it was not. He had laid it somewhat across the wagon. Now he attempted to shove it around so that it would lie straight. I heard a loud discharge. The last thing that I remember about that moment is that I was turning slowly around as I fell toward the earth.

When consciousness returned, I was lying all alone in the awful stillness of the prairie. Gradually I began to try to reason.

"Why don't you get up?" I asked myself.

"How can I get up when my head is shot off?" I thought, and, as that seemed to be altogether reasonable, I lay still.

After a while I decided to feel and discover if my head really was shot off. I put up my hand—and my head was there intact. Then after another while I thought it was time to try whether or not I could get up. I succeeded, but still could not comprehend what had happened. I had only that one distinct impression—that my head had been shot off. Gradually my senses and my common sense came back. The musket ball had ploughed a ridge along the top of my head without fracturing my skull. However, I had more trouble with that skull than I had had with my sore neck.

At last I could walk on, but, only a little way in advance, I found our whole force drawn up in line of battle. Thus we lay till daylight, when investigation proved that the pro-slavery troops had seen us as plainly by that radiance as we had seen them. Thinking themselves nearly surrounded, they had fled back to Lecompton.

We spent several days lying around in camp after that forced march to save Topeka; then [on September 13] General Lane organized an expedition to take a place [in Jefferson County, near the Missouri River] called Hickory Point. We marched up there and formed a line that stretched quite a distance over the prairie to the west of a log house the pro-slavery men held. We fired a few shots from one howitzer we had with us. After some shooting along the line we were ordered away from there and sent to camp on a creek some distance back. I noticed that my Old Titus was tossing his head up and down and would not graze on the grass by the creek. On examining him thoroughly I discovered that he had been shot in the nose, and that a small bullet had gone down through the roof of his mouth and made a spot on his tongue. In spite of this wound he ate as well as ever the next day.

When we had been in this camp only overnight, Lane informed us that a compromise had been reached by the contending forces. Governor Shannon had resigned, and John W. Geary of Pennsylvania had become governor of the territory under a strict pledge that a fair election should be held, and that if the territory were voted free, it should be free. Our side had promised that all armed forces in the territory should be dispersed; and the Border Ruffians had agreed to return to Missouri and the other states from which they had come. Lane said that he was going back East and that every man would have to look out for himself. I went back to Lawrence.

7.

Back to the Wilds

Late in October of that year of 1856, in spite of my recent
crowded months, I was still only sixteen years old, and my zest
for adventure and the wilds was as strong as ever. Among the
newspapermen whom the excitement had brought to Lawrence were [Albert D.] Richardson and [James] Redpath
[noted correspondents both then and later]. Richardson afterward was shot by a man in the Tribune Building in New
York City [and Redpath became the first biographer of John
Brown. Now, when it was rumored to be well for all former
Free State leaders to withdraw from the Lawrence scene], these
two men planned a hunt and engaged me as guide, for I already had some reputation for shooting, and Richardson vowed
he wanted one man along who could hit a buffalo if the animal
came up and stood sideways to him. There was also in Lawrence an Englishman about whom no one knew anything except that he always had plenty of money. He was determined
to join our hunt, and the two newspapermen were equally determined not to let him. They declared that he did not know
how to take care of himself, that if he encountered cold
weather, he would freeze to death, and that they did not want
a lord or a duke with them anyhow. It was known that this
Englishman always took two men along: a Frenchman who did
his cooking, and another of his own nationality who took care
of him and his clothes.

After trying vainly in every possible way to get rid of the Englishman, Richardson finally agreed to let him go on condition that he would take only the Frenchman along. When Richardson owned up to having made this concession, Redpath grew ragingly angry.

"I won't have that helpless lord out with us among wild Indians," he stormed.

I suspect that Richardson was under some social obligation or other to the Englishman, and that now he found himself in a bad fix. Redpath obdurately refused to let the Englishman go. Finally Richardson, in desperation, concocted a plan to rid us of His Lordship. He announced that the night before our trip he, Redpath, and I would collect our supplies and camp out with them on the hill near the town. He told the Englishman we would break camp at nine o'clock in the morning, but at daybreak, long before the Englishman could have waked, he had us up and off.

As always on the first day's march many small problems—the extra horses, the pack animals, and other details—were troublesome all day long. About five o'clock we were forced to camp in order to rearrange the packs and put things into shape for longer marches in the future.

Just before dark up came our friend the Englishman. His Frenchman was driving a cart loaded down with the things that his master "could not do without" on the hunt. Just one sign of good sense appeared: two extra horses were hitched behind. At first Redpath was so angry that I was afraid he would shoot the "lord," but he tamed down a little when he saw how swiftly the Frenchman prepared camp, lariated out the horses, and cooked his master's supper.

Since I had learned from the Indians' talk and from every old hunter I had met that we should find plenty of game out on the Solomon River and along the headwaters of the Republican, I headed our party in that direction. The only provisions we carried were flour, a little bacon, plenty of saleratus, and a good lot of coffee and tobacco. The bacon was for greasing the frying pan to keep our flapjacks from sticking fast.

That Englishman proved to be as much trouble to us as a two-year-old baby. He would not stay with the cart or the pack horses. He kept making side excursions, and as he was not sure whether the sun at high noon was in the north, south, east, or west, and at night did not know the north star from Venus, he kept getting lost. I was always having to hunt him up and bring him back to camp.

One day he came near getting our whole party scalped. He ran across a camp of young Indians who, without the knowledge of their chiefs, were off on a horse-stealing expedition. The young scamps were ready for any sort of deviltry, and I had to use a good deal of diplomacy to bring the lord and ourselves safely out of their clutches. Luckily for us they were Iowas and Otoes. If they had been Sioux or Comanches, our story would have ended differently—and promptly.

After three or four more days of traveling—during which I noticed that the Englishman at last stuck very close to the cart —we reached the buffalo country and camped on the banks of a good-sized stream. The buffalo were there in large numbers, with plenty of antelope and other game. Richardson and Redpath, who wanted trophies to carry back East, took great risks to get heads of big buffalo bulls which had good horns and long, shaggy hair. The Englishman was eager for the head of an antelope—"one of those swift little beasts." I offered to give him a couple of heads, but he wanted to kill one for himself. Again and again I told him exactly how to go about the job, but he never could succeed. One day I went along with him and we shot one, but he never ceased afterward to talk about "the beastly crawling on our stomachs for a mile or two before we got a shot."

Two or three days after we had encamped here Richardson made an astonishing discovery. That Frenchman was a taxidermist and had brought the tools of his trade along in the cart. Redpath was so delighted that he forgave Richardson for having allowed the Englishman to come, because without him we should have had no "Frenchy" along to mount the buffalo and antelope heads ready to show to the city people back home.

Then something happened which I had never before seen on the plains—a heavy fog which lasted almost twenty-four hours, so thick that one could not see a horse four rods away. Early morning fogs are not unknown there, but one so dense and lasting was very strange. I proposed waiting in camp until the fog disappeared, but Richardson and Redpath thought that this would be a fine chance to crawl up on a herd of buffalo or antelope. They insisted that the air would clear soon. We started out, Frenchman and all. After we had climbed the hills and come out on the level prairie, and had pressed on for a while, I noticed that we were crossing our own trail. In other words, we had been riding in a circle.

Though I called Richardson's attention to the proof, he still could not see it. It has always puzzled me why the man brought up in the East cannot see. Richardson dismounted and even then could not see our previous trail until, as he knelt down to look closer, I parted the grass and showed him in the ground the print of a horse's foot.

I proposed to follow that trail back to camp, but all the others were in favor of going on. Redpath announced:

"I'm sure I can hear a herd of buffalo grazing."

"If so," I answered, "we'd better get straight away from here. If they should stampede our way, it would be the end of us."

Nevertheless he, Richardson, and the lord insisted on going on; the Frenchman said nothing; I started for our camp.

At first I followed back on the trail, but it soon became so dim that I could not see it from horseback. I dismounted to follow it on foot, leading Old Titus, but I soon tired of that method. Feeling sure that I recognized a small hill as one that we had come up, I mounted and took the direction I thought would lead me to camp. After an hour or so a drizzling rain joined in with the fog. I finally decided that the best thing I could do was to stop and wait for the air to clear. I unsaddled my horse, took the saddle for a seat, wrapped my blankets around me, and sat there hour after hour in the cold, misty drizzle. That day certainly seemed to me the longest in the history of mankind. Now and then I got up and walked around, trying to find something which would indicate the points of the compass, but I found nothing. Not even a weed grew there— nothing at all but the short buffalo grass.

The day wore away, night came, and still the fog remained. At last Old Titus lay down, and I crawled up to him, spreading my blankets to make a shield from the rain, and went to sleep.

When I woke, the stars were shining, and I was ravenously hungry. Taking the direction from the stars, I started toward the river where our camp was. When I reached the bluffs along the stream and rode up the highest of them to get my bearings, I found that I was several miles above our camp. Just as I was turning away, Old Titus began to show signs of uneasiness. From his actions I knew that Indians were somewhere near, for an American horse can scent them five miles away. My first thought was:

"They're those Iowa and Otoe scamps again."

Then I reflected that perhaps they were Comanches instead and that, if so, meeting them would prove a far more serious matter. I left that high and conspicuous point as quickly as I could. As I came down the hill, I saw a plain trail, apparently much used of late. Ponies had followed it to and fro. Indians were surely encamped in the timber at the foot of that hill. Who were they? To what tribe did they belong?

I walked up and down that trail, studying it as a scholar would try to decipher an almost illegible manuscript. This was what I read. They had been hunting; heavily loaded ponies had been led down the track. That was as plain as if written in capital letters. On one bit of steep path and soft ground a pony had fallen. The imprints of moccasined feet were very clear, but not of Comanche feet, I was sure; for I knew that the Comanches soled their moccasins with "par flesh." I concluded that my best and safest plan was to ride openly into this camp and act as if we were friends.

I made my way cautiously down the hill and out through the heavily timbered bottom land. I saw eight or ten tents and, standing in front of one of them, the old chief, Johnny Cake, the Indian with whom I had stayed on my return from John Brown's "nigger stealing" trip into Platte County.

The Indians, who never shake hands among themselves, still consider that act one of the funniest things in the world, but they have learned that it is the white method of indicating friendship. So now the old chief showed his delight at seeing me by shaking my hand energetically.

"How!" he greeted me. "Come and eat. Give pony to squaw." He led the way into his tepee.

Soon hominy and a bowl of black soup were set before me. As I had had nothing to eat for twenty-four hours, I began hungrily to make way with that food as fast as I could. Presently the old chief asked me:

"Like 'em?"

"Yes," I answered, grudging the time the word took.

After a short pause, during which he watched me eat, he asked again:

"Like 'em?"

This time I used the Indian form, saying, "*Ouda*," with the accent which raised that word to the superlative degree.

A third time he asked:

"Like 'em?"

I laid down the horn spoon, looked him in the face, and told him:

"Yes; it is good. Why do you ask so many times?"

"Grasshopper soup!" he replied. Then he gave himself up to a fit of laughter.

That was his way of getting even for the remarks on Indian habits I had made in his camp two months before. After I had finished the "grasshopper soup"—wholly a joke invented impromptu by old Johnny Cake, for it really was soup made from pounded, dried buffalo meat—I rode away to our own camp.

By the time I got there, I was hungry again. The previous morning, before we had started out into the fog, we had placed about twenty pounds of fat buffalo meat in a trench in the ground, and had covered it with ashes and coals and laid a big sod on top. Now I pulled it forth, well cooked. After I had devoured a lot of it, Indian fashion, I stretched myself out beside the remainder.

The Englishman's voice woke me.

"I told you so," he was saying. "If we had followed our guide and come back to camp, we should not have lain out all night on the prairie in the rain. He came right back and had a good time."

I never informed any member of our party that the Englishman was very badly mistaken.

After we had stayed at this camp until we had frightened away the buffalo and were ripe for new adventures, we started for the forks of Beaver Creek on the Republican River. We had all heard a great deal about this country, where the rivers were described as full of fish, the bottoms as frequently covered with timber rich in wild turkeys, and the plains as the favorite pasturing ground of buffalo, elk, and antelope. The creek had gained its name from the great number of beaver dams along it. The region was a hunting ground for the Pawnees, Omahas, Iowas, and Otoes. As the Sioux also claimed the country and hunted there, it had been the scene of more Indian battles than had all the rest of the Great Plains.

Every hunter and plainsman had declared to us that he had never seen more beautiful country than the Republican Valley. There were no white settlements within two hundred miles; no main trails ran through it. We were not likely to meet any Indians because their summer hunts for meat to dry in the sun and for hides to tan were over, and their winter hunts for meat, robes, and furs would not begin for several weeks. In the heavy timber and along the clear, running brooks we could enjoy a few weeks of wild life which we should never forget, and which even before the next generation would have become impossible. This was the picture which Richardson, in particular, painted for us and which started us on our way in high spirits, resolved to make the most of every moment. No happier group than we five men on that early November morning could ever have ridden across those prairies.

All I knew about the region was the name and general course of each stream, though I had made earnest inquiries of the many hunters and trappers in our Kansas camps. One or two of them had drawn rude maps for me. The Platte River, they said, ran nearly due east from the Rocky Mountains, and, down near the Missouri River, the Big Blue and Little Blue rivers ran south and east. Next to these the Republican River ran east for a long way and then south. Away to the west, but south from the Republican, came, in order, Beaver Creek, Prairie Dog Creek, and the forks of the Solomon River, all flowing east. These were the main ones among many streams. The only rivers of clear water in all that region were the Republican and its tributaries. A plainsman who held those facts in his mind could find his own way over that whole country.

November, we had been told, was a beautiful month on the plains. The days would be cool enough to be invigorating and the nights not too cold for comfort. Breathing the air there was like inhaling the elixir of life. The haze that lay over the plain made the whole day a dream. Mirages would hang in the air; we should gaze on cities or marching armies in the clouds in lovelier pictures than those in the galleries of the Old World. Antelope, buffalo, and turkeys were at their fattest and we need select only their choicest parts to feast upon. There jack rabbits capered over the ground, and prairie dogs chippered about the little fortresses they had built around their holes. So toward those happy hunting grounds we journeyed with light hearts.

Soon we knew that the descriptions had not been overdrawn. From a hill, with the plains running to the horizon on every side and before us a virgin land of streams and forest, we viewed the illimitable stretches long in silence. A herd of buffalo or antelope here and there gave the only evidence of animal life. Southward, above the dry land we had just crossed, appeared a mirage of beautiful lakes and trees. Westward hung the shimmering haze; below were the streams of sparkling water of which we had heard. We sat long on our horses. Then, dismounting and holding them by the reins, we sat on the ground to photograph that scene within us forever.

At last we went down into the valley and made our camp under great trees on the banks of a singing brook, where there was plenty of dry wood at hand and fine pasture nearby. In this hunter's paradise the days flew past with incredible swiftness. We who lived so constantly in the open air did not notice the increasing sharpness in the temperature of morning and evening. We fished, hunted, and trapped, watched the Frenchman prepare our trophies of the chase and, like the nomads of the plains, took no thought for the morrow.

One day when only the Englishman was out hunting, an ominous cloud suddenly rose in the northwest. The temperature quickly fell fifty degrees. A fine snow that cut the face like a knife came whirling through the air. We made such hurried improvements in our camp as we could, to protect ourselves from the cold, and collected a large pile of wood and built a roaring fire. The Englishman came in chilled through and through. Even our generous dosings of hot coffee could not warm him. Meanwhile the day grew colder and colder. At last Redpath suggested rolling him up in one of our big green buffalo robes, with the fur inside. After that process, when we laid him near the fire, he soon got warm, but next morning that buffalo robe was frozen solid around him.

Redpath suggested laying him across the fire to let him thaw out. We tried to chop the frozen bundle open, but the Englishman howled so at every blow that we had to desist. Finally the Frenchman undertook the contract of freeing His Lordship. His method was to take a sharp knife and cut the fur, so that he could slowly bend the released portion backward. He had a long, hard job.

Toward noon of the next day the world grew warm again. Except for the ice in the brook no one would have dreamed by that night that there had been any change from the usual temperature. However, the experience had set Richardson and Redpath to thinking what would happen if we should be caught on the plains by winter—to face weather like that every day. They tried to reckon what time of the month it was, for we had lost all count of the weeks. The only date we were sure of was the day we had left Lawrence. They tried to count up the time we had spent on the trail to our first permanent camp, the length of our stay there, the number of camps we had made in reaching the present spot, and the days we had spent here. The calculations were a sad failure, and only one thing was certain: it was dangerous for us to remain any longer so far from civilization. We decided to start onward the next morning toward the Missouri River.

As we had more meat and buffalo and antelope hides in camp than we could possibly take with us, I went over to a band of Pawnees from beyond the Platte, who had been camping near us for several days and had made friendly advances to us. I told the young chief who led them that I would leave behind us a present for his band, which they must come to fetch as soon as we had started. This outfit, to which we added much that the Englishman decided to abandon, was so rich a gift for the Pawnees that that young leader followed us one camp to thank me and to make us a few presents of Indian curiosities in return. I presented him with tobacco. He accepted it—an act of great significance among Indians—and asked me to visit their tribe later.

We journeyed two or three hundred miles, first following the Republican River, and then across country until we reached a steamboat landing on the Missouri. At that season boats came down the river loaded with furs, but in spite of our hope that one would pass soon none came until we had camped there nearly two weeks. Richardson, Redpath, and the Englishman went aboard, bound for St. Louis.

Beside the hundred dollars they paid me for my services, Richardson and Redpath gave me a highly complimentary letter, recommending me to any party that wanted a good hunter and guide. They also gave me all the remaining ammunition and all the camp equipage except their horses. These they took with them on the boat. The Englishman invited me to visit him in England and gave me one of his cards. I thought it the most curious thing I had ever seen. I merely remember that he had not only five names but a long row of capital letters after them which puzzled me a great deal. I intended to keep it and show it to some lawyer for information, if ever I met one, but during that winter I lost it.

The Frenchman, who had been given the cart and its horses, and I camped together for a few days. Then he packed up his wealth—it was truly great wealth to him—and set off up the river for the Indian agency at the mouth of the Platte.

8.

A Guest of the Indians

Old Titus showed the effects of the hard service he had given me on our long hunt. I bought corn from a pioneer settler who had raised a little; I lariated Titus on the finest grass of the river bottoms and took the best care of him I could; and in a couple of weeks he showed great improvement. Then I began to think seriously about what I should do with myself. Finally I concluded to go back to Kansas. Putting a pack on an Indian pony the Frenchman had given me, I started south. On my way I fell in with a large band of Indians, a mixed lot belonging to the tribes along the Missouri River, who had always been friendly with the whites. For the time being I took up my habitation with them.

There was plenty to eat in their camp, and feasting and dancing were under full headway all the time. Every night the drums could be heard all the night through. After the true Indian fashion they gave no thought to what they should do for something to eat and wear when the morrow came. Their motto seemed to be: "On with the dance! Let joy be unconfined." The swiftness with which the weeks of this happy, unthinking life flew by was amazing.

The real governing power in the band was a man called Village Maker. All except a few members of the Soldier Lodge were afraid of him. He was what the whites call a "medicine man." The Indians said that he had the "power of the bear."

They believed that if any orders he issued were disobeyed, he would pronounce a curse, and then the offender or some member of his family would die, or perhaps would break out with sores all over his body. Therefore, no one dared to disobey any order given by Village Maker.

There were men and women of all sorts and kinds in the village, with great differences in their characters and habits. The young women, especially, varied widely. Some had heavy, very dark, and dull faces, and cared nothing for ornaments or tidiness; others were neat and no darker than brunettes among the whites. Among these last was a girl with beautiful, sparkling eyes and a sylphlike figure, who, though she belonged to a family which, because her father was lame, had no influence, was the belle of the place. Her name, Me-the-um-ba, literally translated means Sunshine.

Another local character was Half Day, an old Indian who was the chronologist of the tribe. When anyone wanted to learn the date of a past occurrence, if he asked Half Day, he received an immediate and correct reply. But Half Day dated everything, not from the birth of Christ, but from a smallpox scourge which had nearly destroyed the tribe. I could never determine whether Half Day's "great sickness" was the severe epidemic of 1815 or the one of 1832–33.

The man among them whom I came to know best was Two Bears, who had the worst termagant for a wife I have ever met in any race of people. He was the storyteller or daily newspaper for the village. He was given presents for telling stories and for dancing at the feasts. He was a fat, jovial old fellow, the most loquacious individual I have ever known, not excluding Indians. I wish, by the way, that I could set some of the white people who think that Indians are taciturn, speaking only when necessity requires it, down quite unobserved among ten or fifteen Indians who have gathered for a social occasion. If in an hour they did not wish they had been born deaf, they would at least be willing to pay a good round sum in order to get out of hearing. I believe that ten Indians can do more talking in an hour than fifty white men in half a day. It is no breach of their decorum for one, or three, or four to break in upon the middle of another's sentence, or for the whole party to speak at once. Altogether they have a jolly as well as a noisy time of it; but let a stranger appear, and the scene instantly changes. The truth is that they have "too great loquacity and too great taciturnity by fits."

Two Bears was a perfect actor and could imitate exactly in his stories the voice of a child, an old woman, or a dignified chief delivering a formal address. After listening to his comic tales for half a winter, I came to the conclusion that all the standard jokes of the white people had been stolen from the Indians, for Two Bears had never been among the whites and could not speak a word of English. Moreover, the story of the man who, seeing himself in a mirror for the first time, made uncomplimentary remarks about that person there who refused to answer his salutation, and other jokes and stories which I had thought to be the exclusive inheritance of white people, these Indians claimed had come down to them from their forefathers. Later experience taught me that it is indeed difficult for a white man to find among all the anecdotes current in literature and travelers' tales any which have not their exact counterpart, though tinged by different habits of life, thought, and expression in the regular catalogue of Indian stories.

One day as I lounged on my robes in my tent, Two Bears pushed aside the door and entered. Seating himself on the opposite side of the fire, his face beaming with fun and good nature, he invited me to attend a meeting of his club.

"These fellows who've been feasting you are too solemn," he chuckled. "They have too much to say about the government. What's the use of all their talk? The members of my club are a different set. We've made a feast for you. You come tonight and we'll have plenty of fun."

His club had a very large buffalo-skin tent, perhaps thirty feet in diameter, with a roaring fire in its center. The place of honor, opposite the entrance, was given to me. First came a dance—something like a cotillion—with the crowning feature that at the end of each set the gentleman was expected to kiss his partner. Two Bears, the first on the floor, danced with whole-souled vigor. The music came from two drums, accompanied by four male and two female voices. At first slow and soothing, it gradually increased in quickness until an almost maddening exhilaration seized upon the hearers.

Two Bears presented to me as my partner lovely little Sunshine, who moved about in the mazes of the dance with fairy-like grace and lightness. Quicker and quicker beat the music, faster and faster flew the feet. Then all at once, suddenly as a flash of lightning, the music stopped! And we? Well, I said before what we did.

Two Bears rushed up to me. "How do you like this? Didn't I tell you we had plenty of fun at my club?"

"This isn't the end, is it?"

"No, the men will dance by themselves now."

"Oh, pshaw!" I objected. "There'll be no fun in that. Let's have some more of this."

Then Two Bears, the old sinner, laughed till the tears rolled down his cheeks. "You're bad," he told me. "Very bad!"

He slipped away, but a minute or two later I heard the master of ceremonies, the old crier, announcing that the dance would be repeated. I looked around in vain for my partner. Two Bears, sitting far back under the very edge of the tent, was trying to look solemn and unconcerned, but his eyes twinkled.

"Where's my partner?" I asked.

"She's gone. You can't have the same one all the time. Go

over there and get yourself one." He pointed to the old women who sat near the door, looking on.

"Get up, you rascal," I bade him. "You've stolen my girl."

Just then I heard a little feminine giggle. I pushed Two Bears to one side—and found my partner hidden behind him. She ran to her place in the set, motioning to me to follow her.

"This dance is different," she instructed me. "You must keep step to the music and try to catch me."

The spectators, knowing what was coming, had all crept away into the borders of the tent, leaving a large clear space around the fire for the dancers. This time the music started off at the double quick. We stood in our places, with partners facing each other, all merely beating time with the foot. As the music grew still faster, my partner looked me in the eye and smiled. Suddenly, at a given signal, she darted backward, holding out her hands toward me. Swift as an antelope, she flew around and around the fire—and I pursued. With eyes and hands she pleaded for me to take her, but ever, as I reached out my own hands to her, she eluded them—and beckoned again.

One by one the Indian warriors captured their coy maidens until I alone was left pursuing. The drums beat in faster and faster time; the victorious warriors shouted and laughed; again tears were streaming down Two Bears' face, and his fat sides were shaking till he was on the verge of a convulsion. But still my coy maiden fled before me. Finally in desperation I leaped the central fire with one bound and caught her in my arms.

"Foul! That's a foul!" screamed the warriors—only they said "bad," but I held onto my maiden until Two Bears took my part, claiming that I had played fair. "For," he insisted, "his feet struck the ground exactly at the tap of the drum. He kept the time perfectly."

Next followed a dance for the men alone—the sort of dance that white people usually see—such as forms a part of the Indians' religious and solemn ceremonies. In this club, whose object was fun, it aroused little interest in anyone. The women, who hardly noticed the performance, were busy hanging over the fire three big kettles of *wabruga,* a preparation of Indian corn. They propped up on sticks large ribs of buffalo to roast before the fire. When the dance had ended and before the viands were fully cooked, we gathered in a circle around the fire, women on one side, men on the other, spectators behind. The men started a wild, exciting song to which the women sang a refrain. At certain places in it the drummers beat the drums.

I know no meat, however deftly prepared, which can tickle the palate like good, tender, fat buffalo ribs roasted before a great wood fire. Each of us had brought along a wooden bowl and a large horn spoon. The bowls were filled with *wabruga,* and I was given a pair of ribs. They measured about three feet by six inches by four inches. They were placed on two upright sticks which were stuck into the ground in front of me. Each feaster, with a sharp knife and a horn spoon, made an immediate attack on similar obstructions set before him. In the course of an hour all objects intervening between the guests and the fire had disappeared from view amid a hum of voices and peals of laughter.

Then out came the pipes and the tobacco pouches; and the convention of the storytellers began. After a two-hour session Two Bears decided it was time for another dance. Everything was shoved far back in under the tent edge, the floor (which was the ground itself) was cleared, the musicians took their station at the right of the entrance, and we were ready.

All the girls had left. One side of the tent had been thrown back a little to enlarge the doorway. A woman's voice, alone, began to sing:

"Come from your hiding,
Come from your hiding
Away in the woods."

Just as the male voices and the drums took up the song, twelve girls ran in and danced around the fire. Outside the tent they had interchanged their clothes, beads, bracelets, and trinkets. Each held a shawl drawn over her head so that it left only one eye exposed. Each of the twelve represented a band in the tribe and had adopted a temporary name. The warriors who were to take part knew those twelve names but did not know which name any girl had chosen. As the girls circled the fire, each waiting brave would select the one whom he supposed to be his former partner and, dancing before her, would pronounce one of the names. If she proved to be his partner and if he pronounced the right name, he led her away to his seat. There he had the privilege of wrapping his blanket around both her and himself while they sat to watch out the game.

The difficulty was that, while a warrior might be pretty certain of his partner, even in her disguise, the name was sheer guesswork. He might have to dance twelve times before he could chance on the right one.

It did not take me long to discover my dusky little sprite among the girls; and I conned over in my mind those twelve names to decide which she had probably chosen. They were: Wild Rose, Fawn, Black Bird, Sunshine, White Bird, Moose, Pine Tree, Eagle's Wing, White Cloud, Swan, Quick to Hear, and Old Woman. They were chosen without logic simply to mystify the guesser.

I had rather a hard time of it. Nine times I made obeisance to my lithe little fairy, and danced the regulation steps before I called her by the right name—Quick to Hear. Though we started for my seat, before we could reach it the other two girls still on the floor were captured. The ungrateful little sprite ran off and left me to sit down alone.

Two Bears, who was sitting close by with his captive all covered up in his blanket, began to condole with me. At last he offered me his own girl, but when he unfolded the blanket, I found instead of a girl a chunk of wood. A roar of laughter greeted this little joke. When it subsided, Two Bears announced that it was time to eat again.

We all sat down in a circle, as before, with our wooden bowls in front of us, and were served with hot soup and with dried fruit which had been pounded in a mortar and mixed with dried buffalo meat. Just as we were finishing the meal, I looked up, and there in the tent door stood Village Maker. His face, as he surveyed the group, wore a kindly smile. After standing perfectly motionless a moment he remarked to us all:

"You have had a good time, but you have stayed too long."

Two minutes later the tent was vacant; silence reigned supreme. As I walked away, I saw in the east the first streaks of dawn. We had made a night of it.

Going to my tent, I wrapped myself in my robes and soon was fast asleep. When I woke, the sun was sinking behind the treetops. I heard drums beating in two or three directions. My first movement was to stretch out my arms. Instantly, at that very slight sound, my tent flap was thrown back and a young man glided in.

"I was the first one in after you woke up, wasn't I?" he asked.

"Why, yes," I assured him, "for I'm hardly awake yet. Why do you ask?"

"Little Chief and Swift Walker both want you to come to their clubs tonight, but I've asked you first."

"I'll go to yours, then."

"Oh, it's not my club. It's Prairie Chicken's. He sent me to ask you."

"Then tell him I'll come."

A woman and a little boy came into my tent, one carrying a large bowl of ground beans (beans that grow underground), boiled with corn and meat, and the other a smaller bowl of soup. All the food was smoking hot, it was a meal good enough for anyone.

When I had eaten, I walked over to Prairie Chicken's club —in a larger tent than that of the night before and with more persons present. They were chatting, laughing, and making merry; some were playing odd and even, some telling stories, some quietly looking on. All the while the drummers were furiously pounding the drums. The guest's place was vacant, awaiting my arrival. I was given dried meat, fruit, and nuts, which I made a pretense of eating. According to Indian etiquette, I carefully put away in my pouch what was left.

The man who sat on my right, and whose duty it was to look after my comfort and entertainment, was the very opposite of Two Bears (who had performed a similar service for me the night before) in both appearance and demeanor. He was tall and sinewy, courtly and graceful. His good breeding would have commanded respect in any drawing room. He wore little paint and few ornaments—only enough not to seem *outré* among his own people.

Soon after my arrival the tent was cleared and the dancing began. First the young men performed, gaily painted and covered with bells. Then followed a masque dance, like the one of the previous night, except that in this case the young men disguised themselves, retiring for the purpose to a small tent pitched close by.

Meanwhile the girls formed a circle and, joining hands, danced around and around. The young men returned, each with his features completely concealed by the head of some animal such as a fox or a bear. The girls opened their circle; the young men passed inside it and stood together. When the girls had circled about them once, a young man parted the hands of two and took his place between them in the ring; another did the same in the next round, and another in the next, until all the men had been taken into the circle.

Then the music stopped. Each young man whispered one of the twelve names into the ear of the girl on his right. If he had guessed correctly, he kept his place in the ring; if not, he must go back into the center. This process was repeated four times, then the young men who had failed to guess right were forced to wear their disguises for the remainder of the night. When the dance closed, four unfortunates were left standing —the butt of numerous jokes which they took good-naturedly and as a matter of course.

As a bit of courteous forethought I had been told that, as this dance was for my especial entertainment, I was expected only to look on. Thus I was gracefully saved from being one of the unfortunates.

In the feasting which followed the viands were much the same as on the night before—except for a great surprise, sprung upon the whole party in the midst of the feast as an honor to the guest. Four women entered with four large bowls filled with genuine white biscuits made out of wheaten flour—almost as rare and costly a treat there and then as peacocks' tongues at the great dinners of old Rome.

After the feast came stories. Near me sat a bright, intelligent-looking girl who wore the tattoo mark of a chief's daughter. She asked me if my own tribe did not know some dances different from those I had seen here. I replied:

"Yes, many different ones."

"Do teach us some," urged a half-dozen Indians at once.

I told them that the great difficulty would be the music, which had a time and movement entirely different from theirs.

"Then teach us the music," begged the chief's daughter. "Persons who sing and dance can learn it quickly."

A drum was brought to me; I whistled a little waltz, keeping time on the drum. As they seemed delighted, I repeated it several times. Soon the drummers caught the movement, but the female singers made an utter failure of it. Just then someone called out:

"There's a girl here who says she can sing that!"

"Where is she? Come out here!" cried three or four at once.

The girl came forward and sang the tune to Indian words. I was astonished.

"Where did you learn that?" I demanded.

"When we went to visit the Cataho." She named a tribe who lived far toward the west and of whom I had never heard.

"Where did they learn it?"

"I don't know. They said it was one of their songs."

"But the words! When did you learn those?"

"The words are nothing. I made them up myself."

"Well!" I said to myself. "This beats all! A wild Indian girl singing a waltz tune learned from other wild Indians! Surely there's nothing new under the sun if this isn't new."

Afterward I found out that it was not new; some of the Rocky Mountain Indians have a waltz time to some of their dance music.

The girl sang, the drums beat, the male voices soon caught the movement. Here was the music for a waltz—and I was in a pretty predicament. I had had no thought of teaching these Indians to waltz, but now I saw no way of escape.

"Teach us the dance! Teach us the dance!" came to me from all sides at once.

They had cleared the floor; everyone was waiting; I could do nothing but go ahead. Taking the chief's daughter by the hand, I led her out from among her companions. In less than ten minutes we were whirling through the tent in the ecstatic delight which youth, health, and the waltz, combined, alone can produce. The whole group was wild with excitement. Other couples tried it; and soon the tent was filled with pairs of Indians whirling around in a half-civilized, half-barbaric style that seemed to take all our senses away.

The news that a new dance was going on brought in scores of spectators. More wood was piled on the fire, the edge of the tent was thrown up all around, to give a better view to those who could not get in. At first these onlookers merely beat time to the music with their feet; then, two by two, other couples, some male and female, some with both dancers of one sex, joined in. More singers caught the tune, more drums were brought out; the crowd increased until half the village was waltzing around Prairie Chicken's tent. Everywhere were shouts of laughter, screams of delight, the racket of drums. Finally the old men and women, long sound asleep in their tents, wakened by the uproar, came crawling out to see what had caused such a hubbub at midnight in their peaceful camp.

When they saw their daughters enfolded in the arms of young men, threading with flying feet the dizzy mazes of the waltz, their first impression was that we were all drunk. One old woman caught her granddaughter and, pulling her away from her partner, gave her a good shaking.

"I never expected to live to see our family so disgraced," she wailed.

Next day nothing was thought of or talked of but the new dance. The young people were mad over it; for three weeks they did nothing but waltz. White people sometimes say that a tune is "worn out," but I do not believe that that is possible, for if a tune could ever be worn out, there would have been nothing left of that poor little waltz after the first week.

From the start the older folk had looked with disfavor on the new dance. Gradually the opposition to it grew so strong that a general council was held to decide what should be done. Here the waltz met its fate. The old, wise men decided that it was "dangerous and indecent." They prohibited it in their tribe for "as long as the grass grows and the waters run." But the young folk, as they went back to the simple games and dances of their forefathers, bade good-by with many a regret to that bit of civilization.

It was now near the middle of a very severe winter. Provisions grew scarcer; the invitations to "come and eat" were extended less often. Food in an Indian village always belongs to the women, who distribute it as best suits themselves. They look after their children first—then, if anything is left, the men get it. Soon nearly everything eatable had been consumed, and no one had enough food except when some small hunting party which had been fortunate enough to get an antelope or an elk came back. These men who brought in meat were hailed as heroes, and for days were made much of by those who had been hungry. For some time now many families had been waking up in the morning and finding nothing at all in the tent to eat. Things had come to such a pass that the greater part of the tribe were begging from each other.

9.

We Seek Buffalo Meat

One day I heard the old crier going around the camp, calling something which, so far as I could make out, was that Village Maker had summoned a council to decide when the winter hunt should begin. No one seemed to notice the old man as he made the circuit of the camp four times, steadily repeating that one set of words, but after his fourth round I saw the chiefs, carrying the great pipe, gather in a tent. Then in a long series of ceremonies which lasted four days everything was done which they believed would insure the success of the hunt. I had no part in these ceremonies and, in spite of the Indians' politeness, I could see plainly that they did not want me to go on the hunt. All those four days I had very little to eat, and probably should have had nothing whatever but for the kindness of Meepee, my partner Sunshine's mother.

Three or four more days passed in making preparations, and during them the Indians were running hither and thither all the time in a continuous uproar. I noticed that one of the members of the Soldier Lodge, although he was not a chief, seemed suddenly to have become the greatest man of the village. All sorts of honors were paid to him, his food was cooked and brought to him before anyone else was served, and he always had several courtiers close to him, waiting to obey his slightest command. Then I learned that he had been made the *nudunaga*, the leader appointed for the hunt, whom it was death to disobey.

One morning all the Indians began to move up the river—some on foot, some on horseback, some alone, some in squads—gaily painted young men, finely mounted, and older men who trudged along in the rear through the snow, yelping dogs, scolding women, and ponies laden with tent poles and camp equipage. No uninitiated observer could have dreamed that such a cavalcade had a leader and a perfectly planned organization. They did not even march in ranks, for some followed the main trail, some started off nearly at right angles to it, some lingered far behind. Yet each one knew the exact spot in relation to the others where he or she would sleep that night.

After traveling about twenty miles the foremost Indians reached the designated camping place before sundown; the last ones did not arrive until nearly midnight. About a third of the band had no regular tents, so these unfortunates—and I was one of them—scraped away the snow from the leeward side of logs or thick bushes and, wrapping themselves in blankets or robes, slept in the open air.

Those of us who had no womenfolk had rather a hard time of it. We slept in the snow; we had nothing to eat, because all the food belonged to the women, who gave it away, when they did, with an air of importance which indicated that such poor, helpless creatures as men would all have starved to death long ago if the women had not taken care of them.

Next morning I went to the tent of Two Bears, because he had his wife with him, but while I was still outside, I heard her scolding him fearfully. She told him he was a lazy, good-for-nothing old rascal who did nothing but dance and eat.

"Look at our pony!" she stormed. "Our only pony! It's so poor it can hardly walk, just because you've been too lazy to take care of it! All winter long you've kept it tied up while you were at dances. I expect it will die before we get back from the hunt!" And so on, and on.

Through the tent flap, which was drawn a little to one side, I caught sight of Two Bears sitting by his fire and answering back not one word. While I stood there, one of my young friends came up and suggested:

"Go on in there."

"I rather think I won't," I told him.

"She'll give you plenty to eat."

"She's more likely to tell me to clear out."

"Then I'll go in." And in he went.

Without waiting to see the result I walked on. Though I stood for a while near two or three different campfires, no one told me to "come and eat." Presently I saw the women taking down their tents and the men mounting their horses. The order to move on had been issued. I drew my belt up a notch or two, mounted Old Titus, and rode along. Hunger seemed to heighten my every sense until no sound or motion within the range of my sight or hearing escaped me. We were marching northwest, and all day long a snowstorm beat in our faces.

Once I deliberately wandered far off the route in search of game, and stopped for more than an hour in a patch of rushes to let Old Titus feed. When I picked up the trail again, I saw just ahead of me five or six women trudging along through the snow. Another followed them a good way behind.

I heard one woman call back to this loiterer:

"Hurry up, Daughter! It's not very far to camp now!"

All the women carried packs on their backs and showed that they were wearied by walking through the snow against the wind.

As I rode up, I saw that the lagging one was that fairylike little Sunshine, who had been my partner at Two Bears' dance. She could barely stagger along. Indian etiquette, which deems it an unpardonable crime for a young man to address a girl on a trail or highway, forbade my speaking to her. I rode past all the women and dismounted. When the main group reached me, I said to the nearest of them:

"Mother, the young girl is exhausted; she can never walk to camp. Take my horse. He's strong and he has just had a good meal of rushes."

The woman held up both her hands and bowed her head, thus giving the Indian gesture of thankfulness.

"My son," she replied, "we were afraid and tired out."

I handed her the rein of my bridle and walked on. In a few minutes the women had used their hatchets to cut two long poles, had fastened them, one trailing back from each side of my saddle, had tied a blanket between them and had placed Sunshine and their packs upon this travois. Then they marched swiftly after me along the trail. I saw that because I was weak and faint from lack of food they could travel faster than I, so I stepped to one side and hid in the bushes to let them pass.

Few of us reached the camping place that night until after dark—and I was one of the last of all to arrive. I sat down by a big fire which some of the young men had built. They soon went away to rest, and I sat on alone; but just as I was preparing to lie down, I heard the welcome words:

"Come and eat."

I followed a vanishing form through the darkness until I reached the group called "End People." There against a sheltering bank Sunshine and her family had built a roof of branches with a fire in front of it. They had felled quite a large cottonwood tree, and Old Titus was foraging on the bark of its limbs. Though not a word was said on the subject, I knew from the seat I was requested to take that for the remainder of the hunt I was to be the guest of that family.

A great pile of *nuskeda*—sweet potatoes which grow in wet, springy places and are not injured by frost—was in one corner of the bower. It was the search for these roots and the task of digging them that had delayed the women, who also had brought them many miles through the snow in their packs. A good supply of these potatoes was roasting in the fire, and I soon received more than I could eat. Both from etiquette and because I had no idea whence or when my next meal would come, I stowed what was left of my portion in my pouch. Such reasons are the basis of the custom by which every Indian, when given food, always carries away with him all that he cannot eat on the spot.

We had many callers that evening, and all were fed. Though the sleeping place assigned to me later was as sheltered as possible, the night was so cold that, when the fire burned out, I woke. I rose to pile on more wood and then, after waiting to warm myself, lay down again. In the morning I found that, while I slept, someone had spread another blanket over me. I folded it and laid it by the pile of *nuskeda*. While I was in sight, no one touched it, but after I went away, its owner came and got it.

That day we pushed on, traveling steadily until late into the night. Even then no regular camp was made and no tents were pitched. Instead, tent skins, robes, and blankets were spread around three great fires, and we all lay down in circles with our feet toward the warmth. After sleeping only two or three hours we hurried on. Very few had eaten anything that day.

By two o'clock in the afternoon the advance group reached a thickly timbered spot and made camp in the dense forest. A stream dashed by over a sandy bed; there were large quantities of dry wood lying about. Nearby was a low bottom, almost surrounded by hills and covered with a dense growth of the rushes which would fatten our horses more quickly than any amount of grain. And now the buffalo could not be far away.

I was among the first to arrive, but as hunger had made me restless, I mounted Old Titus again and rode across a low range of hills to a much larger stream. All the time I was straining both eyes and ears in search of game. I realized that I was the best-armed person in the whole party because I had not only a good breech-loading Sharp's rifle but also two six-inch Colt revolvers, one of the best weapons ever invented.

Toward night I saw one single turkey track. I hitched Old Titus and crept silently through the bushes, following that track for over half a mile until I found the flock roosting in a low tree. I took out both my revolvers and cocked them; I also cocked my rifle and laid it by my right side. Then I fired three shots in rapid succession and got two turkeys. The rest of them flew a short distance and alighted in some low undergrowth. Again, noiseless as a panther and alert as a famished wolf, I followed. Taking out the turkey bone I carried for this purpose, I sounded a call on it. I caught answers from two or three directions. So I prepared my weapons as before and kept on calling until the turkeys drew near enough for me to shoot two more of them. Then I threw all four birds across Old Titus and rode swiftly back to camp.

Although my adopted family had not arrived when I had ridden away, I knew exactly where to find them. When I reached camp, nearly everyone was asleep. Only one woman, Sunshine's mother, Meepee, sat by the fire in front of the little tent and the shelter of boughs.

"Mother," I told her, "I've brought you some meat."

At first she looked incredulous, but when I pulled my four turkeys from Old Titus's back and threw them at her feet, she raised her hand to her mouth and made the peculiar intonation by which Indians express surprise. Then she darted into the tent and returned with Sunshine and another woman. In a moment they had unsaddled my horse, spread a robe for me on the ground in front of the fire, and arranged my saddle for a

pillow. One of the women led Old Titus away, the other two
skinned two of the birds, and in less than ten minutes they had
the turkeys roasting before the flames.

The next morning before daylight two or three groups were
sent out to look for buffalo. These scouts were forbidden to kill
or attempt to kill any game, and were under strict orders, if
they made a discovery, to return to camp with the report, so
that all the hunters might start out together with an equal
chance of success.

Very early I was invited to the tent of the *nudunaga*
who gave me food and presented me with an eagle feather,
the regulation honor conferred upon the man who has brought
in the first game on a hunt. Everywhere, I found, I was received with great respect, and some of the Indians were inclined to apologize for the shabby treatment they had given me
for the past few days. We did not know then that on this very
day a further bit of sheer good luck was to place me temporarily
almost on the pinnacle of local fame.

About noon one of the scoutgroups reported that it had discovered buffalo five miles to the southwest. Instantly the camp
was thrilled with exactly such intense, deadly excitement as
one sees on the stock exchange when prices fluctuate wildly
and men's fortunes are lost and won with every click of the
ticker. We saw before us, not sport, but a most serious business,
with life itself hanging on the issue.

Some of the Indians were pale and trembling; some were
dignified and moved with unusual slowness; some ran about,
hardly knowing what they were doing. The *nudunaga*, who
was the first to mount, sat quietly on his horse until, amid much
confusion, all the hunters were ready. Some carried rifles, some
bows and arrows, and a few had revolvers. As we rode out of
camp, the women followed us afoot. Four men were sent to a

hilltop to make smoke signals to call back all the other scouts.

Because the wind blew from the north, the *nudunaga* made a detour to bring us up to the buffalo from the south. He kept us constantly in ravines and under cover of the hills. Just as we swung northward, I saw five antelope, who stood still, some thousand yards away, looking at us. I asked a member of the Soldier Lodge if I might shoot at them.

"No," he answered. "They're too far away and you might frighten the buffalo."

After a moment I rode up to ask the *nudunaga* for permission to fire at them, explaining that, as the wind was blowing toward us from the buffalo, the latter could not possibly hear the report of my rifle. In substance his reply was this:

"My friend is young, but he should not be foolish. It is impossible to kill an animal so far away. Why should you waste your ammunition when you can get no more until you return to the trader? However, if you wish to be foolish, you may fire once."

I leaped from my horse, raised the rear sight of my target rifle to its highest point, and took aim, more at the center of the flock than at any one animal. Then I carefully raised the gun to a point which I judged was twenty feet above them—and fired. One antelope fell; the rest fled. Though my success was the veriest accident, I did not tell my companions so. I merely left them to form their own conclusions.

The amazed *nudunaga* looked from me to the dead antelope, which was only a speck on the white snow. He exclaimed:

"Men have told me of guns that shoot for miles, but I never believed them. I always thought they were liars!"

Meepee, as the mother of my family, was so wild with delight that it took a sharp reprimand from one of the Soldier Lodge members to keep her quiet. She and another woman started off at once to bring in the game. That night she told me that the bullet had struck the antelope on its jugular vein, and had penetrated the flesh only a little more than an inch. This shot was the first step toward my being admitted later to several of the Indians' secret societies.

We had reached the base of a low, pointed bluff which rose up out of the plain. Atop of it, where the wind had blown the grass clear of snow, a herd of buffalo was feeding. Thus far on the hunt the Indians had followed a go-as-you-please method; now everything was reduced to the strictest order, with death as the sure penalty for disobedience.

The "head soldier" of the expedition advanced up the point of the bluff to a position which commanded the valleys that diverged there, one on each side of the point. The *nudunaga* now divided the hunters into two equal parties, one led by him, the other by a soldier. Then each division, governed by signals from the "head soldier," who, watching both bands, could thus direct them to keep abreast, advanced silently up a valley. Therefore, when at last we all were given the signal to charge, we dashed upon the herd from the rear and from both flanks simultaneously. The buffalo, thrown into great confusion, ran into and over one another for a few frantic moments—which the Indians used to every possible advantage. Then the whole herd rolled away northward.

For a white man, mounted on a good horse and armed with revolvers or a repeating rifle, to kill a buffalo requires very little courage or skill, but for an Indian, though mounted on the best of their ponies, to kill a buffalo with a bow and arrow requires bravery, skill, and great strength of arm. I deserved no credit for killing seven buffalo that day, while the *nudunaga* killed only three, but it is the way of the world that I received the greater glory.

About two hours after the first shot had been fired, the *nudunaga* recalled his men by blanket signals waved from the highest point in the vicinity. He did not want the buffalo

chased out of reach. Meanwhile the women, who had followed
our ranks, had been skinning the slain animals and cutting up
the meat. Poor old Meepee! I shall never forget the look of
triumphant joy that lighted up her honest old face, so wrinkled
with toil and bronzed and hardened by exposure. And how
little Sunshine's eyes were sparkling! With what eagerness she
helped her mother!

"You are brave!" she told me. "Very brave! Why didn't you
tell us that you could hunt before we started out?"

Meepee's family owned only two ponies, both too old to be
of much service, and her husband was lame. Nevertheless,
poorly mounted though he was, he had killed one buffalo with
his bow and arrow. I told Sunshine:

"Your father is far braver than I. He is old and lame—and
yet with that poor old pony and a bow and arrow he killed
one buffalo. I am young. I have a big horse, two revolvers, and
a rifle."

As I did not see her father anywhere, I asked her where he
was.

"He's gone to camp," she answered, "to get another pony;
there's more meat here than both of ours can carry."

So I told her to take Old Titus and load some of the meat on
him while I returned to camp on foot. Soon after I reached the
shelter, Meepee and Sunshine came leading in the three horses
loaded with meat. Meepee, with two other women to help her,
then started back with the horses for another load. Sunshine
was left to take care of the meat they had brought in already.

Next morning a mountain of meat—more than Meepee had
ever had in all her life before at one time—lay piled beside our
little tent. I well remember with what a royal air she gave away
large quantities to those unfortunates who had not succeeded
in killing even one buffalo.

That was perhaps the proudest moment of her life. Her husband was lame, her family poor; heretofore she had been a

recipient and not a donor. But a donor is the highest position an Indian can achieve. Now she was the disburser of bounteous gifts. She stood at the summit of housewifely distinction. Though many years have fled since then, it is even now a great comfort to me to think of Meepee's moment of happiness. From that day on she exerted herself to show her gratitude in every possible way. She would not let me do the slightest service of any sort. If she saw me carrying a stick of wood, she would take it from me, reproaching me for disgracing her by doing work which was her duty to do.

According to Indian custom the robes would be my especial property—not given away while on the hunt, but retained by the hunter himself. Meepee and Sunshine toiled at them night and day to prepare them for my use. Though a great deal of hard work goes into merely tanning a buffalo robe, Meepee was not satisfied to stop there. She ornamented them with paint, beads, and porcupine quills, which, seldom carried on a hunt and hence hard to obtain then, she chiefly begged from the other women.

For days thereafter we remained in camp. The women dried and smoked the meat, and worked on the robes; the men feasted, danced, made arrows, and tended the many traps set both in the stream near us and in the larger one to the north. It is very hard work to tend traps, for those who own them must "make the rounds" every day, walking several miles through snow and often wading through wet and marshy places. The women did not do all the work by any means; on any hunt there is a pretty fair division of labor between the two groups.

10.

Two Bears and I Become Koo-Bay

One day our scouts reported buffalo about ten miles to the northwest on the divide between two streams. Though the news caused great confusion and hurrying to and fro, there was none of the wild excitement of that first discovery, when many had eaten nothing for two or three days and the life of the band had depended upon success. Now that we had plenty to eat, the hunt was a mere matter of business.

We rode upstream under cover of timber and hills until we reached a point southwest of the herd, where the wind blew toward us. There the *nudunaga* called a halt, and sent a soldier to crawl up the bluff, peer over its top, and return to tell us how far away the herd was. He reported that it was at least two miles beyond the crest of the bluff and that the land between had no ravines or depressions to serve us for cover. He had hardly finished speaking when everyone but the head soldier and the *nudunaga* broke out into loud and excited discussion. Most of them talked in a high falsetto, a dozen at a time. I soon found out the trouble. Many of them were mounted on very poor and weak ponies. If we all rode to the high ground and made a dash for the herd, only those who had the best ponies would get any buffalo. On the other hand, if we went back on our tracks in order to approach by a ravine to windward of the herd, the buffalo would probably scent us and be off before we could come within reach of them. Nevertheless the men who had weak ponies were advocating the latter plan.

After they had talked and talked till all were out of breath, both parties appealed to the *nudunaga*. I had noticed that, though he took no part in the discussion, he listened very closely to every word. Now he sat silent in his saddle for a moment, while all the hunters kept absolutely still. Then with a gesture he brought the head soldier to him.

"My son," he questioned, "if we ride up slowly from this side, do you think we could drive the herd right down the bluffs, and then overtake it in the deep snow that the wind has surely been piling up over there?"

Not another word was said; our whole party started off uphill. My post was on the extreme left, and near me rode Two Bears on his discouraged-looking old pony. One glance at it confirmed the soundness of his wife's prediction that it would die before we got back from the winter's hunting. Its rider was as jolly as ever. He asserted that he was going to pick out the finest buffalo in the herd and run it down, just to show me that pony's speed.

"I brought along some meat," he added.

"I suppose you thought you wouldn't get back from this chase before spring," I chaffed him. "If I rode that horse, I'd carry a week's provisions every time I went out."

"I'll tell you a secret," he confided. "I'm going on the war-path. On this horse I can reach the Sioux in three days, dash into their camp, cut out ten or fifteen horses, and be gone before they can wake up. You've never seen him run."

"No; and I don't think anyone else has for the last twenty or thirty years."

"Have some of this." He took from a fold of his blanket about five pounds of jerked meat. "You'll be hungry before you get back."

He cut the piece in two and gave me half.

"Where did you get it?" I asked.

"Meepee gave it to me."

"How many arrows have you?"

"Four—only three of them are not very good."

"How many buffalo do you expect to kill with those arrows?"

"Maybe one."

"Why didn't you make more while we were in camp?"

"I was going to, but Black Eagle and Prairie Chicken both killed buffalo the last day we were out, and each of them had a feast and a dance, and that took two days, and another day I went with No Knife to look at his traps."

"What did you do all the rest of the time?"

"I was tired and rested."

"If I should lend you one of my revolvers, do you think you could kill a buffalo with it?"

"Kill one buffalo? Why, I'd kill six! You just let me try!" His eyes sparkled and his face gleamed with joy at the thought.

"Then here it is."

He thrust the revolver into his belt. Excitedly he urged his pony into a trot and pushed ahead of the line until one of the soldiers called to him:

"What do you mean? Have you gone crazy? Get back with the others."

Two Bears came back even quicker than he had gone forward. We all were proceeding uphill very slowly, obeying the signals of the leader. The buffalo, who were still feeding, did not seem to notice us until we were quite near. Then they suddenly galloped off, going over the bluffs toward the north. Our whole party dashed after them, and in a few moments the best-mounted riders overtook them. The herd broke up into scattered bunches. I chased after a few who went to the left. When they had run along the top of the bluff for some distance, they plunged down a ravine, which soon turned sharply. There a buffalo, blinded with the snow, rushed pell-mell against the bank ahead of him—and wheeled at bay. Before I could check Old Titus's speed, I was almost onto the creature.

Titus leaped to one side into a gully and sank into ten feet or more of snow, where at first he plunged about frantically. Then he lay still in despair. About a hundred feet away stood that old bull, glaring at me with bloodshot eyes. I knew that if Titus made the slightest motion, it would promptly be all over with us. Down that old bull would charge, and we should be smothered in the snow. After studying me for a long moment the bull turned away to walk on down the ravine. As he rounded the bank, he presented his side to me—and I sent a rifle ball through his heart.

Then I began to tread down the snow around Old Titus to give him a firm footing for climbing out of the gully. After a few exhausting minutes I stopped to take breath. Glancing up the ravine, I saw Meepee and Sunshine coming on their ponies following my trail, ready to take care of the game they were sure I should kill.

When Sunshine saw me, all covered with snow, tramping up and down there like a man in a treadmill, while Old Titus floundered about beside me, she began to laugh. Meepee, turning on her in a rage, struck at her with a riding whip.

"You're the most ill-mannered thing I ever saw in my life!" she scolded. "Instead of sitting there laughing, you'd better get down and help that horse out."

Sunshine's answer was a most unearthly scream. Instantly she, Meepee, and their two ponies came tumbling into the deep snow on top of me. Ten or twelve more buffalo had come rushing down the ravine behind them. As the bank on the other side was steep and high, my gully was the only refuge.

For a moment I thought that my time to start for the happy hunting grounds had arrived. One of the ponies was directly on top of me, but fortunately, after two or three breathless struggles of mine had failed to free me, he rolled off of his own accord, and I could lift my head up out of the snow. Full of wrath, I crawled up to higher ground, but I had hardly taken one good breath when I heard a new noise coming down the ravine.

"Ho!" I thought. "Now for more buffalo!"

So I leaped back again into the snow and sank in it to my neck. Then I looked around to see Two Bears coming, pounding his pony and swinging his revolver. His fat sides were shaking; his eyes were wild with excitement. On that down grade the old pony was making considerable speed. Two Bears did not notice us in our gully until I called to him. Then, when he saw my head just sticking up out of the snow, and the ponies and the women floundering around beside me, he pulled up his pony and actually shook himself off it in a fit of laughter.

"Oh!" screamed Meepee. "You bad, fat, old big-eyed thing! What are you standing there laughing for?"

"You're the meanest man I ever saw," Sunshine added, joining in.

"Come help us get these horses out," I ordered, "or I'll take that revolver away from you!"

Two Bears laughed helplessly on.

"I wish his wife was here," Meepee exploded. "She'd make him start pretty quick."

"Oh, I'm coming," Two Bears gasped, "just as soon as I hitch my horse."

"What's the use of hitching him?" she retorted. "He wouldn't run away if he could and couldn't run away if he would."

Finally Two Bears calmed down, and after half an hour of hard work we had all the horses out. Meepee and Sunshine halted their ponies beside the buffalo I had killed. Two Bears and I rode on down the ravine.

"Let me go on ahead," Two Bears begged. "It's only fair. You've killed one buffalo already. Let me have the first chance."

"All right," I agreed. "You go on; I'll wait here till you have a good lead."

Two Bears rode down through the ravine and out onto the broad bottom land where there stood a grove of timber. Through this grove ran another deep ravine, very steep on the near side, but with an easier slope to its opposite bank. As I rode slowly after Two Bears, I watched him trying to cross the gap. Just when he had made the descent, with that steep bank behind him to stop his turning back, he glanced ahead up the opposite slope. There at its top stood a shaggy old buffalo, looking down at him. Two Bears jerked out his revolver, half cocked it, and began to pull at the trigger with all his might. He did not know that a revolver will not go off at half-cock.

"*Pazhe!*" he sputtered. (Thus a very angry Indian always contracts their lone swear word, *pe-ah-zhe*, which means "bad.") Then, addressing the old bull, who seemed to be complacently studying the situation, he began a formal speech.

"My friend, I know you own this country and all the grass that grows here. I have heard of you and have come a long way to pipe-dance you. I have come a long way, for I want us to be friends." Here he gave another hard pull at the trigger. "Now if you'll just walk away so I can get out of this ditch, I'll go with you and we'll make a lasting peace." Another jerk at the trigger. "And neither of us will ever go on the warpath again. I will eat nuts and birds' eggs and wild potatoes—and you shall have all the grass. My friend, we shall be brothers, not enemies."

The old buffalo shook his head but stood still.

"I am a great chief," Two Bears went on. "I have four hundred lodges in my band, and all the tribe shall make peace. We all have heard of you and admire you very much. We will never harm you." He turned the revolver bottom side up and jerked the trigger again, saying, "I speak the truth."

The old buffalo turned to walk away. I shot him through the heart and he fell in his tracks. Two Bears rode up the slope and stopped there, looking down at the dead bull. In his excitement he had not heard the report of my rifle, but he was at no loss to account for that buffalo's death.

"I was *koo-bay*," said he.

What shall I say to the reader about *koo-bay?* There is in English no word or combination of words which can express its meaning. More than that, even the idea it represents was never conceived by a white man. *Koo-bay* has been translated as "medicine," "magic," "power," "miracle," "witchcraft," "holy," and many other words. Every Indian tongue has a word of the same meaning, but so far as I have been able to investigate the subject, no written language, ancient or modern, has any equivalent word or phrase.

If one wishes to conceive the true meaning of this word *koo-bay,* let him put aside everything suggested to his mind by the words magic, sorcery, witchcraft, necromancy, conjuration, or enchantment. When an Indian says that he is *koo-bay,* no other Indian would think of him as assisted by God, evil spirits, good spirits, or the devil. These have no connection with *koo-bay;* yet a man who is *koo-bay* has the power to do supernatural or miraculous things.

"I was *koo-bay*," announced Two Bears. "I turned this mad buffalo away, and he lay down and died."

"He didn't die until I shot him," I asserted.

"You didn't shoot him. I was *koo-bay* and killed him."

"But don't you see the blood coming from his nose? Come on this side and you can see the bullet hole."

When he came around and saw the hole, his surprise was intense.

"I didn't hear you shoot," he insisted.

"Well, I did shoot, and that was what killed him."

"I was *koo-bay*, or he never would have turned away when I was in the ravine."

We stood arguing there for some minutes. That he should have turned the buffalo away by *koo-bay* seemed to him wholly natural and normal, but that I should have fired my rifle so close to him and he have failed to hear it he considered a matter which could only be accounted for by the interference of the *wa-nach-e* (ghosts).

We rode away across the bottom, while the wind blew nearly a gale from the northeast. We saw a few buffalo going along up the other side of the river, keeping under shelter of the bluffs. Most of the herd evidently had gone downstream, for every now and then we could faintly hear a shot in that direction.

"How many are there in that bunch going up the river?" I asked.

Two Bears, looking at them more carefully, answered, "About ten."

"They're mine," I told him, "and I shall kill every one of them.

"I'm koo-bay," I continued very slowly. "You see that timber far away on the other side of the river. I will send the buffalo there and make them stand still while I shoot them."

"But those trees are nearly half a camp away," he protested.

"My horse is koo-bay too, and he will go there while you go back to where Meepee is. Tell the women to come right on after me and leave the buffalo that I killed last. He is old and tough and his robe is not good. These that I shall kill are young and tender and their robes are good."

Two Bears rode away without a word.

Putting Old Titus to his best speed, I rode up the river, keeping those buffalo in sight. Though it was farther to the timber than I had thought, the buffalo, as I had foreseen, went into it for shelter from the cold wind. They passed around to the southwest border of the grove and stopped in a bunch together, with their heads turned away from the wind. As I was south of them, I had their sides toward me. After hiding my horse, I crawled up to within three hundred yards of them, but could not go any nearer without risk of being seen. I intended to practice tactics which every old hunter knows. I realized that while the wind was blowing such a gale and roaring through the trees behind them, they could not hear the report of my rifle. If one of them dropped, the others would merely think that it had lain down. I aimed at the one in front—and saw the snow fly up at least two feet ahead of it. I had not allowed for the variation caused by that strong wind. It was a clean miss. However, if I had shot at a rear buffalo, I should merely have wounded one of those in front, and then they would all have been off and away together. In my next shots I used more judgment—and nine of the group had fallen, one after the other, before the remaining four started off. Two Bears had been wrong; there were thirteen of them instead of ten.

11.

Promoted

I built a big fire and waited for Two Bears, Meepee, and Sunshine. None of them arrived until long after dark, and then, instead of Sunshine, who had been sent back to camp with my first buffalo loaded on her pony, came Two Bears' cross old wife.

The two women, setting to work with their small axes and large knives, soon finished a comfortable little house to shelter us men. They themselves did not come inside because they had nine buffalo to skin and cut up. If these were left intact until morning, they would be frozen as hard as stone. As the women skinned each buffalo, they threw its robe around our bush tent, so that before morning we had the warmest place in that whole region to live in. Those two women must have worked nearly all night, but when I woke in the morning, they were sitting on the far side of the fire, talking in whispers so as not to disturb me, and roasting the choicest bits of the buffalo for my breakfast.

While I was eating, Meepee disappeared—yes, disappeared is the proper word, for it has often seemed to me that Indians do not go away, but vanish. One moment you are talking to a warrior; the next moment you look up and he is gone. The moccasin makes no noise, neither does the opening or shutting of the tent door. The only way to be sure of an Indian's presence is never to take your eyes off him.

Meepee did not come back for nearly two hours, and then she looked decidedly weary.

"Where have you been?" I asked her.

"There's a place about half an hour from here where wheat grass grows. I took the horses there to lariat them, but I had to tramp a trail through deep drifts."

"You'd better lie down and sleep now."

"I will for a little while," she agreed.

As she lay down, Two Bears woke up. His wife cooked his breakfast and gave it to him, telling him all the while what a mean, lazy, good-for-nothing, fat old thing he was. He ate and went to sleep again, but she continued to scold him long after he was snoring.

Meepee slept less than an hour, then she rose, brushed her hair, and asked me what she should do. After a moment of surprise at this new importance of mine I told her:

"There are nine buffalo. I give Two Bears' wife four of them and you five."

Both women raised their hands, bowed their heads, and thanked me.

"Now," I added, "I'll go back to the camp."

"Why not stay here in the tent, today?" Meepee suggested. "Having killed so many buffalo, you must be tired."

"What will you do?" I asked.

"We'll go back to the camp and bring some women here to help us cure the meat and tan the hides. But we'll leave you plenty of wood here to keep you warm."

For an hour or so I smoked and rested. Then I tired of it. The only sounds were the wild howling of the wind and the snoring of Two Bears. When I went out of the tent, I could see only the treeless stretches around us and the bluffs beyond. Though the sky was clear and the sun was shining, the air was so full of drifting snow that the landscape looked dreary and indistinct. All was loneliness and desolation. I went back into the tent; Two Bears was still sleeping.

"Wake up!" I shouted. "There are ten thousand ghosts wailing around here."

Two Bears slowly raised his head and glanced about the tent. "Where is she?" he asked.

"Oh, get up! She's gone back to the camp."

"Good!" he ejaculated.

Then he took his pipe, filled it, and handed it to me to light. Pretty soon he began to laugh.

"What are you laughing about?" I questioned glumly.

"I was remembering how Chazaninga got us all into a pretty scrape last year."

"How?"

"The Comanches invited us to visit them and pipe-dance— so about four hundred of us went. We had the same *nudunaga* as now. It was eighteen camps to their village. When we got there, they treated us well. They gave us about three hundred horses as presents, and eighty more in exchange for goods we had brought. We were camped right inside their village. One night Chazaninga, who is very young" (and by "young," an Indian means "silly"), "in company with three others about his own age, slipped out of camp, stole about seventy-five horses and started home with them. Next morning, when the Comanches discovered their loss, they took from us all the horses they had given us and all those we had bought, and told us to go home. On our way we overtook Chazaninga and his helpers. The *nudunaga* took all the stolen horses away from them and distributed them among the rest of us, and had those four young fellows whipped."

"Served them right," I commented.

"The Comanches have been very bitter against us ever since," Two Bears went on, "and the *nudunaga* is afraid we may fall in with some of them on this hunt. Now and then they come up this way to kill buffalo."

"I wish they would come," I growled. "Anything would be better than lying here listening to that wind shriek. Let's go out and hunt jack rabbits."

"It's too much trouble," Two Bears objected.

"Then come look for the Comanches."

"Wait for Chazaninga; he'll go with you. He wants to kill a Comanche and seize his pony. He wants a wife."

"Why doesn't he get married, if he wants to?" I asked rather snappishly. I was losing patience.

"Because he has nothing to make presents with. He hasn't even one pony."

"Let's go hunt turkeys," I suggested, utterly bored.

"I'm too tired. You go, and I'll keep up a good fire to warm you when you come back."

As there was plainly no hope of getting him out of that shelter, I started out alone. When I left, Two Bears was sound asleep. I thought that the prospect of a good fire on my return was rather poor.

As I did not know where Meepee had left Old Titus, and was too lazy to follow her trail to look for him, I went off afoot and out of temper. As a result I shot badly and missed several antelope in succession. When at last I started back with the wind in my face, it was fearfully cold and growing colder. My feet were safe in well-furred buffalo-skin moccasins, and my hands in a piece of good fur, but I soon realized that in spite of my closely drawn blanket my face was freezing. In a sheltered spot I rubbed it with snow. Then I hastily built a fire and beside it, taking out my pouch, I covered my face with a thick coat of paint, which Meepee had given me. Now I could face that icy northern blast without harm. The heavy covering would not let my animal heat escape.

When I reached our shelter, I scarcely knew the place. I found eight tents there instead of one. Meepee had brought along her own relatives, her husband and his relatives, and Two Bears' kin besides. Chazaninga was one of the group. They all had heard of our store of meat and robes and had bright dreams of more to follow. All were feasting and having a good time. Meepee's husband met me and led me as his guest to a place especially prepared—a new, medium-sized tent covered with tanned skins. The snow around it had been cleared away. Inside it the ground on one side was covered with robes, on the other with dry grass. In the middle burned a roaring fire. On the outside of that tent my deeds since the start of the hunt were shown in picture writing. Other brave deeds still to be performed appeared there too. For one thing, I was pictured as starting on an expedition with nineteen warriors—twelve on horseback, seven afoot.

All these Indians were treating me after a new fashion. They addressed me by the very high title of "father" instead of by my former one of "friend." I was told that after I had eaten and rested, a council would be held here in my tent. The choicest food obtainable was brought to me. Then I slept, wrapped in warm furs.

As soon as I woke, all the men assembled for the council. The pipe had been passed around, and a middle-aged man rose to speak. He announced that the *nudunaga* had thought it best to divide the old camp into three parties—one to stay where it was; one to go over to the river to the south, two camps away; one to go farther up this river. My present companions, who made up this last group, had talked the matter all out already and had chosen me to be their *nudunaga*.

I replied that I was too young to assume such a position, and that it would be unbecoming conduct, seeing that there were others among them much older and wiser than I. To tell the truth, I had no mind to face the requirements of that honor, for

I knew that the leader of such a party must defend it, if need be, with his life. Moreover, no movement of any sort could be made without his orders. My final argument to the Indians was that, as the group included two or three members of the Soldier Lodge, it was the duty of one of them to become the *nudunaga*. That council was a long one with many speeches. One Indian, Wahan, insisted strongly that my refusal proved that I was wise and the proper one to lead them. Finally they offered, if I would accept, to take the necessary steps for admitting me to the Soldier Lodge, the secret society to which only their bravest men were admitted. The head soldier in a tribe has more power than any of its hereditary chiefs. I finally accepted on this basis. In due time I became a member of the lodge and learned there the most important part of what I know about the real life of the Indians.

Meanwhile, however, I realized fully that my election as *nudunaga* was promoted by the Indians' self-interest, for they are as self-seeking as other races. Unfortunately, like all uneducated people, they frequently do not know what their own best interests are. Thus because my breech-loading rifle was the first repeating arm they had ever seen, and because I had some skill in shooting, they believed that I could kill more buffalo than all the rest of them together. Now the *nudunaga* is expected to be liberal and, after a successful hunt, to give away almost all his own store. If I continued to be simply the guest of my adopted family, that family was likely to return home the richest in the tribe; but a *nudunaga* must treat all alike and could not confine his gifts to one family.

As soon as I had accepted the position, I began to exercise my authority, largely from curiosity to see if each of my orders really would be obeyed implicitly.

My first problem was settling a family quarrel. An Indian had struck his wife for accidentally spilling hot soup on his foot. I ordered him to go back to his tent and make his wife a present for having struck her when she did not deserve it. He obeyed me instantly.

As Two Bears and his wife were merely staying in a tent with some of his relations, I ordered him to put up a tent of his own. He went to find his wife and told her:

"The *nudunaga* says to put up our own tent."

"That's just what I told you, you lazy thing," she retorted. "But you would have me come in here, when I wanted to make my own tent."

Though I had expected a torrent of scolding to follow, she then went silently to work with all her might to pitch her tent. It took her an hour to scrape away the snow, put up the poles, place over them the heavy skin covering, and build the fire. It is work that no Indian man ever tries to do—and if he did try, the women would not allow it. When all was done, Two Bears' wife began to scold again.

"You miserable old Estinika!" she raged. (Estinika is a character in all the old legends who is always a fraud and a cheat. Indians apply the word to monkeys.) "You miserable old fraud!"

Two Bears silently pulled away at his pipe.

"There's not another man in the tribe who has not more than one wife!" (That was a sheer untruth.) "But you are so bad! bad! that you make me pitch the tent and do all the work alone and won't get another wife to help me. You mean old Estinika! I'll kill you!"

Thereupon she seized a stick and began to belabor Two Bears over the shoulders. He smoked on and did not move a muscle. When she tired of vainly pounding him, she ran screaming out of the tent, mounted the old pony, and told the world that she was going back to her relatives.

Two Bears refilled his pipe and smoked on. She rode off, fast as she could go. An hour or so later she rode back, went into the tent, and began cooking just as though nothing had happened.

Young though I was, I had sense enough not to try to exercise my new authority on that woman.

Yet whether official rank among the Indians is of life tenure, like a hereditary chieftainship, or held for only a few days, like the leadership of a hunting party or a band on the warpath, the incumbent of the office receives honor, obedience, and deference which gratify that ambition to rule which is instinctive in their race. My own official life was very brief. Three days later, with the coming of milder weather, many buffalo were reported on the south side of the river; I started out with "nineteen men and twelve horses," as the picture writing on my tent had foretold. We found a herd of countless thousands quietly feeding on the short buffalo grass. I called a halt, ordered a return to our camp, and sent runners to the old camp to ask the *nudunaga* to bring all his horses and men and join with us in a general attack. My own followers, though they obeyed me perfectly, never wholly forgave me for what they counted as an act of inexcusable folly. Why should not our band have attacked that herd alone, killed a large number of them, and then have had the glory of giving them away? My failure to do this was something they simply could not comprehend. Wahan and Chazaninga were especially bitter toward me. The only one with a word of excuse for me was Two Bears.

"Why shouldn't he?" he argued. "I suppose he was tired."

When the old *nudunaga* arrived the next morning with his own band of hunters, he took command of the whole party— and my little interval as ruler ended.

That day's hunt succeeded amazingly well. We drove a large herd of buffalo over a precipice where, as they fell to the bottom, they were smothered and killed by the score. We camped at this spot for several weeks while the women dried the meat and prepared the robes. At last, just as the earliest hints of spring began to appear, we started back—every woman, child, horse, and dog loaded down with every pound that each could carry. Even the little dogs that were hardly larger than big cats were loaded too. All the men except the *nudunaga* went afoot. Our cavalcade stretched out over the prairie for nearly two miles. Though our progress was slow, we traveled about twelve miles the first day.

12.

We Lose Sunshine

The next morning Two Bears' old pony would not get up. He had notions of his own about what he should and should not be required to do. One of these notions was that when he was overloaded one day, he would not work the next. Therefore Wahan and his family, Chazaninga, Meepee and her family, and a few others remained there also with Two Bears and his wife to take a day's rest while the tribe moved on; I, of course, stayed too.

While I was sitting in Meepee's tent that forenoon, Chazaninga came in. He was a tall, spare man, with an air of command and a dignity of carriage that compelled respect from the younger men. Sitting down beside Sunshine, he wrapped his blanket around both her and himself. As Meepee did not look displeased, I knew that Chazaninga had somehow arranged for the presents of which Two Bears had spoken. I got up and went out of the tent. Mounting my horse, I rode away down the river.

Later I lariated Titus and vainly stalked some tantalizing antelope afoot, crawling up within range again and again, only to have them scamper off. I did not give up the chase until they had gone altogether out of reach. As I started back toward Old Titus, a black cloud rose in the west. By the time I reached the horse, the wind was blowing a gale and the rain was coming down in torrents. I made a little tent of my blankets and sat down on the ground to wait till the deluge stopped. Then I decided that it never would stop. Down it poured just as steadily as ever. At last I mounted and rode toward our camp.

About a mile short of it I saw a little boy running wildly down the bottom land, and I rode toward him to ask him what the matter was. He hid from me in the tall, dead grass, and though I searched for him for ten or fifteen minutes, I could not find him. I rode on to our camp. There I found the dead bodies of Wahan, of four women, and of two half-grown boys. They all had been scalped. A hasty search of the ground showed me that the murderers were ten in number, that they had carried away a prisoner, and that they had not been gone over two hours.

As I turned to leave the spot, I saw another body, a little to one side, lying face down in a pit that had been made by the women for smoking skins. The body had a ghastly wound in its right shoulder. I turned it over to see who it was: it was poor old Meepee, still alive but unconscious. In the pit underneath her were three children, safe and unharmed. When she revived later on, she told me the story.

When she had seen the foe close upon them, she had thrown those children into the pit, and flung herself down over them, feigning dead. Two of the attacking party had noticed her as she lay there and one had asked:

"Is she dead?"

The other, answering, "I'll see," had plunged his knife into her shoulder. Because the brave old woman had not moved a muscle, the fiend had turned away. Why he did not scalp her was always a mystery to us all.

In a few minutes I had made a travois, and fastened it behind Old Titus, and placed Meepee and the children on it. We started on the trail of the main body at a brisk walk. In the bottom I halted to send the children to call the little boy who had hidden in the long grass; when they failed to find him, we pushed on.

Toward noon I saw ahead of me a strange-looking object that moved in the same direction as ourselves. When we overtook it, I found that it was Two Bears, carrying his wife on his back. She was desperately wounded, and he had carried her nearly ten miles. He was almost exhausted and the perspiration was running down his face in streams. After we had added her to the load Old Titus was dragging, we had to proceed so much more slowly that it was midnight before we reached the main camp, pitched in a wild, lonely spot at the foot of a hill, and reported the massacre.

Five minutes later the whole camp was wailing. Several men climbed to the hilltop and lamented there all night long.

Everywhere there was uproar and confusion. I sought the *nudunaga* and described the exact appearance of the scene of the murders, and told him that a prisoner—who must have been Sunshine—had been carried off. Remembering Two Bears' story of Chazaninga's horse stealing the year before, I suggested that this might have been a Comanche raid.

"But where is Chazaninga?" the *nudunaga* asked.

"Sure enough," I admitted. "I forgot about him."

"The tenth trail you saw must have been his, tracking after the rest. You should have known his moccasin print from a Comanche's."

"And Meepee's husband? I saw nothing of him."

"He has just come into camp."

Already a war dance was under way. The young braves danced around a pole, stuck in the ground, which had a number of old scalps tied to it; they were going through all sorts of bodily contortions and working themselves into a state of frenzy. Then the *nudunaga* ordered the dancing to stop. For two hours before daylight there was no sound to be heard except the wailing of the men on the hill.

I was very weary. I had had neither food nor sleep for forty-eight hours. I had no tent to go to, for poor old Meepee was dangerously wounded and her tent was destroyed; so, wrapping my blankets around me, I lay down to sleep in the open air.

Oh, that deep dreamless sleep of the tired and healthy young! My rounded and hardened muscles found the ground an easier couch than a bed of down would be to me today. My pillow was a saddle, my only roof the deep blue sky. I had four hours of absolute oblivion before I woke to find the camp already moving. A woman stood beside me. She held in one hand three pairs of moccasins, and in the other a bag of provisions.

"Meepee," she told me, "bade me give you these. She said you must be hungry and you will need the moccasins before you get back. Be brave."

Meepee in all her fever, pain, and sorrow over the loss of her daughter had thought of me as one who had no kindred in the tribe, and had begged these things for me.

As always for a little while after the main body moves on, the old men were lingering to smoke around the campfires. On the hilltop one lone figure stood motionless and clear-cut against the sky, gazing fixedly toward the west. Afar I could hear the people who had gone ahead of us, wailing for the dead. Then a young man in war paint rode up to me with a message:

"The *nudunaga* asks if you will go with the party after the Comanches."

"Yes," I answered.

"Then mount your horse and follow me."

Just around the hill I found a party of about fifty men, finely mounted and almost all well armed. We rode away toward the scene of the tragedy, each man going as he pleased, to the right or the left or following a good way behind. A mile or so farther on we saw a horse jogging slowly toward us down the trail, which it followed with its nose close to the ground. We did not catch it as it trotted along past us.

"Two Bears will be glad when he sees that pony," said a young man who rode near me. "He wanted so much to come that he nearly cried—but he had no pony."

"It's a good thing," I remarked, "for that pony would die before it got halfway to the Comanches."

We pushed on to the scene of the disaster. Here the *nudunaga* halted and, taking three of his most experienced men—and inviting me to join them—went forward to examine the ground. The dead still lay there, unharmed by wolves. The men, giving them only a glance, hurried forward to examine the trail. I showed the *nudunaga* the route they had taken. He took one quick look at the moccasin tracks and exclaimed:

"*Wach!* These are not Comanches! They're Sioux!"

After going forward a few rods more he stopped again, pointed to a footprint, and said, "Chazaninga!"

Then we all galloped half a mile to a clump of timber where we knew that the Sioux must have left their horses before they crawled up to the camp. Several of our men pointed out the trail of the captured prisoner and, to the left, the track of the captured horses. A consultation followed in which everyone but the *nudunaga* joined. He, as usual, listened attentively to every word but said nothing.

13.

On the Warpath for Revenge

To go on the warpath against the Sioux was an entirely different matter from fighting the Comanches. The former numbered many thousands and were the bravest, most warlike, and best armed of all the tribes. They domineered over the whole country from far south of the Platte to the British possessions in the north, and from the Rocky Mountains to the Missouri River, where they had a foothold on even the eastern side of its upper reaches. A few other tribes along the Missouri River had escaped extermination through alliances, first with the tribes to the east and then with the whites, but the Sioux were still masters of a vast region. They called themselves, not "Dacotah," as the whites believe, but "Lacotah," which means "The People," as if there were no others. Many French traders, most of whom had married Sioux women, lived among them and kept them supplied with the best arms and quantities of ammunition. Our nudunaga and the members of the Soldier Lodge knew all these facts.

After everyone had said every word he had to say, the nudunaga arose to make a formal speech. He gave a detailed account of all the past atrocities the Sioux had inflicted on this tribe and on other tribes with which it was affiliated. Then he related the brave deeds which he himself and some of those present had done. He ended by saying that though the Sioux were many and we were few, we could not stand beside the bodies of our dead and refuse to avenge them. If we did, God would send a curse upon the tribe, and it would disappear from the face of the earth.

After that, though nothing more was said and no orders were issued, each man began to strap his accouterments on his horse. Very soon we all were mounted and were following the trail. In that starlit night two men who ran on foot ahead of us had no difficulty in tracing the track; when they grew tired, others took their places. At daylight we halted, fed our horses, and then pushed on. About noon the trail turned almost due north from its previous western course.

"We'll camp at the Hidden Grove," a dozen exclaimed at once as they saw the runners make the turn.

The Hidden Grove was unlike any other place I have ever seen on the plains—a great circular depression of twenty acres or more, with perpendicular banks and heavily timbered. One might ride within a quarter mile of it without seeing it. It lay about thirty miles north of where the trail had turned, and we reached it just at dusk.

Early in the afternoon the trailers had missed Chazaninga's tracks; therefore, the nudunaga had sent parties to right and left to search for them. Before night we discovered that two of the Sioux were also missing. Fresh trailers who had just gone on duty had been the first to notice it. The two men whom they relieved, and who had not noticed where those Sioux had turned off the trail, received a terrible reprimand from the head soldier. Though we halted and sent trailers back over two or three miles, they returned without having discovered anything.

Shortly after we reached the Hidden Grove the men sent out to look for Chazaninga's trail came in, reporting that they had found it and that Chazaninga in turn had come upon the trail of two Sioux. The latter, they said, had stalked an antelope and killed it. While they were skinning it, Chazaninga had crawled up and shot one, and had killed the other after a hand-to-hand struggle. Then he had taken their horses and passed on northward, keeping west of the Hidden Grove.

A great storm was now coming up. The wind roared over our heads through an inky blackness brilliantly pierced now and then by vivid lightning. The woods were thick with birds and wild animals seeking shelter. When the sharp, frequent peals of thunder had lessened, the night was made hideous by the howls of a thousand coyotes. Our terror-stricken horses huddled together. Each man made himself a little booth of branches and long grass, just large enough to crawl into for shelter from the rain and cold.

After an hour of storm the clouds passed over; the stars shone out bright and clear; the bedlam of wind and beasts died away. In tomblike silence each man was soon asleep in his tiny wickiup.

About midnight I was wakened by a howl of disgust and anger from the man in the booth nearest me.

"What's the matter?" I questioned sleepily.

"A snake," he grunted.

I knew his voice and that, because he belonged to the Inshtasunda, snakes were things he must not touch. If he did, some calamity would surely befall him or his family. Though the sky had clouded over again and rain was drizzling down, I heard him wriggle out of his shelter.

Nevertheless in the morning we all heard someone snoring in the deserted wickiup. When we quietly tipped it aside, there lay Two Bears, sound asleep. He had followed us and, reaching camp late, he had somehow identified the Inshtasunda man. So by pushing a snakelike crooked stick into that wickiup, he had ousted its occupant and appropriated his shelter.

"How did you get here?" I asked him.

"On my own pony. Didn't I tell you I was going to ride it on the warpath against the Sioux?"

That old pony stood with the other horses, looking no better and no worse than on the morning when, by merely refusing to get up, he had brought on the massacre—and this war.

Soon we were on the march again, but because the storm had nearly obliterated the trail we had to proceed slowly. However, by midday we had passed clear across that rain-beaten region and found a plain trail again.

By three o'clock we had reached the banks of the Platte River at a spot where it divides into many branches. From the southernmost to the northernmost bank lies a watery expanse of more than five miles. As there was danger of quicksand, we dismounted and plunged into the stream instead of riding. In some places the water was not more than ankle deep, in others we had to swim for short distances. Whenever we reached an island, we remounted and rode across it to the next branch of the river. Finally, when we reached the extreme northern bank, we could not discover any sign of a trail, though we searched up and down the stream for five miles. Then we tried again and again to pick up the lost traces in the hills. There was no trail anywhere.

Though the nudunaga said nothing, I could see that he was greatly exasperated. While we still searched the banks of the Platte, night closed down. Every moment lessened our chances for overtaking the Sioux war party.

Though we lariated our horses and lay down, each near his own animal, I doubt if anyone slept. Every man there felt personally disgraced. Where could those Sioux have gone? We had seen where they had first entered the river and where they had crossed each island. They had not gone back, because we had searched the southern as well as the northern bank of the river.

After I had lain there a while, Two Bears came over to me and announced solemnly:

"I know where those Sioux are."

"Where?"

"The fishes ate 'em."

"You're a fool," I told him.

"I've seen the Platte fish swallow a man many a time."

"You never saw a man who could tell as big lies as you can."

"One might as well tell lies as to get angry and say nothing, like the nudunaga," Two Bears asserted. "I tell you he's pretty angry. Won't they laugh at him when he gets back and they hear how he lost a trail and couldn't find it again! If I were he, I'd never go back. I'd go and live with the Comanches."

"I wish you'd stop talking."

"Anyway," he insisted, "I'll tell you one thing. I'm going to find that trail in the morning myself."

I would not listen to him any longer. Over and over I was saying to myself, "Where can those Sioux have gone?"

When I had fallen asleep at last, I was roused by a whisper from Two Bears: "See there!"

I looked through the dark to where he pointed. A young man was stealthily leading away a horse. At some distance from us he mounted and rode up the river.

"What does that mean?" I asked.

"*Ethopenhamuzzhe*," said Two Bears. That is what an Indian always answers when mystified. It means "I don't know."

"Where do you think he's going?"

"I don't know," Two Bears repeated.

Four or five more men departed in the same fashion, but all I could get out of Two Bears was "*Ethopenhamuzzhe.*"

Then suddenly he exclaimed, "*Ethopeha!*" (I know!)

"Tell me, then," I urged.

"Those young men, who are very much ashamed because we

lost the trail, are going far out to see if they can't find it as soon as daylight comes."

"Does the nudunaga know?"

"They don't care for the nudunaga. If he can't keep as big a trail as that one was, he's no good."

"I'm going too," I decided. I quietly led Old Titus out of the camp, mounted him, and rode down the river—simply because I had seen no one else go that way. Knowing that the bank had been thoroughly searched for a long distance, I pushed on as fast as I could nearly until dawn. By then I was some ten miles from the camp, so, halting to wait for full daylight, I led my horse to a low spot and lay down. Soon I heard a noise. Looking up the river, I saw Two Bears following me. I felt exceedingly angry; when he came up, I accosted him very roughly. He only laughed and told me:

"Don't be angry. We'll find the trail."

Daylight showed me a stream flowing into the Platte a half mile ahead. I rode along the riverbank searching for the trail. Between me and an island in the Platte flowed only a narrow stream of water, perhaps four rods wide. As I rode along, I happened to glance across it and saw something hanging on a twig close to the water. It took me only an instant to fasten Old Titus by twisting my lariat around some tall, dead grass and to plunge across the stream.

I found there a small piece of Sunshine's dress, tied to the branch by a peculiar knot which could almost be made with one motion of the hand. Evidently the Sioux had waded down through that icy water for nine or ten miles to hide their trail. We had known from the trail record that Sunshine had walked much of the way to the Platte. Now I knew that she must have waded down it, or else she could not have fastened that fragment to so low a bough.

Back I hurried to Old Titus and rode him down the river,

certain that I should soon find the place where the Sioux had
emerged from it. But when I came to the stream which I had
noticed earlier, I found the bank so steep that I could not cross.
Just as I was about to plunge into the Platte and skirt the mouth
of this creek, I heard a fierce yell to the north. When I looked
around, I saw Two Bears signaling me with his blanket. The
Sioux had followed up that creek itself for more than a mile
and then had come out on its eastern side. Two Bears had
found the trail.

"I am a great man! I am a great man!" proclaimed Two Bears.
"I told you I'd find the trail—and I found it. I'm a great man.
I'll tell it at every dance." He began to sing with all his might.

Just then, far to the north, we both saw a little cloud of smoke
no bigger than a man's hat.

"*Pazhe!*" growled Two Bears in a great rage. He had stopped
his song and was shaking his fist at the smoke.

"There it is again," I exclaimed.

"It's the nudunaga's signal. He's found the trail himself. We'll
have to ride hard to overtake him."

Hitting his pony a tremendous blow with his whip, he was
off as fast as he could force the poor old beast to go. As the
Sioux had made no further efforts to conceal their trail, we
could follow it most of the way at a gallop. Two Bears' pony
now fell into a jog trot, a steady gait of about seven miles an
hour, uphill and down, always at the same rate of speed. He
carried two hundred pounds. By midafternoon my Old Titus
was getting fagged; the sweat had been dripping from his quiv-
ering sides for hours. But the old pony was in the same condition as when we started. On he went—trot, trot, trot, seven
miles an hour.

I dropped into the rear, loosened my saddle cinches, and
gave Old Titus a free rein. He struggled on; sometimes he fell
into a walk. At last I got off and ran behind him. The old pony

jogged along the same as ever. The sun went down and the stars came out; still on and on went the old pony. Wearily Old Titus followed. Finally he staggered, trembled, fell to his knees, rose again, dragged on a short distance, and fell exhausted. The old pony disappeared over a roll in the prairie, still going at the same rate—seven miles an hour.

As I sat by my worn-out horse, alone on the prairie, with no prospect of joining in the fight which seemed close at hand, I had the most gloomy thoughts. Soon more Indians, who had been still farther behind, passed by. One of them stopped an instant to tell me that this trail followed a divide, and that if I went either east or west for two or three miles, I should find water.

It was nearly dawn when I got Old Titus back onto his feet and led him slowly eastward along the divide through a brief shower of rain to a beautiful valley with large groves of timber and a clear, flowing stream. Soon the sun came up over the hills, sending great roseate beams to the zenith and turning the drops on the winter-dried grasses and the delicate new growth to a mass of glittering diamonds. The first birds of spring broke forth into song, rabbits sat up and looked steadily at me with great brown eyes, and antelope nearby raised their heads and gazed at me without fear. Prairie dogs, lured out by the mild air, capered and played around their homes, paid short visits to their nearest neighbors, and scampered back to chipper to their wives and children. An old owl, who sat on a dead cottonwood, silently examined the scene before him, preparing for his day-long sleep. A few prairie crocuses had just shoved their purple, leafless blossoms through the earth. The calmness of peace was everywhere, and I stood amid it all—alone.

I could see far down the valley, where the stream wandered through groves and level stretches of meadow that were tinged with that beautiful pale green which only the early spring prairies can show.

I gazed long at the scene, but at last turned from its charm to face the pressing needs of the hour. My horse was weak and thin. Because his covering, the typical coat of all American horses, was not half fur like that of the Indian ponies, the winter had borne hard upon him. My life depended on his life. So it was with many a pioneer of that frontier, who must always preserve his span of horses if he, his wife, and his children were to survive.

First, therefore, I looked for forage for Old Titus. The new grass was still too short to help much, but I found some reassuring patches of rushes. A week among these would put my good horse into sound condition. Next, what about myself? Should I dare to make a fire, or would some war party be sure to see its smoke? Must I still continue to live on dried meat?

On our second resting day, while I was walking along at the foot of the bluffs on the west side of the stream, I came to a gulch. It had perpendicular banks, and a great cottonwood had dropped across it. After looking at the fallen monster for a few moments, I walked on, but as I returned along the same path, that tree again caught my eye. Some of its limbs near the center of the top were discolored by smoke. I climbed up to them and found underneath them a round hole in the ground, which also was smoke-blackened.

"That looks like a chimney!" I exclaimed aloud.

Then I explored underneath the tree. There I found the entrance to a dugout, but its door was shut and fastened with a padlock. I broke the door open and discovered a large room. At its farther end was the fireplace which had blackened that chimney hole. On one side stood a rude bedstead, on the other a large oaken chest, heavily bound with iron and locked, like the door, by a padlock. There were some stools, a bench, a few dishes, and camping utensils. To judge by the dry mold which had accumulated on everything, a long while had passed since anyone had been there. In a corner stood a primitive cupboard; I opened its door. Its upper shelves were filled with bottles of drugs, and its under shelves with medical books.

Then I examined the chest more closely, although its padlock resisted all my efforts to break in. Determined to follow up every clue to the mystery of this place, I took the final resort of turning the chest onto its back and building a fire atop of its hasp and padlock. At last I could open it. Within, wrapped in skins and furs, I found the skeletons of a woman and a tiny baby.

I closed that chest, placed it in the farthest corner and sat down to think. But though I sat there a long time, no possible explanation of such surroundings presented itself to my mind—and none has come to me since.

"At any rate," I told myself, "here is a good shelter while I have to stay in this valley, and I'll make the most of it. I can even have a fire in here at night without anyone's being able to see it."

When I went out again, a cold wind was blowing from the northwest, and a sleety rain was falling, mixed with snow. Poor Old Titus stood all humped up, shivering with cold. As I came near him, he neighed piteously and rubbed his nose against me.

"You honest old fellow," I said, as I stroked him, "you've always done your very best for me. You followed the trail just as long as you could stand up; and when you had fallen from weakness and exhaustion, you rose and struggled on till you could go no farther. You shall have the very best place I can fix for you."

So I made him a shelter under the boughs of the cottonwood and close to the steep bank. I carried him bundles of rushes and wheat grass. Whenever I came near, his eyes sparkled and he rubbed his nose against me. For months I had observed the Indians talking to their domestic animals and reasoning with them as they would with persons, and I had often thought that those animals understood a surprising share of what they heard. So here, alone in the wilderness with Old Titus, I was not lonely. I had a friend.

For three days the storm of sleet and snow raged on unabated, but Old Titus and I were comfortably housed, he in his shelter and I in my warm dugout.

At last the storm ended, the sun came out, and everything grew bright and beautiful, but when I walked on the hills I could not see any human being or any human traces.

14.

The Pawnees Cross the Trail

I stayed two days more in that valley before I packed my things. Then as I was about to mount and ride away, I saw a horseman coming down the opposite hill. The next moment I knew him for Two Bears, and ran forward to meet him. He was haggard and half starved, but his old pony looked the same as ever. We did not speak at first. I merely pointed to a patch of rushes nearby. He dismounted, took off the forked sticks which the Indians call a saddle, turned his pony loose, and followed me to the dugout. After eating some of my jerked meat he filled his pipe and passed it to me. Then he spoke for the first time.

"The nudunaga is no good."

I took a few whiffs of the pipe and passed it back. After he had smoked a while, he volunteered what had happened since we parted.

"We followed that trail all night and till noon of the next day. There the Sioux had made a camp—but a party of about a hundred Pawnees had come upon them and killed everyone in it except Sunshine. They carried her off to make a sacrifice of her. They'll take her to their village, put their old men to guard her, and feed her all she can eat. When she gets fat, they'll kill her. Then they'll all rub their guns, bows, and arrows over her burning body so that they'll become *koo-bay*. We'll never see Sunshine any more."

Then he began to wail. For more than an hour he sat there

with great tears running down his face, slowly swinging his body backward and forward, and lamenting after the fashion of his race. Then, as his weeping turned to wrath, he pronounced every curse known to Indians on both the Sioux and the Pawnees. Finally he fell asleep, exhausted.

While he slept, I was busy forming a plan for rescuing Sunshine, for I knew well that every word of his prophecy as to the fate awaiting her was true. The Pawnees would sacrifice her exactly as he had described, not from revenge or because they were cruel—for the Pawnees were a generous, kindly people—but because they hoped in that way to obtain supernatural power and, by becoming *koo-bay*, to be able to protect their wives and children from foes who were always seeking the lives of their tribe. However, it still was only a very few months since one band of Pawnees and I had met and parted on the best of terms, and since they, laden with gifts from our autumn hunting expedition, had invited me to visit their tribe.

Two Bears slept long. When he woke, I asked him about the rest of our party. He said they were one camp north and would go in a day or two to the Big Woods on the Platte to rest their horses for a few days.

"They are all cross and angry, and it will go badly with any Pawnees or Sioux they may meet. They will not return to the tribe until they have killed somebody."

"What are you going to do?" I asked him.

"I knew I'd find you either here or over in that other valley, so I came along. Now let's go back to our village. I'm tired and I want to rest."

"No," I replied, "we'll go on to the Big Woods. I want to see the nudunaga."

"The nudunaga is bad! He's no good!" asserted Two Bears very vehemently. "Dubamonie thinks he's a great man, but no one else thinks so."

That was the very first time I had ever heard the nudunaga's name, but now Two Bears was trying to be as insulting as he could toward our leader. Therefore he called him by his personal name instead of his official title—as unpardonable an insult among the Indians as it would be on the floor of the United States Senate.

"What's the use," Two Bears continued, "of following such a man? He lost the trail. He couldn't catch the Sioux. He's afraid to fight the Pawnees. He's no good at all! That's what all the men think, and they'd put him out if they weren't afraid of him. Once, on the warpath, he pronounced a curse on a man—and in three days that man died. Like Village Maker, he has the power of the bear."

"Well, I'm going on to the Big Woods," I asserted, "and you can go home if you want to."

"It's a long day's journey from here to the Big Woods," he grumbled.

"I'm starting in the morning," I insisted.

The next night we found the whole war party in the Big Woods—morose, ill-natured, disappointed. Not one of them had achieved any glory. All they knew of Chazaninga was that he had followed the Pawnees.

I called a council. When a large fire had been built and the Indians had seated themselves in a circle around it and the pipe had been passed, I rose and made the following speech:

"We have been on the warpath for many days, but we have not met our foes, for they, being afraid, ran away. We should not be discouraged; our horses were weak and poor and could not go fast. They will soon be strong again. Let them rest and feed here for a few days. I have a thing to propose. The Pawnees are friends of mine. They have invited me to visit them and pipe-dance. You stay here for ten days and I will go to them. When I return, I will bring Sunshine with me, and we will go back to the village rejoicing."

Everyone present gave a grunt of approval; they had not expected any such proposition. When I sat down, the nudunaga rose and replied:

"What you have said is good, but the time you allow is too short. Your horse is poor. It will take you four days to get to the Pawnees, four days for the ceremonies, and with fresh horses, if they give them to you, three days to get back. We will wait twelve days for you."

"I must go alone," I announced. "No one must follow me." And I looked very hard at Two Bears.

The head soldier rose and replied in a tone of command, "No one shall follow."

On the fourth day in midafternoon I entered the Pawnee village. Evidently something was wrong. When I rode up to the head chief's lodge, he was not there, and though I stood for some time holding my horse, no one came to welcome me. I realized that a council was being held and that there was subdued general excitement everywhere. Before long, however, the head chief came walking rapidly toward me and began the usual formal conversation.

"Where are you going?"

"I come to pipe-dance the Pawnees," I answered.

A woman led away my horse and I walked into the lodge. There I was seated in the guest's place of honor, and the lighted pipe was passed to me. The women stirred the fire and brought out their daintiest edibles. Soon a bountiful feast was set before me. Meanwhile, by Indian custom, not a word had been spoken —a truly refined courtesy, for I was tired, hungry, and needed rest. When I was through eating, the chief told me:

"Your tent is ready."

It had been newly erected for me beside his lodge, a fire had been built, and numerous robes and furs had been spread on the ground. For as long as I should remain there this would be my home. Almost at once other chiefs and headmen began to drop in. By evening the pipe dance was under full headway.

It was nearly the close of the third day before I became fully convinced that Sunshine was not in that village; and I could not surmise what had become of her. On the morning of the fourth day, the chief's eldest son, who had turned out to be that young leader of the previous autumn's hunt who had accepted tobacco from me and had urged me to visit them, invited me to contend with him in shooting at a mark. This was a genuine compliment, because ammunition—the very life of the community— was exceedingly difficult to obtain.

After a few shots I asked the young chief:

"What became of that girl the Pawnees captured from the Sioux?"

"She's gone." He looked very confused.

"Gone?" I exclaimed in amazement. "Gone?"

"Gone."

"Gone where?"

He did not answer me for some time. At last he said, "I'll tell you all about it."

The story he related is known among all the tribes along the Missouri River. I have since heard it among the Omahas, the Otoes, and elsewhere.

The chief's son saw Sunshine when she was brought into camp, pale and weak. When they took her from the horse on which she had been tied, the men had to carry her to the lodge where she was to be confined. The six old men who had been detailed to guard her sat in the tent with her day and night, and the women brought her much to eat.

The chief's son noticed that after the first two or three days the old men grew sleepy and careless. He then took two of his father's best horses and tied them not far from the lodge. On the fourth night, while the old men slept, he stole Sunshine away from them, led her to the horses, mounted her on one of them, gave her the lariat for leading the other, and told her to ride for her life. When one horse grew tired, she was to ride the other.

The next morning there was a great uproar in the camp over her escape, and the head chief accused his son of having aided her. The young man frankly confessed:

"Yes, I did it. That girl had never harmed the Pawnees; and you cannot tell for certain that, if you had killed her and burned her body, any blessing would have come upon your weapons. They might not have killed any more surely than if you had not done so. I had pity for the young girl, and I let her go."

Because more than half of the chiefs and people sided with the head chief's son, the council had decided to take no action on the matter. So already Sunshine was far on her way toward home and was safe from all present danger.

I knew that Chazaninga must be somewhere near, watching his chance to steal horses or to release Sunshine, so I told the young chief all about our chase after the Sioux and the events which had brought Sunshine to their camp. Now the Pawnees were hereditary enemies of the Sioux, but were on friendly terms with the Omahas, the Otoes, and the other tribes along the Missouri whose members had made up the band with which I had journeyed. When I mentioned Chazaninga to the young chief, he exclaimed:

"*Wah!* I know where he is. When I was up the river yesterday, I saw a man far off with three horses, but I thought he was one of our own men."

That night the young chief and I slipped out of the village and found Chazaninga. I told him that the Pawnees who had captured Sunshine had given her two horses and started her homeward, that our party was waiting in the Big Woods, and that he had better join them there.

Next day, when we told the Pawnees the whole story, they all felt well satisfied. Their medicine man declared that the young chief must have been aided by the spirits in discerning what was not known to the rest of them, and that he would live to be a great and wise leader of the tribe.

15.

Vengeance on the Sioux

I left the Pawnee village that morning with a present of five horses, two of which were well laden with gifts of furs, robes, blankets, provisions, and other valuables. The third night after this I reached the Big Woods. The nudunaga with two others had been absent for three days but had ordered the rest to remain where they were until he returned.

After I had eaten, the whole war party gathered around the campfire to hear my news, but while I was still relating what had happened Chazaninga arrived. He was haggard and thin, his moccasins were worn out, and his blanket was in tatters, but he had brought the two horses he had taken from the Sioux and he wore their scalps dangling at his belt. Therefore, by Indian reckoning, he had captured all the honors in the affair.

For the sake of maintaining my own standing in the tribe and of conforming to Indian etiquette I distributed to those who had befriended me or who were in the greatest need most of the presents I had received from the Pawnees. Next day the nudunaga returned with the news that a large party of the Sioux, evidently going to the Arikaree to hunt, had crossed the Platte two camps west of us. He proposed to take vengeance on them for our dead.

Though we were up early the next morning, we were ordered to hunt instead of setting out after the Sioux. We spent several days in securing and preparing meat for transportation.

How we wished that we had brought some of the women along! Our warriors were pretty awkward at that work. When at last we were ready to start, we were divided into three grades: first, soldiers; second, baggage carriers; third, servants. That is the literal translation of the terms the Indians used, but, to tell the truth, the "servants" held rather the posts of quartermasters and commissary sergeants.

For several days we all traveled southwest in very leisurely fashion, but when we reached the headwaters of the Republican River, the nudunaga divided the party and sent the baggage carriers south to the headwaters of Beaver Creek. Among these went Two Bears. I had given him one of the Pawnee horses, and the nudunaga did not seem to have a high opinion of his fighting qualities. The soldiers, stripped of everything but their arms and one blanket each, pushed on due west. We traveled night and day, stopping only to let our horses feed. The last day we had nothing to eat but some wild turnips which we dug up from the prairie with our knives.

A little before sundown we halted in a deep ravine to wait for darkness. As soon as night had settled down on the broad, silent prairie, we pushed on. We had seen the trails of the Sioux everywhere; we all knew that we were very near them. At three in the morning we rode out on a little hill—and there in the valley below us lay the Sioux camp, a circle of tents upon which the stars shone down and in which a thousand or more Sioux were sleeping without thought of danger.

When we had retired behind the hill, the head soldier came along and ordered one to "Stand here," and another to "Stand there," until we were divided into two equal parties. Many had no guns but were armed with bows and arrows. Then the nudunaga came slowly along our lines. He placed all the men who had guns, including me, on the north side of the line. Then he gave his orders.

"The men with guns will go as near to the north side of the Sioux camp as they can without arousing the dogs, and will wait there. All the Sioux horses are picketed on the south side of the camp. The men who have no guns will leave all their own horses tied together in charge of two men. They will creep in on foot between the Sioux horses and the camp. As soon as they hear firing, they will cut the picket ropes and stampede the Sioux horses toward the south. The two men left with the other horses will then rush them forward so that all can mount and drive the Sioux horses toward the head of Beaver Creek. Then these are your orders: push the herd on as fast as possible and, unless I overtake you, do not stop when you reach our servants and carriers but still push on toward the Missouri River and our own villages."

Then he turned toward our line of guns and commanded, "Follow me."

Each Indian had thrown off his blanket and fastened it to his saddle. Each was naked except for his breechcloth and moccasins. Our ponies seemed to understand what was happening, for they passed over the prairie noiselessly. We advanced in absolute silence.

When we had reached the position he wanted, the nudunaga halted us with a motion of his hand, which he held out at a right angle to his body. He rode a little way ahead and to one side to a spot from which he could overlook the whole camp. He sat there on his horse a long time, motionless and silent as a statue, looking steadily forward. Then he came slowly back to where we waited on foot and, riding to the right of our line, commanded:

"*Kaka!*"

A yell—wild, fierce, revengeful—burst from every throat. The air was rent with it. Simultaneously we poured a volley into the nearest tents. Yell followed yell; volley rang upon volley.

Instantly the Sioux camp showed inextricable confusion. We could see the women and children fleeing toward the brush that bordered their tents on the west.

In the dim light I could distinguish a tall man moving among the Sioux and shouting commands to them in a language I did not understand. But our nudunaga understood it. He rode in among us calling:

"Go back! Go back!"

All but one of us turned to go. Chazaninga, though he had a gun, rushed forward with a bow in his hand. He seemed to clear the distance between us and the Sioux with the speed of an antelope. Though he was shot at from every side, on he went until six great Sioux rose up together in front of him. Because they tried to take him alive, he escaped, after striking two of them with his bow. A frantic yell of rage went up from that Sioux camp. They were disgraced forever—and Chazaninga had won the greatest glory possible for an Indian to attain. *He had struck a living enemy with a bow.*

Though Indian law requires a nudunaga to defend every member of his band, even at the risk of his life, our nudunaga was under no obligation to save Chazaninga, for he had disobeyed orders.

A fleet-footed Sioux, tall and powerful, bent on retrieving the disgrace put upon him and his tribe, dashed after Chazaninga. Because they ran in a straight line between the fighting forces, neither side could fire at its foe without killing its own man. The Sioux gained on Chazaninga, and would soon have struck him with his bow if our nudunaga had not dashed forward. Mounted as he was, he offered a fair target for the Sioux bullets and arrows. Before he had gone many rods, his horse reared, plunged forward, and fell. Instantly the nudunaga sprang up, leveled his rifle, and fired. He missed, and the Sioux warrior was upon him. He warded off the first blows with his uplifted gun, then both he and the Sioux drew their knives for the final effort. The Sioux made fearful thrusts; sometimes he crouched low and sprang like a tiger. The nudunaga appeared to fight on the defensive, retreating as opportunity offered. At last, when all the Sioux's attempts at a final stab failed to succeed, he drew back a few paces and began to fix an arrow in his bow.

With one bound the nudunaga was upon him, and the two men rolled together on the ground, indistinguishable to the onlookers on both sides. For a moment all the yells and war whoops ceased. Suddenly the nudunaga rose and ran toward us.

All this time both sides had been firing at each other.

A dozen men stretched out their arms to receive the nudunaga, who was covered with blood. He was taken to the rear, where our horses had been kept during the firing, and was placed on a horse. He ordered us all to retreat as fast as possible. In a few moments we all had mounted and were riding away—and the Sioux, whose horses already had been stampeded by our southern band, could not follow us.

When we gained the hilltop, dawn had broken. Far to the south we could see the great herd of horses which the other half of our party was driving along. Henceforth our nudunaga would be the greatest man, not only in his own tribe, but in all tribes that were hostile to the Sioux. He had reached the very highest pinnacle of Indian fame, for he had attacked an overwhelming force, had captured all their horses, and had not lost a man. No matter how great a victory a chief may win, if he loses many men, he gains no glory among the Indians.

But the nudunaga's success would not bring him rank and pay, as it would have brought him among the whites. Though he had been severely wounded, he would receive no pension. His authority would cease with his return to the village. He was not a hereditary chief; he would take his place in the tribe merely as a private Indian. Though lawfully all the captured horses were his, he would give away every one of them to his followers, for Indians are esteemed among their own people, not for what they possess, but for what they have given away. His only reward would be a place of honor at the feasts, dances, and ceremonies of his own tribe and of any other tribes he might visit.

We overtook the herd of horses, found our baggage carriers at the appointed place, and at last regained our village, where we then spent many days in rejoicing and dancing, gift-making and gift-taking. The tribe was wealthy now, as the Indians count wealth, and all present were as happy as children on a holiday—all but two of us.

Meepee, who had recovered, told the following facts to Chazaninga and to me.

"When Sunshine got home, she lay in the tent for many days, and Village Maker came to see her. He said that she was very sick and might not live. Two white women, who were visiting the missionary's wife, brought Sunshine many of the good things to eat that the white people cook. After she got better, they wanted to take her home with them. At first I said no, but Village Maker told me: 'If she stays here, she will die.' I let her go, and she is to stay with the white people for two years and go to school and learn all the white people's ways."

Chazaninga and I were not happy.

16.

Civilization Reclaims Me

After my autumn, winter, and spring of hunting and following the warpath my hair had grown until it reached my waist and hung in a great mass down my back. I had not seen a barbershop or a pair of shears anywhere on the Great Plains. A butcher knife, even though whetted on a sand rock, was not a good tool for cutting hair.

My cap was made from a half-tanned beaver skin; my shirt and leggings were of antelope skin; my blankets were in rags and strips, sewn together here and there with horsehair; my moccasins had been patched so often that the original material had almost disappeared. Now I borrowed a pair of shears from the missionary and persuaded an Indian to cut my hair as close to my head as possible. Several good buffalo robes of mine, which the women had brought back from the hunt and stored for me, as well as four or five ponies I had acquired, I swapped with the trader for such articles of white man's apparel as he had in stock. I also purchased a new saddle girth, new stirrup leathers, a bridle, and some ammunition.

I had begun to tire of life in an Indian village, with its continuous feasting and its drums that beat all night long in each part of the camp where dancing was going on. Feeling that I had had enough of the wilderness to satisfy me for the present, I turned Old Titus's head eastward and went back to the law office in Winterset.

When I, now seventeen, reached that western part of Iowa, however, I found it overrun with horse thieves. The Winterset citizens, who were determined to eradicate this gang, heard rumors of my adventurous year, so they promptly came to me with the proposal that I should help them to capture the outlaws. They wanted me to pretend to join the thieves and thus gain information which would enable the citizens to break up the whole criminal organization and capture its leaders. I consented and soon became a member of the horse-thief band. Before long, however, those outlaws discovered that they were being betrayed. In a piece of pie which I ate at a hotel in Winterset, I was given a dose of strychnine which, if I had not had an iron constitution, would undoubtedly have ended my career then and there.

As it was, I came so near to dying that one of the doctors actually pronounced me dead. I lay for several hours in that condition. After weeks spent in bed, I got onto my feet once more, but for seven years afterward I was subject to severe spasms and twitchings which kept me to a large extent an invalid. For that reason I never succeeded in passing a medical examination for military service.

From this hard experience I reaped one benefit. When the doctors failed to give me the relief I longed for, I borrowed from one of them all his books on nervous diseases. Then I realized that, to make any headway with these, I ought to know anatomy and physiology. Therefore in the next two or three years I read almost all the standard books on those subjects and attended two courses of medical lectures. By that time I probably knew as much about calomel, quinine, blistering, bleeding, and opium as most of the medical fraternity of that day. Though I had followed this path only in search of a cure for my own needs, I later found that knowledge useful in helping others.

Because I no longer could shoot with skill or endure the privations and hardships of wild life, I began studying to complete my education. I added to the standard algebra, geometry, Latin, and Greek of the day Commonstock's *Philosophy*, logic, rhetoric, Paley's *Evidences of Christianity*, and Watson's *Theological Institutes*. I studied these subjects first at a private school and later at [the then newly founded] Mount Union College in Ohio. To get there, I started out on foot, but as I crossed Iowa, I began giving talks and lectures on Kansas and on my life among the Indians, so that I finally reached the college in comfort and with some little cash in my pockets.

While I was a student at this college, I had my last interview with Old John Brown. The college was conducted under the auspices of the Methodist Episcopal Church and was thoroughly abolition in its sympathies. Because I had been with John Brown in Kansas, I was somewhat of a hero there. East of Mount Union was a Quaker community made up wholly of abolitionists. They invited me to visit them, and I, half-starved student that I was, accepted eagerly. Their tables were always bountifully supplied.

One day [in 1859] one of these Quakers came to my room and asked me if I would be willing to meet John Brown again. I told him I should be delighted to do so. He then said that Brown would be in Cleveland, which was not a great distance from my college, on a certain night and that if I would go there I could have a talk with him. After giving me definite and minute instructions for finding him the Quaker told me that I must call there only after dark, because it was necessary that Brown's presence in that city should be kept secret.

I found Brown in a small story-and-a-half house on the outskirts of Cleveland, in a bare, desolate room which had a cheap soft-coal stove in the center, a table, and three or four chairs. The only light was a single tallow candle. Beside it on the table many pages of manuscript were spread out. Brown was much

as I had known him in Kansas three years before, except that
his hair was grayer.

He told me that he had formed a plan to capture Virginia
and make it a free state. The manuscript on the table contained
the future constitution of that state and the laws for governing
it. He read the former aloud to me and gave me a summary
of the laws. Then he told me that with a small party he would
capture Harpers Ferry, where there was an arsenal with a large
amount of arms. He would hold the place, and Negroes would
flock to him by thousands. With the help of these Negroes, who
would be fighting for their own liberty, he would capture the
whole state. He did not directly ask me to join him, but he laid
his whole plan before me.

I told him that an attack on the state of Virginia would be
an entirely different matter from such fighting as we had done
in Kansas. There we had had at least a claim to being the right-
ful government, but no question whatever existed about the legal government of Virginia.

I also told him that if he were captured, he would be tried
in the United States courts and would be hanged for treason.
He answered that it mattered nothing what happened to him
—that God used His instruments in His own way.

Then I pointed out to him that his plan was wholly imprac-
ticable. Even if he should capture the arsenal, and even if the
Negroes should flock to him by the thousand, he could do nothing with them. Probably not one of them had ever been allowed
to handle a gun. They would not know which end of the
weapon to put forward. I told him that I could take one company of trained soldiers and whip five thousand of them.

His only reply was:

"You never showed any lack of courage while in Kansas."

When I was in Boston in 1894, Dr. Edward Everett Hale
told me that he knew of two other men to whom Brown had
made the same proposition. I said to him that I had some doubt

about including an account of this interview with Brown in any reminiscences I might write, because I could furnish no proof to sustain it, but Dr. Hale told me that it most certainly should be included because perhaps other men had memoirs to be published in the future which my account would support.

On October 1, 1861, I married in Freedom, Pennsylvania, Amelia Owen, an English girl who had recently come over with her family. She was so different from the women I had known in my pioneer life that at first sight her indefinable look of refinement and culture literally overwhelmed me. She had lovely rosy English coloring, large brown eyes, a lithe, faultless figure, beautiful white rounded arms, and dimpled hands. But she talked so earnestly to me about my life among the Indians and the Government's harsh treatment of them that my embarrassment soon passed away. I began to ride over that way often on my beautiful, fast, but very vicious horse.

Amelia herself was a fine horsewoman. The first time she consented to ride with me, as we paused at the window looking down at the horses who stood hitched at the gate ready for us, she asked me to let her ride mine. With my arms still aching and my hands swollen with trying to hold him, I laughed at her.

"He's never had a woman on his back. He'd delight in nothing better than biting your head off."

"Oh no!" she protested. "You misrepresent the poor horse."

I realized then that it was no use to argue with her. In fact, there was always something about her that one could not argue with. There are women who never say a cross word, who never try to command anyone or make any actual demands, and who seem utterly gentle and weak; yet strong men bow before them, eager to learn and carry out their wishes. These women wield an indescribable power, and whenever this power is backed by a kindly or inspired purpose, the good that one of these rare beings can accomplish in life cannot be estimated. Such was the spirit I recognized in Amelia Owen as she turned to me now with her pretty, pleading look.

"Come!" she urged, and led me to the gate. There she walked straight up to that big wild brute, and patted him on the neck. "I'm really very timid," she confided to me, "but all horses are my friends."

Dazed, I watched that "cussed" bay put down his head and nuzzle her shoulder.

"See," she insisted. "He's all right. He likes me. Now let me ride him."

"That's out of the question," I told her. "He's so hardmouthed that even I can hardly hold him."

"It's only because you're not kind enough to him. He's such a fine horse that he could gallop over a mountain without effort." She kept on stroking his docile head with her dimpled hand.

Then, after she had ordered a servant to change our saddles over, I helped her to mount. Off walked the horse meek as a lamb. I, too, was mounting, to follow, when suddenly I saw the wind blow her long English riding habit right under the bay. He gave one plunge forward, then reared on his hind feet. I caught the old gleam in his eye. The next second he was gone like the wind.

Though I flung myself into my saddle and lashed the mare I rode to a breakneck speed, I could not begin even to keep up. I could only see, far ahead of me, that the girl was sitting firm and upright, with the reins wrapped around those small, delicate hands of hers.

On and on went the bay and his rider—down through the village where people stared after them—across the bridge—and up a rocky road along the mountainside. With his light load he steadily drew away from me, but I forced my pace ruthlessly. I had only one thought—to save the girl. As the bay swung around a point of the mountain, I caught a glimpse of her, still sitting firmly in the saddle, and sawing at the brute's mouth. Near the top of the climb I passed an old farmer who called out to me, "Hurry up, or that's a dead young woman sure!"

Though my mare was getting winded and was dripping with sweat, she made the summit. I saw the bay fully a thousand yards ahead, going down the descent in long, steady leaps; and Amelia Owen still sat firmly in her saddle. Then trees and turns of the road hid them until I, too, reached the foot of the mountain and followed their tracks to a long level lane. There I saw them again—the bay still dashing ahead, Amelia still sitting straight in the saddle. But now they were going right against a strong wind. Her riding hat blew off, but she did not turn her head. They vanished around a bend. Suddenly, as I raced after them, I saw them coming back. She had managed to swing the horse around, and she still kept her seat. Here was my chance. I checked the mare and, as the bay came up to me, I turned beside him, dropped my rein, and caught him by the bits. He lifted me clean out of my saddle, though the bits cut into him till the blood flowed out of his mouth. But finally he came to a dead stop.

For the first time I looked up at the girl's face. She was white as a ghost except where a little red stream trickled down her cheek from the lashing of some branch. I threw the bay's reins over a fence post and helped her to dismount. She almost fell into my arms. While I still held her, she looked down at her hands—each marked with a deep white circle where the rein had wrapped it tight.

Neither of us ever could remember the first words we spoke, but I know that after a moment or two I told her shakenly:

"You're brave enough to be the wife of a frontiersman!"

"Do you think so?" she asked.

"Yes, indeed I do."

There was a pause. Then she said earnestly and with dignity: "That would be an honor for any true woman."

I took her in my arms and told her all, then and there—and she was content. I changed over the saddles at last, and we rode home side by side—slowly, hand in hand. We had come twelve miles, and we kept meeting new groups hurrying in search of us. By the time we reached the village everyone had turned out to meet us.

Twenty years afterward I adapted this incident to use in a novel—so that it should not be forgotten by our children.

Immediately after our marriage we again turned our faces toward the setting sun. Then for nearly ten years I simply played my part in the humdrum round of civil life.

I turned to journalism, and before long had held every position on a daily newspaper from assignment reporter to editor in chief. Whenever a man gets into the newspaper business, he acquires the journalistic disease, a malady harder to overcome than the opium habit. If any man ever recovered from that disease, there are no records to prove it.

17.

The Indians Try New Paths

Meanwhile I always anxiously watched from afar the harsh changes which the slow closing in of civilization, especially in every region on the western bank of the Missouri in Kansas and Nebraska, was bringing to my old friends, the Indian race. Their former way of life was done—and their new life was almost unendurable. About a dozen years after I had left the wilds, I heard that some little time ago the tribe which I had known so well had been obliged to take up its quarters on a reservation not impossibly far from my own beaten track. Early that spring I went to call on them.

In spite of the old rules of Indian etiquette I carefully sent no runner and no advance presents of tobacco ahead. For I had heard that these Indians now were very poor, and, knowing their tradition of generous gifts for visitors, I did not intend that any old friend of mine should give me his last pony and last blanket and then should get sick and die from cold and exposure. I had heard of exactly such cases in this cruel adjustment stage between the old, openhanded ideals of the easy-come, easy-go hunting and raiding days and the new, stern conditions of a restricted life. All I wanted to do was to meet again those friends of a happy year and yet not accept a present from a single one of them, no matter how deeply my refusal might wound his feelings.

I found the country cultivated right up to the reservation line on every side. The only land now open to the use of the Indians with whom I had roamed here over broad, free plains was a tract, about thirty miles long and twenty miles wide, of the poorest soil in the state. This chiefly took the form of high, gravelly hills, interspersed with narrow valleys which were cut by deep creeks and impassable gullies. The agency was located in the most inaccessible spot on the reserve. Here there were five or six residences for the white employees, a blacksmith's shop, a sawmill, and a government storehouse.

As I rode in toward a border town to approach the reserve, I noticed on the outskirts a small group of Indians who sat under a tree. They had a little fire beside them where something was boiling in a camp kettle. The seven men, two women, and three children all were dirty, ragged, and lean. I dismounted and strolled over near them, but they took no notice of me. All of them were looking too eagerly toward the town.

Soon an Indian woman and a young girl, each with a small pack on her back, came hurrying out from the last houses onto the open road. The Indians underneath the tree kept growing more and more excited. As soon as the newcomers could possibly hear, one of the men called loudly, "What did you get?" The women, not wasting breath on words, hurried into the group, laid down the packs and opened them. I sauntered past. I could see spread out there some dingy meat, evidently waste from a butcher's shop, some discarded scraps of stale bread, and other stray odds and ends of food.

The women popped the meat hastily into the kettle, which evidently had held only boiling water. After a few moments of stewing, barely enough to warm the meat well through, the party devoured every scrap of the food ravenously. I walked away into the town.

Looking back a few minutes later, I saw the whole group climb into a rickety old wagon drawn by two miserable ponies.

As they drove by, I stood on the sidewalk and heard young boys hoot at them. A man called jeeringly:

"Hallo, John! Want to sell them ponies?"

The Indians, looking neither to the right nor the left, rode slowly through the town and on out of sight. And though from the first I had known the leader of that party, I let them go and made no sign. He had not recognized me in my civilized clothes and with a full beard. And I, who had known him when he was proud and highly honored, was anxious now, in what should have been the height of his prime, to spare him the pang of my seeing him there and thus. For the leader of the forlorn little group was Dubamonie, the tribe's former nu-dunaga.

While I followed his wagon outward toward the reservation, I felt a wave of fury toward our government's whole Indian policy. Could it be God's will that men like Dubamonie, brave, generous to a fault, dignified, intelligent, faithful to every trust, loving their families and children and every inch of their native plains, should become beggars and gradually be swept off the face of the earth?

Must they make room for a race of sordid people who were subordinating every noble instinct to a ruling passion for accumulating property? For example, that town which I had just left was mostly owned by one man.

"He makes all the poor men work for him," I thought, "for they have to pay him rent for his lands and houses while he lives luxuriously and does nothing. Now if he were an Indian, he would give every man in the place a house and would keep only the poorest one for himself. If Dubamonie had kept all the property he gained as a leader in the hunt or on the war-path, he would be richer than this local Croesus. Which is the finer man of the two? Yet Dubamonie is hooted there in the streets where the rich man always rides along with a sort of triumphal progress, like a great lord."

Then suddenly, with a quick revulsion of feeling, I turned my wrath upon the Indians.

"Where did you come from," I asked them all mentally, "that your nature is in so many ways the exact opposite of the white man's? Your ideal is giving—and there is nothing so foolish. You've given away a continent, though the whole world agreed that it was yours in fee simple. Even if you feast a man who's already rich, you come home a beggar because you've given him everything you own. I've seen an Indian proudly acquire a blanket, a cow, or a horse; and soon afterwards I've asked him where it was. He's given it away.

"Oh, you fools! Will you never learn anything? Do you enjoy going around as beggars and being hissed at? When will you learn *not to give?* In that failing you Indians are all alike from the Atlantic to the Pacific. If one of you by working hard has gathered a little stock of provisions, he calls in all his neighbors. Then you all eat up every scrap of it in one huge meal.

"When white missionaries come to you, one of their favorite texts is: 'God loveth a cheerful giver.' Can't they see that that text was meant for white people, not for Indians? The Indian missionaries ought to preach: 'Cursed be the man who gives away anything.'"

Riding along a faint wagon track, I entered a little valley. In the bank was a sort of dwelling, half dugout and half log cabin. To one side was a small field where a man and a woman were at work, the woman holding the plow, the man driving. As I drew nearer, I heard the woman scolding at a fearful—and familiar—rate.

"Why can't you make them go straight?" she demanded. "How do you suppose I can hold the plow when the horses keep going this way, that way all the time? You never were good for anything and never will be."

"I can't make them go straight," he grunted. "It pulls too hard."

"If you'd ever been any good at all, you'd have had two big horses instead of these two little ponies. These can't pull anything. There! Look! Whoa! You awkward old thing! What did you fall down for? Get up; don't just sit there! Here! Come hold the plow and I'll drive!"

The man struggled up slowly, but just as he took hold of the plow handles, one of the ponies lay down and began to roll. This frightened the other pony; he began to kick. The woman screamed; the man yelled, "Whoa! Whoa!" The kicking pony, catching his hoof in the harness, fell over the pony who was down already. Then both ponies kicked wildly, and the two Indians kept on calling, "Whoa! Whoa!"

I, still unnoticed, selfishly hung back, waiting to see what would happen next. The ponies, tiring, gradually quieted down, and at last the Indians got them onto their feet again.

"It was all your fault," the woman stormed. "If you had only looked where you were going and hadn't fallen down, we shouldn't have had all this trouble."

Just then I rode up to them. I had guessed right; they were Two Bears and his wife, trying to farm. I simply cannot describe their delight at seeing me again.

"Come and eat! Come and eat!" they both urged me at once, and led me into their miserable little hut.

Inside of it I saw a stove, a homemade bedstead, and a few worn blankets and cooking utensils. Around the stove were scattered a lot of *nu,* or *nuskeda* peelings, evidently the refuse of several days. I noticed in a corner a heap of those same almost tasteless wild prairie tubers. There was nothing else at all to eat in that hut, but outside of it I had seen a little tent or coop of bark and sticks three or four feet high. In this were three chickens, which the wife must have used great care and watchfulness to preserve from the weasels and other animals who always come crowding into a reservation as soon as the wild land around it is built up.

Two Bears' wife slipped out of the hut. From the door I saw her approach the coop. I knew that she meant to kill those treasured chickens for me to eat. They were all she had left, and no doubt she had often gone hungry for days that winter so as to preserve these for raising more the coming summer.

I ran out after her.

"Mother!" I called. "Don't kill the chickens! Keep them to raise a new brood. You've plenty of *nu* in there. I like those—they'll be a change for me. I'd much rather eat *nu* than have you kill those chickens. You may not be able to get any more for two or three years."

I shall never forget the look of humiliation which swept over her face.

"I never thought you would talk to me this way," she answered plaintively. "You've come on a long journey to visit us. We're poor and we can't make you nice presents; but if I should not give you something to eat, what would happen to me? I'd rather die than bear the shame of it."

In less than a minute she had killed all three of those chickens. After we had eaten them, I went out with Two Bears to see his field—of about ten acres. He was very proud of it. He showed me where he had been plowing. I stooped to examine the plow.

"Why!" I exclaimed. "No wonder those ponies wouldn't go. Your plow's running beam deep."

"It won't go any other way," Two Bears admitted sadly. "See, I've put the doubletrees down to the lowest notch."

Then I realized that the plows given out to the Indians were made for horses, not for ponies. So when the Indians were forced to hitch up their ponies, the collars hung so low that the plow dug down in clear to the beam.

When I asked for news of my other special friends in the tribe, the answers were not cheering. Kind old Meepee had died not long after I left, from the effects of the wound she had received in the Sioux raid while she guarded the three children who were hidden in the pit. Chazaninga, restless and angry because Sunshine had been taken East by white women, had joined other tribes in their battles against the whites. Before long he was captured and imprisoned; and while in prison he was visited often by a prison missionary who could speak his language. Later, when freed, he went back to the missionary and asked to be made a member of that church. After long training he finally was ordained as a minister. For some years now he had had a little Indian congregation of his own far up the Missouri. He had never married—an almost unheard-of thing for an Indian of those days.

These facts interested me deeply, partly because they were so totally unexpected. A few months later I was present at the huge yearly encampment of all the Christian Indians in the northwest. When the meetings had come to an end and all the farewells had been said and my tent was the only one left standing, I saw a tall, dignified Indian approaching me, leading a horse. I noticed that he moved with a peculiar grace which somehow seemed familiar to me.

Pausing before me, he said quietly, "You were present when Sunshine was captured and her mother was wounded."

I looked him steadily in the face, held out my hand, and said, "Chazaninga!"

He did not take my hand, but turned away as if to hide some intense feeling. Then, after a moment, he answered sadly:

"The old life has passed away. I try now to live the new life."

Without another word he mounted his horse and rode away.

And what of lovely little Sunshine herself? Two Bears and his wife could tell me only the main facts from the Indian viewpoint, but gradually I heard the whole story from others who could understand the drama of it far better. Here it is.

Sunshine's terrible experiences as a captive and her serious illness afterward which finally had led to her going East to learn the white people's ways had happened in 1857. Five years later the stage landed in the center of a little isolated prairie town two well-dressed, ladylike Indian girls who looked frankly appalled at finding no one there to meet them. They had trusted the head of their Eastern school who, according to Eastern ideas, had notified each home in ample time. Now they had only ten cents in money and knew nowhere to go. For five years they had lived the completely sheltered lives of cultured women in a civilized state, yet here they were, suddenly stranded in a totally strange place.

Some of the town's shabby loafers, noticing how pretty Sunshine was, began to try to scrape acquaintance. For refuge the girls hurried into a little bakeshop close by, where they spent their ten cents for crackers. The fat, not overneat woman in charge of it proved to be kindly. When she fully understood the situation, she stormed about the school which had launched its innocent girls forth so recklessly and with so little regard for the probable delays which would be caused by the agency's constant carelessness in handling Indian mail and by the Indians' need to hunt up an interpreter. Finally she took both girls to her own home, fed them generously, and sheltered them for two days until someone came for them.

Early in the afternoon of that second day Sunshine saw an Indian driving a team of tired pinto ponies that were hauling a heavy lumber wagon. She watched him first drive to the stage stop and then, still in his wagon, go wandering up and down the street, trying to peer into the stores as if searching for someone. Yet he asked no questions; perhaps he did not know a word of English. Hesitatingly Sunshine left the store and went across the street to see if she could help him. The other girl, Nellie, stood watching from the doorway.

This Indian was a greasy-looking man with a red cotton handkerchief tied round his head. He was clothed in a filthily dirty once-white shirt and an equally dirty cotton sheet worn as a blanket.

In the bottom of the wagon under the full blaze of the sun which beat down on her uncovered head sat his wife—patient, dirty. Beside her were piled a tent-cloth, black with smoke, an ax, and a camp kettle. Tied outside the wagon were eight smoke-stained tent poles.

As the Indian saw Sunshine's graceful, fashionably dressed figure coming toward him, he climbed politely down from the wagon, and stood staring into the face which five years of absence from the prairie sunshine had left hardly darker than any white brunette's. What did this white woman want of him? Then their eyes met—and the old tenderness suddenly shone out in both faces. They did not shake hands or kiss; such was not the Indian way. He merely said, "My daughter." The tears ran down his face and hers. With very little food he had driven forty miles across the prairie to fetch her.

Sunshine, however, still looked at him incredulously. Five years ago she had left her father, Light of the Sun, as a man who, though poor because he was lame, still was reasonably respected in the tribe, and who was decently dressed in native clothes which Meepee toiled hard to keep always fresh, whole, and clean. Now Sunshine could recognize only his eyes—and a pair of beautiful beaded moccasins which Meepee once had made for him, his sole visible link with the old days. And she realized now that the dirty woman seated stolidly in the wagon was her new mother, with whom she must live until she herself married.

Very quickly Sunshine and her plainer, dark-skinned companion, Nellie, seated in the wagon among their trunks and satchels, were starting on their way to the reservation. Luckily Nellie's father, a French half-breed, lived on a creek road into which they could easily turn aside, so that Sunshine could leave Nellie safely at home instead of stranded there in the town for no one knew how long. The kindly bakeshop woman, her arms akimbo, stood looking after the girls with tears in her eyes.

Five miles out of town Light of the Sun drove his team aside into a little grove of box elders and cottonwoods. His wife clambered down, unhitched and unharnessed the ponies, turned them out to graze, and began to set up the tent. Sunshine and Nellie stepped forward to help, but the woman, eying their neat dresses with evident awe, waved them aside. They gave in willingly. It was so long since they had done any such labor that they feared they would be slow and stupid. But they gathered some dry sticks for a fire and, while the woman kindled it, Sunshine took the camp kettle down to the creek to fetch water. Before she succeeded, she had sunk into the sticky mud over the tops of her shoes.

The woman had taken from the wagon a gunny bag from which she drew out a few hard, brittle strips of sun-dried beef. With a knife drawn from her belt she whittled these into long pieces which she dropped into the camp kettle. While this was boiling, she made coffee in a smoke-blackened coffeepot. After the meat had boiled for half an hour, she sharpened a stick and with it she picked out pieces to divide among the four of them. There was no bread, no vegetable or fruit, no balanced diet such as the girls had been taught to enjoy at school.

The sight and still more the smell of that boiled dried beef brought back to each girl a flood of memories of her own early childhood and of happy days on the annual buffalo hunts. It was all that Sunshine could do to keep back the hot, scalding tears of longing for her own mother, Meepee. How different her welcome would have been from the best this utter stranger could give! Yet the woman was trying to be kind. Of the two tin cups she gave one to the girls, the other to her husband. Only when all the rest were satisfied would she pour out the dregs of the coffee for herself.

In the morning they all ate more of the beef and started on. Within two miles they met Nellie's father coming for her. He had not heard of her arrival until the night before, but then at once he had set off anxiously and had driven all night. He transferred Nellie and her things to his own neat, sturdy wagon. Soon afterward he halted at a branch in the road. The girls told each other a sad good-by—and parted, never to meet again while both lived.

Plain, dark Nellie fortunately went to a prosperous home in a log house of several rooms, with her own loving father, mother, and brothers and sisters. Though the housekeeping often was a very casual effort, the house was well furnished, and stood almost on the reservation line, next to a compact white settlement. As a half-breed, Nellie's father had resisted the Indian traditions of big feasts and ostentatious giving and had lived thriftily. Therefore he was scorned by the Indians as stingy—in their eyes the most despicable of traits. But he now owned a large herd of horses and lived with his family a life into which Nellie's broader training and new dainty ways dovetailed perfectly—to the pride and happiness of all concerned.

Far out across the prairie rode charming little Sunshine in the grubby old lumber wagon, well aware by now that her father was disappointed in her having come back "so much like a white woman," and wondering what lay ahead of her. The old free life of the camp and the plains lingered in her memory with charm, but she knew that in this region that life already was gone. Late in the afternoon they reached the home in which she must face the new ways—a small log hut, partly underground, with one door, one little square window which did not open, and a roof of sods. Around it, scattered along a small creek, lay the rest of the village, mostly formed of houses like Light of the Sun's. The tiny settlement was twenty-five miles from the agency and forty from the stage route. The only reminders of the old days which Sunshine saw in it were two large tents, some twenty feet in diameter. It also had an assembling place for the whole village in the form of a great mud lodge, built to hold three hundred. All the bottom land along the creek was planted with little patches of vegetables and corn.

Sunshine's trunk, landed in the hut's one room, seemed to take up most of it. And as soon as she had unlocked it, the girl made the gesture which was to typify the rest of her life there. She raised the lid, took off the hat of civilization, which five years in the East had made a matter of course to her, laid it inside the trunk, and left it there—forever.

After a very slender supper the stepmother offered Sunshine two blankets. Rolled in these she lay down on the dirt floor and slept. Next day a few relatives called, but as there now was no food at all in the house, for either them or their hosts, they did not stay long. In the afternoon all three hungry Indians went eagerly to visit relatives who would be able to offer them the food they needed so badly. So at last they were fed.

When night came, drums began to beat in one of the big tents close by. Someone was giving a dance and a feast. Sunshine, conforming to local style, drew a blanket over her head and went with the other women to stand outside and look on. When she came back to the stuffy little hut, she could not sleep against the noise of the dance, which went on nearly all night. She lay there on the hard floor, thinking sadly of the quiet in the long, airy dormitory at the school, with its rows of cool, clean beds. Next day she learned that at the dance several Indians had earned new influence and the admiration of the whole band because they had given away every last thing they owned.

No one in that whole village could speak or read English. There was no school anywhere near. Except for Sunshine's own scanty schoolbooks, now buried deep in her trunk, there was never a book or a newspaper or anything else to occupy an eager mind which for five years had devoured every scrap of human knowledge that could be reached along its path. Except for a little work in Light of the Sun's small field in the early spring there was nothing at all, here in another woman's home, for Sunshine to do except now and then to tan a hide and to make ornamental moccasins and bead necklaces. Nothing at all. And she had nowhere else to go. In her one promised letter to Nellie she poured out her whole troubled heart, but she never wrote again.

Meanwhile into a very similar village some fifty miles to the north a young, pleasing white woman with plenty of means had come as what we today would call a settlement worker. She planned to board in the only respectably built house and learn the language, but within three months she had almost driven the woman of that household frantic by constantly asking the Indian name of everything in sight. Just then this harassed mother heard about Nellie and her fine education, so she sent an interpreter to tell her boarder, whom I will call here Miss Green, about this rare chance to learn the tribe's speech properly from a girl who could speak both languages well. Before long Miss Green had engaged Nellie to live with her there in the village in a new house to be built especially for their needs. Miss Green planned this new home as the center of her activities for the tribe.

Soon the old missionary from the agency, who with a young Indian helper held monthly services there, asked Miss Green whether, in case his church were willing to build an addition to her house for use as a schoolroom, she would take charge of it. Miss Green refused the task but offered Nellie as the teacher. The school thrived, all the more because Nellie and Miss Green managed by all sorts of ingenious schemes to entice the young Indians into giving up the paint habit, and won the girls over to wearing hats as an obvious symbol of welcome to the new ways.

At the end of the year Nellie married the missionary's earnest young helper, White Ghost, with the warm approval of Miss Green, who arranged for them to live there with her and for Nellie to go on teaching the school. So a couple of years slipped by.

The fourth summer after the two girls had come back from the East, Miss Green with Nellie and White Ghost went to the big annual Christian meeting. Miss Green was a guest in the resident missionary's own home. One morning as she passed through the kitchen she saw a poorly dressed Indian woman sitting on the floor and burdened with a tiny baby strapped to her back. The woman's head was bent forward. She slowly swayed back and forth.

Miss Green spoke to her, but she took no notice. Then Miss Green knelt beside her and, looking into her face, found it thin and haggard, with deeply sunken eyes. Lifting the little baby from the tired back, Miss Green was horrified to see that the tiny thing was literally mere skin and bones. Hastily she called the missionary's wife. Meanwhile the Indian woman had leaned her head back against the wall and let her hands drop helplessly at her sides. The missionary's wife ran for the doctor. Miss Green quickly found some food for the baby and began feeding it.

The doctor hurried in and examined first the woman and then her baby. He gave the mother a stimulant and, certain that she, poor soul, could not understand him, did not hesitate to say frankly to Miss Green:

"This Indian's dying of consumption. She may rally for a few days, but I think she'll die before morning. The child has no disease—it's simply starving. Pour a lot more of that strong beef tea into it. It works well with these young Indians."

After she had settled the woman cleanly and comfortably in bed, Miss Green sat down beside her with tear-filled eyes. At last she began to sing in a low voice in the Indian tongue:

"Nearer my God to Thee,
Nearer to Thee."

The woman's eyes opened heavily. She said in slow but perfect English:

"It was a long way and I was very tired, but I knew I was going to die."

Miss Green listened, amazed. The Indian went on feebly, as if fumbling for half-forgotten words:

"My baby was hungry all the time. I had no food for it. I knew if I left it with them when I was dead, it would die too. I carried my baby all the way—to give it to the missionaries—so it might live. I saw you feeding it. That made me—so happy."

She lay a moment with closed eyes, and then whispered slowly and weakly:

"The way—was—v-e-r-y—l-o-ng."

Miss Green bowed her head on her hand. When she looked up, the woman was dead.

When the missionary came home from the afternoon meeting, he found Miss Green alone with the dead Indian.

"Do you happen to know who this woman was?" she asked him.

He took the cloth from the worn face and looked down at it pityingly.

"Yes," he sighed. "I know about her. She was sent to school in the East and was well educated. Then she was returned to her band. They all were blanket Indians and had kept all of the old customs they could. This girl's father sold her to a man for his second wife. I heard he got ten ponies for her. Then, because she wasn't strong and had lost the knack in doing things well in the Indian way, her husband constantly abused her and half starved her."

Just then Nellie came in. She went to the bedside, looked down at the haggard dead woman, and burst into tears. Turning away, she sobbed:

"Oh, Miss Green, that's poor little Sunshine."

That night a great silence fell on the big Christian encampment, for everyone had heard Sunshine's pathetic story. The Christian Indians made all the arrangements for the funeral services the next day, and an Indian minister volunteered to preach the sermon. The whole service was in the Indian language. The tall, dignified, graceful preacher gave out his text. Soon the whole congregation was in tears, which gradually gave way to a look of hope and joy. With his last words they all rose to join in the Indian words of the hymn:

"In the cross of Christ I glory."

Sunshine's body was laid to rest with the full service of burial on the top of the highest hill in the neighborhood. That night was still and clear. Long after midnight Miss Green and Nellie —the white woman who had pitied Sunshine and the Indian girl who had loved her—sat together by an open window looking up at the hill, and watching where, silhouetted against the northern sky, a tall Indian stood beside the grave, as motionless as the great boulders scattered about him.

"Who was he?" I asked Nellie when I met her at the next yearly encampment after my call on Two Bears. She, who understood better than anyone else the whole tragic little tale, had just told me her version of the final years of the joyous little friend of my youth. "Do you think it was her husband?"

Nellie shook her head.

"I really don't know why he did it," she admitted, "but it was the preacher."

I, too, felt puzzled by that lonely watch on the hillside until the next day at the close of that same meeting, as I have told already, I spoke for the first time in years with Chazaninga.

18.

Revolvers and Bibles

In 1871, while collecting religious news for the St. Louis *Globe*, I reported a Northern Methodist Episcopal Conference in northern Missouri. I heard a presiding elder state that their denomination had not one preacher in either Platte or Clay counties, Missouri; in fact that he could not induce one to go there, because they all knew how the natives hated Northerners and Northern institutions, and because they feared the robber bands of the James brothers and the Kansas Red Legs. Afterward I told that elder that, if he would license me to preach, I would serve in those counties in spite of the Jameses and the Younger crowd and Red Legs and all the other rebels. So he recommended me, and the bishop appointed me as a preacher.

I bought a circus tent in St. Louis to hold three hundred people. I put it and my wife aboard a steamboat and told the captain to land us in Clay County. He set us ashore near an abandoned fort, garrisoned long before the Civil War. We camped there several days while I tried to hire some farmer to haul the tent inland to a little valley. As no farmer would have dealings with a Northern man, I had to fall back on persuading one of the "poor white trash" to tackle the job.

We had brought with us a primitive little melodeon, and my wife, who had a splendid voice and was a skilled pianist, could somehow lure out of it a passable accompaniment for her singing. At first the natives merely hung around the entrance to listen; gradually they ventured in. Before long I had a large congregation every evening.

One afternoon three heavily armed men rode up to the tent and dismounted. I shook hands with them as they hitched their horses, and invited them in. After we had all exchanged a few commonplaces, I asked my wife to play and sing. One of the men asked if she knew a certain old hymn tune. As it was new to her, she asked him to hum it. Instead, he whistled it through —and she promptly played it back to him.

"Sing the words," I told him. "She'll play an accompaniment." It went well, and after one hearing she sang each chorus with him. When the other men asked her to choose a song for them, she gave them: "Home, Sweet Home."

A touching silence followed—until one stranger muttered, "Jesse, this thing is all right."

He thrust his hand into his pocket, drew out two or three silver dollars, and dropped them into his hat, which he then held out to the others. Each tossed half a handful of silver into it. Finally he carried it to my wife and poured the contents into her lap, explaining:

"That's to support the Gospel."

They had hardly ridden comfortably away down the winding road under the trees before a native hurried up to demand: "Do you know who those men were?"

"I do not."

"The Younger brothers and Jesse James!"

Soon afterward the James gang robbed a bank in Liberty, Missouri, and carried off a good sackful of cash. I happened to be there that very day—so naturally I joined the posse to follow them. We overtook them in a schoolhouse, probably halting to divide up the loot, and they fled to a cornfield, where they dropped behind the shelter of a rail fence and began to shoot. We had ten men to their one, but our crowd, I soon learned, were not fighters. I begged them to charge and attack, but they would not even follow my lead. All I achieved by riding on ahead was to get my horse shot. The outlaws stole away, and fled across the Missouri to the Sand Hills.

Several weeks later I was riding along beside a fence that was lined higher than my head with weeds and brush. As I turned a blind corner, I came square on Jesse James. His horse was halted, his revolver drawn. He "had the drop on me." Looking me squarely in the face, he demanded:

"I want to know whether it's war or peace."

"Under the present circumstances," I answered, "I'm for peace."

He laughed, and then asked, "Are you going after us any more, or will you stick to that preaching business?"

I replied that I was so disgusted with that Liberty posse that I had long since made up my mind to have nothing more to do with them.

"Just think of it," I concluded. "Five of you fellows held off fifty or sixty men just as well armed as you were."

He told me to ride on.

My wife and I and our tent traveled all over Platte and Clay counties. Today's dwellers in that land of peace can hardly imagine the state of society there after the war. Murderous gangs overran the country; bloody crimes were constantly happening. I always went armed, and I addressed our congregations with a revolver either lying beside the Bible or equally ready to my hand elsewhere. Our tent was attacked several times, while our hearers took to the brush until the shooting stopped. In each emergency my wife was as brave and cool as a man. Almost always there were a few men, mostly Union sympathizers, to stand by me, but twice I was left to fight it out alone. Probably all that saved our lives was my reputation as an expert shot. At any rate, my enemies never combined to charge me in a body, and they seemed to view my revolver with decided respect.

During those two Missouri years I received practically no salary. Wherever we went, our entertainment was provided for us—that was all. I earned our living by writing for the newspapers—and it was a very poor living.

In that country of malarial diseases, too, where there were no educated doctors and the local healers relied on blistering, bleeding, salivation with mercury, and sometimes on quinine up to fifty grains at a dose, I found that prescribing for the sufferers without a fee was merely a regular taken-for-granted side of a Methodist circuit rider's work. Because careful observation taught me that healers' methods were worse than useless, I discarded them all—and most of my patients got well. For instance, a young man in Harlem, where we were living, sent for me to save him in a bad attack of the same malarial fever from which his brother, using the regulation treatments, had died a week before. My simple directions and prescriptions cured my patient in only a few days.

Just then I heard that a former Civil War bushwhacker, one Lige Schofield, was in a little town nearby, and that he had decided that it was time to rid the region of me; so he sent me orders to "clear out within twenty-four hours" or else he would "put me fuller of holes than a skimmer." I had had several such warnings before, but somehow this one particularly exasperated me; so I bade its bearer tell Lige that he had better go to the mourner's bench that very night, get religion, and join the church, because the next day I was coming to his town and would make sure that the region was rid of him.

Harlem had a "local preacher" named Bill Price. When he heard what I was planning to do, he offered to go along with me. Next day, when we reached Lige's town, I took up a position where I could not possibly be attacked from the rear, and where any front or flank attack would expose the attacker to my fire. Then I sent Bill Price through the town to tell the natives that I was there to see which would emigrate—Lige Schofield or I. Bill faithfully started on his errand but soon came back to report that I was a day late. When Lige had heard my answer, he had "skipped the town."

On our way back to Harlem, Bill again begged half jokingly for my best revolver. Now, like all machines, revolvers have individual qualities. Two of the same pattern from the same firm may look exactly alike, but a man can work best with his own familiar tool. But Bill, like old Two Bears fifteen years before, held the notion that with my revolver he would surely shoot just as I did. I knew better, and refused again.

Next day the father of my recovered malarial fever patient called to give me twenty-five dollars in gold. With this to add to some small savings from my newspaper work I decided to leave Missouri and go to western Nebraska, then newly opened to settlers. So we packed our big tent and scanty household goods, but before we left, I gave both my revolvers to Bill Price. In those two Missouri years I had never owned a suit of clothes that was free from bullet holes. In all the years after I discarded deadly weapons no one ever shot at me.

19.

We Face the Famine

Back after sixteen years to the old hunting grounds on the Republican River! There along the valley where the Sioux, Pawnees, Omahas, Iowas, and Otoes had fought their battles for unnumbered years I found great changes. A large tide of immigration was flowing in. Land speculators and owners of townsites were issuing enthusiastic bulletins and seeing wealth ahead. I was assigned as minister to Republican City, close to the middle of Nebraska's southern border—just where I had hunted with Richardson and Redpath.

Already thousands of prairie acres had been planted with corn and wheat by eager young folk, mostly from the Northern states, but many from all over this country and Europe. Some, though they evidently delighted in acquiring Western mannerisms and speech, were finely educated. In they poured, seeking homestead claims—chiefly as poor folk who owned only a "team," a very few household utensils, and scanty provisions which would barely last until their own first crop. Always hopefully they built their sod houses or dugouts and turned over the raw prairie soil, certain that the region would somehow raise enough to feed its still-meager population until next year provided larger fields.

Soon a cheery hospitality drew them into one big family who together looked forward—with good reason—to building themselves and their children permanent homes there. Hardships existed, for 1873 was not a good crop year even for experienced settlers. Much of the cheerfulness hid want, but the ills seemed only temporary.

Even I did not realize quite how hard things were until one day when I "took dinner" potluck with one of my church officers and he apologized for the "slenderness of the repast." It was only flour-and-water cakes; and such delicacies had been his family's chief fare for six months. I soon learned that this was only one case among many.

Meanwhile my wife and I traveled up and down that valley, holding tent meetings where no religious service had ever been known. Even the villages had almost no ministers. Usually we pitched our tent on some hill or rise where it showed up for ten or fifteen miles and brought the people crowding to us.

By late June 1874 the crops were growing splendidly in spite of drought. For months the whole valley had been doing without meat, but each family felt sure that soon it would be gathering the golden grain which would buy food and clothing. Then within the space of one July day an unprecedented disaster literally descended on that entire section of Nebraska and parts of adjoining states, so that every settler faced starvation.

We were "taking supper" with a family we loved dearly. Suddenly I saw the mother's face grow blank; she pointed to the northwest. As we all looked, we saw immense clouds rising swiftly. Then we heard a roar and a rush.

Grasshoppers! Inconceivable millions of them! They instantly filled the air! As I shaded my eyes with my hand and looked toward the sun, the gossamer wings produced an effect I can never forget. The air seemed filled for a mile upward with flakes of snow. Though the cloud itself passed slowly onward, the ground already was spread thickly with those living creatures—all eating. Instantly they began to devour every green thing except the buffalo grass. Any animal which could not live on that grass alone died soon. Then the pigs and the chickens, brought hopefully across hundreds of miles for fine breeding stock, had to die too. Men looked each other in the face and grew pale. They could have fought marauding bands of Cheyennes or Sioux, but these small insects they could not fight.

In no time all up and down that valley those honest, brave, patient, hard-working men, women, and children—my own congregation whom I knew and loved—were hungry, hopelessly hungry. The cupboards of the "soddies" and dugouts held nothing at all but flour, and little of that. And now all hope of more was gone. On such a diet, already too long continued, the people sickened and died, literally from starvation for want of fitting nourishment. Families which had been dragging along on a tiny ration of boiled wheat reached the end of that supply.

Melancholy days followed. Thousands of weeping women and white-faced men left, but thousands more had to stay. How could they get out? No money for railroad fares, no livestock to transport them, no provisions to feed them if they set off afoot! There was genuinely nothing for them to do but stay there and starve. Weeks dragged along without relief or hope, a horror for which there was just one cause—the greed of speculators who forced the newspapers to misrepresent the true facts. For their own selfish interests they were willing to let thousands of American men and women suffer and starve. Reports of famine in Nebraska would keep new settlers away. The value of townsites would crumble. Those speculators controlled the whole local press. Nebraska papers, even outside of the stricken zone, suppressed the bad news for fear it would damage the standing of the unharmed counties.

Gradually my wife handed out to the sufferers nearly everything in our own little cottonwood shanty. When a baby boy was born in a gulch dugout near us, she cut up her only woolen skirt to make clothes for him. One morning I asked her:

"How long can you make our own provisions stretch?"

"About two weeks," she answered.

Neither of us had a cent left, but at least we knew that we should be kept from starving. The real estate men were so anxious for us to stay on right there that winter that they promised to keep us supplied with food. All the local storekeepers who had small stocks of goods on hand were townsite speculators too. But I knew these promisers did not speak from religious zeal. They merely knew it was good advertising for a town to have a church and pastor. The moment I suggested asking famine help from the East they opposed me vehemently. Nevertheless I forced into print here and there some plain statements from persons who had nothing whatever to eat and from doctors who had attended cases who died of starvation.

My effort to appeal to the great American nation for aid brought down on me a flood of abuse and insults from the untouched sections of Nebraska—especially Omaha. The state officials, too, grew furious with me, but all the clergy backed me up and sent out appeals of their own, as well. Then the Nebraska papers promptly denied up and down that any sort of help was needed.

Soon cold weather struck. One day a man came to us through eight inches of snow, dressed in rags, shoeless, with just cloths wound around his feet. He had come fifteen miles afoot. All we had to give him was fifty cents in cash, but with this he at least bought flour for his starving family. So with that small return for his thirty-mile round trip of torture he started home, almost heartbroken with anxiety for the future. And all around us graduates of fine colleges were dreading the harsh Nebraska winter, almost naked, starving. Strong men risked death from hunger exhaustion. I decided it was time for me to start action elsewhere.

One day when the stage came through, I halted its driver. "I want to ride over to Kearney," I told him, "to the railroad to fetch help for these starving people. I know it's a fifty-mile trip and I haven't a cent to pay for it—but all the same I'm going somehow."

"All right!" He motioned me to climb up beside him.

When he stopped at the halfway station for dinner, I walked out over the prairie to make myself forget that I could not buy even a scrap of food. Suddenly I noticed that I had strolled right out on top of a dugout built into the steep bank of a draw. The household inside, hearing me up there, all turned out—and recognized me. They had visited one of our tent meetings.

"Please come in," the father begged. "This morning I managed to trap half-a-dozen prairie chickens. There's plenty to eat!"

That was a wonderful dinner.

As our stage reached the railroad at Kearney, I noticed the private car of the Burlington road's directors standing on a siding. I climbed aboard it and found the Road's powerful friend, J. Sterling Morton, and some of the higher railroad officials inside. I told them all flatly that they ought to do something at once for the settlers over on the Republican River.

"Your railroad is more interested than any other corporation in keeping those people right here in Nebraska," I argued. "If you leave some of them here to starve to death, and the rest manage to get away to tell how and why those others starved, it won't be long until your road won't have any passenger traffic or any freight traffic either."

For these were all businessmen; naturally I must talk to them from the business angle.

"Ten years from now," I told them, "if you let this famine go on, your cottonwood ties will all be rotted, your rails will be two streaks of rust, and your Burlington Railroad stocks and bonds will be worth just what they'll bring as waste paper."

"What do you want us to do, then?" Morton asked.

"I want this railroad to send those sufferers some meat and vegetables."

Morton nodded and went out. Later I learned that he at once bought a quantity of bacon and potatoes and a keg of pickles and ordered them sent to the Republican Valley. Meanwhile the officials invited me to ride in their private car to Omaha. There I went to a small hotel kept by an Irishman and told him squarely that I had no money at all. Then I explained my errand. As I described actual scenes, I saw tears in his eyes. He assured me instantly:

"You can stay at this hotel just as long as you wish without any charge."

On inquiring everywhere what was being done toward relief I learned it amounted to mighty little. Because no grasshoppers had invaded the Missouri Valley, the public there did not dream how serious the disaster was elsewhere. A relief committee with an ex-governor as treasurer had received a few small offerings of money and goods, and the use of a storehouse which held a very few old clothes. That was all. But I myself could not achieve any more. No one believed my reports. Meanwhile I had to live and support my own family, so I decided that my wisest course was to hunt up a job and wait to strike hard when enough of the truth began to leak out to support my statements. That time was bound to come. I heard that a small daily paper, recently started by some striking Omaha printers, thought it might use a reporter. I turned in a sample write-up of the state fair, only to have the editor tell me that he was tired of his job already and preferred to set type, so I must be editor. As the pay was good, I sent for my wife and our two little girls.

This opening solved our own problem, but it did not lessen our heartache at the letters from our Republican Valley people. I could not sleep for thinking of them, and though I accomplished nothing by my efforts, I kept hammering at that Omaha committee, warning them that thirty to forty thousand Nebraska people must be helped promptly either to stay or go. But not one real preparation for relief was made.

Suddenly one day General Ord, the local military commander, asked me to give him all the facts I could. Coincidently an immigration agent who had been especially bitter toward my appeals returned from a trip of his own through the seven Republican Valley counties—and began eagerly to endorse every word I had said. Right there he had found 2300 people who for seven months to come must be given rations which, even with free transportation, would cost nearly $116,-000. His report set other groups to investigating.

Abruptly the authorities woke to the horrible truth that not seven but thirty-six counties were destitute. With their best efforts they would be able to issue to ten thousand starving people only half rations of the coarsest food—flour, onions, sauerkraut. Worse still, they shared at last the dread which had haunted me for months: that soon if even those poor rations were to fail for just one short week, the ten thousand people would die—and already winter was actually here.

Easterners could not dream what that thought meant to experienced plainsmen, especially in those early days of Western railroad construction. At any moment a blizzard might close down all traffic for ten or twelve days under impenetrable snow. Unless supplies were brought together and rushed out to distributing centers at once, the lives of more than half of Nebraska's citizens would be at the mercy of the weather. Only prompt help given now could ward off a national calamity. This was the factor which the many tenderfoot Eastern-reared speculators and newspaper owners refused to admit—even now, when the disaster they themselves had caused loomed right over the district.

A few days after our first talk General Ord detailed Major

Brisbin to go East for the Nebraska Aid Society. He raised money in Cleveland, Buffalo, and elsewhere, but not enough to matter. Some condemned army clothing which was distributed counted for nothing among so many. And impostors, always alert, turned up everywhere, begging funds which they serenely pocketed.

I decided that different means must be tried. With the Aid Society's endorsement I could go out at last and tell what I personally knew. Backed by General Ord, I went to Chicago, which, as the center of a vast grain trade, could readily sympathize with this tragedy. There the president of the Board of Trade agreed to let me talk to the board myself, but he warned me not to expect any cash. The busy traders would stop for no one. Still, my effort might attract public interest and thus encourage help elsewhere.

On December 22, 1874, I went with the president to the little stand set above the howling mob of traders. When he rapped loudly with his gavel, all eyes turned toward us. Without waiting for his introduction I called at the top of my lungs, "Listen!" For five minutes I described actual sufferings which I myself had seen. In the sixth minute a Nebraska Relief and Aid Committee took shape and began to scoop in money and checks. The ninth minute trading started again, but the new committee already held $3500 for the fund.

The very next morning every Chicago paper printed a long dispatch from Omaha denouncing me as a fraud, and denying that any Nebraskan was suffering at all. As previously arranged, I met the new committee to draw up plans. I asked what they thought of those dispatches. A spokesman answered that a man who positively refused personally to receive or handle one cent of money when it was thrust upon him, or to allow anyone to pay his hotel bill, simply could not be a fraud.

I assured them that the Nebraska headquarters, too, were trustworthy, especially now that an army quartermaster had charge of all shipments. "He picks up every pin and button," I told them, "and it goes onto the lists and is charged and receipted for."

That Chicago committee went right on collecting and forwarding money and pushing the relief work until they had shipped to the Nebraska Aid Society several carloads of supplies, including clothing, shoes, and bedding. Meanwhile I went up to the Milwaukee Chamber of Commerce in another grain center. This, too, responded promptly and generously and started a successful appeal to the public. These various contributions greatly relieved the famine temporarily, but nothing relieved the onslaughts I now had to face from nearly all the eighty-odd papers in Nebraska. No name was too vile to apply to me. And when I reached home I found the printers' strike over and their daily paper ended, but I promptly secured work on the Omaha *Bee*.

Though the press still stormed at me, no one could now hold down all the truth, for the famine naturally grew steadily worse. Soon General Ord detailed three army quartermasters to make a thorough survey. They brought back affidavits from 49,000 Nebraska residents who declared under oath that, unless helped promptly, they must go or die. Then General Ord urged me to go East again, but those state-wide insults had been too villainous. I felt I could not stand any fresh attacks. At last a notably honest and educated Easterner, Rev. G. W. Frost, who knew the West, consented to make the trip—on condition that I would go with him as chief speaker. After I had held out for another day or two, the thought of my Republican Valley people forced me to go—if General Ord would give us an official commission.

We found eager, responsive audiences in Detroit, Buffalo, and Utica. At this last meeting two senators spoke and Governor Seymour of New York State presided. Afterward he took

me out to his farm with him for two days. At Troy, where the
meeting was held in the opera house with the stage full of dignitaries, I felt myself on alien soil. Everything was so very
polished and cold and aloof. Mr. Frost spoke politely as an
Easterner to Easterners. I saw little chance of a good response.
So at the first pause I sprang, unintroduced, to the front of the
stage and plunged ahead in impulsive Western fashion.

"I don't pretend to be civilized," I told them. "I only know
that mothers are clasping their starving children to their bos-
oms out on those wind-swept plains—that there's no food in
those dugouts and sod houses. They are American citizens; they
love God and read their Bibles the same as you do. They've
not asked for help; they suffer in silence. But I ask you to help
them."

Before I had finished telling actual cases I had seen, people
began to throw money and pocketbooks onto the stage. A man
in back shouted, "There's half-a-dozen here who want to give!
Start someone round to take up a collection!"

Then, as the committee leader protested that he had secured
the opera house on his guarantee of no collection, a notable on
the stage jumped to his feet and called out, "Let those who
made a pledge like that keep it. I wasn't a party to it and I'm
not bound by it!"

He grabbed up a bunch of dignitaries' hats from a table behind him and dealt them out to the group on the stage, saying:

"Go down there and get what those people want to give!"

Back came the hats piled up with bills, checks, and jewelry.
If I remember rightly, it amounted to about three thousand dollars. That was just one instance of what the East was ready to
do for the West, once it had a fair chance to understand the
need.

The climax of our trip was to have been a huge New York
meeting, but just as all arrangements were completed, General

Ord peremptorily called us back to Omaha. There he told us his reason:

"I wouldn't suffer men under my orders to be the targets of such abuse as the Nebraska papers were heaping on you."

However, in our thirty days out we had raised some $80,000 in cash, and also many carloads of supplies; more contributions in money and goods kept coming in all winter from along our route. Though the total could not end all the suffering, it did enable the people to keep their homesteads, and thus it saved Nebraska from losing many years in her development. For though the speculators and their hired papers firmly refused to admit the fact, nevertheless if those people had starved to death unhelped, naturally, as I had told J. Sterling Morton months earlier, the tragedy would have become notorious, and many years would have passed before other settlers would face risks to fill the vacant places.

20.

Sent to Old Spot

At first after the grasshopper war, though I earned our living by writing, I continued my religious work, beginning with a crowd of newsboys at the Omaha Union Depot, where the general superintendent lent us a room for our meetings. Soon some families nearby joined us in organizing a church. I discovered a girl whose voice had wonderful upper and lower registers, though it was poor in certain middle-register notes. When I planned songs for her which avoided those notes, she drew a crowd. To keep up the good work, I wrote, first, some original music and then a cantata for her, all suited to her needs; these brought her success. Before long, by writing music, giving concerts, and other devices, I had raised enough funds for a small church and a parsonage.

One day one of the many army officers who had become my friends asked me if I knew the real character of a man who had some authority over me in the Church. As I looked blank, he referred me to records at the army headquarters where the story was on file. After reading it, I felt that duty compelled me to lay the matter before an ecclesiastical court, but that court refused even to hear the evidence from the official record on the plainly stated ground that the Church considered that all army officers were wicked, and that their testimony was unreliable.

Thereupon the man himself charged me with slander. In the

long run we both were acquitted, but I withdrew from that church. I did this with a clear conscience because coincidently I turned over to the Church the property, valued at many hundred dollars, which my efforts had secured. Also, I realized that for my religious labors of some five years I had never received, all told, enough to support my little family completely for even three months.

At last I was left free really to follow the newspaper profession, and I went at it hard and struggled steadily ahead in it through nearly three years of night work, of being practically a stranger to my wife and my two little daughters. Finally I became assistant editor and principal editorial writer on the Omaha *Herald*. Meanwhile I kept up my interest in Indian affairs and my army friends. High among these I rated Brigadier General George Crook, commander of the whole department of the Platte, with his headquarters in Omaha.

So far as I have heard, he was the only other white man who ever was made by the Omahas a member of the Soldier Lodge, the great Indian secret fraternity into which I had been taken in 1856, when I wintered with the Indians. Because we both remembered the painful initiation ordeal and understood some of the hidden mysteries of Indian religion and thought, we were conscious of a unique bond between us.

I was one of the few white men who realized how in the terrible crisis year of 1876, after Custer's defeat, Crook accomplished something which he himself appraised as the most valuable service of his whole life, for he prevented what undoubtedly would have been the greatest of all Indian wars. I myself often heard him express surprise afterward that no historian had ever recorded that fact. For he—and only he—made possible a treaty which soon brought all those hostile Indians back to their reservations and restored peace throughout the whole region of the Dakotas, Wyoming, and northern Nebraska. As part of this treaty, thanks to Crook's special personal authority and skill, Spotted Tail's band of five or six thousand Brûlé Sioux were safely landed at the Rosebud Agency, their third location in eight years.

They had surrendered their lands in the Black Hills by the treaty of 1868; had been relocated on the Missouri, where the whites had proved hostile and the facilities for getting liquor were dangerously many, and had then been removed to Rosebud, where the land, though apparently barren, had its possibilities and suited their wishes. Unfortunately, later in that same difficult year of 1876 the still-new Indian commissioner, who was sure he knew far more about Indians' needs than General Crook or the other army men who had spent thirty years on the plains, ordered Spotted Tail's band to go again to the Missouri, just above where the Niobrara joins it. He justified this removal by a recent act of Congress which had set on foot a new puss-in-the-corner game for the "men in Washington" to play with the tribes and the reservations.

Spotted Tail and his chiefs naturally were furious at having their earlier treaties repudiated. They firmly refused to be moved because it was too late in the year for the whole tribe, with its old, its sick, and its children, to undertake that long journey. Scores of them would die. So all Crook's recent fine work for peace seemed likely to go for nothing. In fact "Old Spot," as the West called him, declared out-and-out that the government had shown so much bad faith that there was no use in even attempting any more contracts or treaties.

"The best thing to do," he insisted, "is to take to the warpath, flee to the Bad Lands, and fight it out to the bitter end."

Naturally the whole affair worried Crook's entire department. That removal order would cause them another long, hard, deadly winter campaign which would cost the country millions. Crook vainly pulled every possible wire to have the order rescinded. When the whites failed him, he went to see

Spotted Tail. Then from Rosebud itself he sent Washington such vigorous protests and prophecies of trouble ahead that he partly succeeded. The Washington group agreed to let Crook make a new contract for only a temporary removal. All the tribe's winter supplies, they explained, had been shipped there to that Missouri location. They could not be shipped to Rosebud by railroad so far into the winter season. If only the Indians would come and join their supplies, they should surely return to Rosebud in the spring.

Canny Old Spot said at once that this was just a scheme to get the tribe moved, whereupon this agreement, like all the treaties, would be repudiated. However, if General Crook personally would promise that in the spring Spotted Tail and his band should surely return to Rosebud, he would go. But he added casually that possibly this removal might end in an even bigger war than if they fled now to the Bad Lands, because soon the Missouri bank opposite the new reservation would be lined with whiskey shops to supply his young men freely. Then war and murder would follow—yes, plenty of both before spring.

Yet, when General Crook gave Spotted Tail his personal word of honor, confirmed in writing, to do everything in his power to hold the men in Washington to their promise, Old Spot yielded reluctantly. The report of the army officer who conducted that march is filed in Washington. His record of that journey of the sick and the old, the women and little children, through terrible cold which brought suffering and death, is one of the most horrible of all the cruel stories in the War Department's abundant archives. But the Indian commissioner had had his way; he planned to keep on having it.

In February 1877 the commissioner formally announced that he himself soon would travel westward to hold a council with Spotted Tail and induce him to stay right there on the Missouri.

The day General Crook heard that news he came to see me, heartsick. He had given those Indians his word; now he felt sure that this new treachery would result in a general war that would involve all the northern tribes.

He came again a few days later—and that is how I personally shared in a near-tragedy which mercifully turned into a comedy. At last I can tell it because all the other chief actors are dead. General Crook asked me, his fellow-member of the Soldier Lodge, to go secretly with a message from him to Spotted Tail.

I was to tell Old Spot that General Crook truly had kept his word and done his utmost to hold the "men at Washington" to their promise, but now the commissioner himself was coming to persuade the Brûlé Sioux to stay there. I was to urge Spotted Tail to refuse even to discuss that proposition at all—and to make some sort of a demonstration which would strike terror to the hearts of the "men from Washington." I gladly undertook the mission, agreeing to Crook's firm demand that I should be very cautious not to let anyone, either white or Indian, learn who I was or what my purpose was.

Soon I sat one evening in Spotted Tail's tent, delivering Crook's message to him. I had grown so rusty in using the sign language that I dared not rely on it completely, but I could at least let him know that my errand was very important indeed and ask for a reliable interpreter who could keep a secret. He provided one. Then I not only repeated Crook's message in full, but I added on my own account a warning to make the biggest "bluff" he had ever played. I knew the old chief was no novice at poker. He understood just what that term "bluff" meant.

Therefore in May, when the commissioner and his entourage arrived, Spotted Tail's stage was set. On the sunny side of a large frame building the Washington magnates assembled for their council with the Indians. These last, with every brave present, were dressed for their roles. Covered with war paint, they looked as frightful and dangerous as possible. The interpreter was the Rev. Alfred Riggs, who, born among the Sioux, did more effective work than anyone else for their advancement.

The white participants in the council, the "men from Washington," were not imposing. The commissioner was perfectly bald, lacking even those three hairs which cartoonists like to implant on all bald heads. He spoke first, assuring the Indians that it would be much better for them to remain there than return to Rosebud. The government, he said, intended to give them many presents of horses, wagons, plows, cattle, household furniture, and provisions. Now how much easier to bring all those goods straight here by water rather than send them the many miles to Rosebud in wagons. In short, his eloquence—and sincerity—matched the speech Two Bears had made to the old bull buffalo long ago.

When he ceased, Old Spot rose up, large and commanding.

"I have made," he exploded fiercely, "many treaties with men who came from Washington. Never has one of those been kept. All the men who come from Washington are liars, but the worst liars among them are the bald-headed ones! This last treaty must be kept!" He brandished his copy of it in the air. "If everything here is not on wheels and moving inside of ten days, I shall turn my young men loose, and they will make a desert of all the country between here and the Platte!"

I have never seen the commissioner's own official record of that speech, but that is how it was reported to me—on the best possible authority. I was told, too, that "the commissioner turned pale as death, and some of the others still paler." At any rate they got back across the Missouri as quickly as they could. And before the ten days were up "everything was on wheels" and was actually moving—although it traveled only ten miles before camping for two weeks to wait for more supplies for the journey.

The night after that council I, a visiting reporter, slipped into Old Spot's tepee. He greeted me most cordially and asked me, laughing, "Did I do it right? I was a little afraid I had overdone it."

The Secretary of the Interior's 1878 report of the incident, as quoted in Helen Hunt Jackson's *Century of Dishonor*, stated: "The Indians were found to be quite determined to move westward, and the promise of the Government in that respect was faithfully kept."

When I saw that report, I felt that I should like to watch a poker game between Old Spot and that Secretary of the Interior.

21.

The Poncas Need Help

At nearly one in the morning, March 30, 1879, almost two years after my last talk with Spotted Tail, I was working hard in the *Herald* editorial rooms. My chief was away, and I was carrying his share, too. Suddenly General Crook came in. I could see by his face that something had gone very wrong.

"During twenty-five or thirty years that I've been on the plains in the government service," he told me, "I've been forced many times by orders from Washington to do most inhuman things in dealing with the Indians, but now I'm ordered to do a more cruel thing than ever before. I would resign my commission, if that would prevent the order from being executed—but it would not. Another officer would merely be assigned to fill my place. I've come to ask if you will not take up the matter. It's no use for me to protest. Washington always orders the very opposite of what I recommend."

Then we two, the only white members of the Soldier Lodge, began a talk which did not reach its full result for over seven years.

Someday a historian will take up the tale of those years scientifically, examining the United States court decisions in the cases which I was the means of bringing to trial, and searching the records in Washington and the newspaper files which told the daily events. Finally he will write a permanent, reliable account of a very vital chapter in our nation's history.

For at long last the outcome of General Crook's appeal to me was that our government reversed its hundred-year-old policy toward a whole race of people. Here I can touch only a few high spots of my own personal share in the struggle.

In the spring of 1877 the department at Washington, which had been busily shifting tribe after tribe down into the newly formed Indian Territory—now Oklahoma—had tackled the Poncas. These were a gentle, friendly band of 710 Indians who owned outright through title in fee simple their own reservation on the Niobrara River, up by the Nebraska-South Dakota boundary. From these Poncas, more than half of whom were women and children, the farms they owned and loved had been harshly taken away. Most of the homes and practically all the farming tools were either destroyed or sternly removed. Then the whole tribe had been driven down by soldiers to a certain unwholesome tract in the Indian Territory. On that heartlessly cruel journey many of the tribe had died. The Department of the Interior's annual report for 1877 tells the pitiful day-by-day story of that exodus.

This removal had been carried out in spite of the protests of experienced officials and Western legislators. No provision whatever had been made for sheltering the tribe in the wild tract where they were left at last; not one dollar had been appropriated for feeding them. Worse still, malaria raged there, and the water proved actively poisonous.

Finally the chiefs' frantic pleas had won for them a slightly better wild tract, but by 1878 all their cattle had died. Out of the 710 Poncas whom the soldiers had driven southward from the Niobrara only 430 still lived. One of the last to die had been a sixteen-year-old boy, son of Chief Standing Bear who had seen all his other children except one little girl die since the soldiers drove them from their Niobrara home.

On that March night of 1879 General Crook showed me an order he had lately received through the War Department from the Secretary of the Interior:

"Thirty Ponca Indians have left their agency in the Indian Territory without permission. I respectfully request that the nearest military commander be instructed to detail a sufficient guard to return these Poncas to the agency where they belong."

General Crook at once sent soldiers to Decatur, Nebraska, where the runaways had taken refuge with the Omaha tribe on its agency. The thirty men, women, and children who, led by Standing Bear, had traveled all the hundreds of long miles back from the Indian Territory now were held under arrest at Fort Omaha.

These were the basic facts of the pathetic story which General Crook told me that night with force and deep feeling.

"You have a great daily newspaper here which you can use," he argued finally. "You're perfectly acquainted with all the crimes of the Indian Ring at Washington. I ask you to go into this fight against those who are robbing these helpless people. You can win; I'm sure of it. The American people, if they knew half the truth, would send every member of the Indian Ring to prison."

"General," I answered, "if I once went into such a fight as that, I should never give up till I won or died. It would require at least five years and would cost thousands of dollars. I should have to abandon my profession here as a newspaperman—right now when after five years of hard work at journalism I'm just getting where I can command an honorable place in it. You're asking a great deal of me!"

"I know I am," he agreed, "but no matter what we do, all that any of us can get out of this world is what we eat, drink, and wear, and a place to shelter us. If we can do something for which good men will remember us when we're gone, that's the best legacy we can leave. I promise you that if you'll take up this work, I'll stand by you."

As we left the *Herald* office that Sunday morning, we saw the first streaks of the spring dawn in the east. I slept a couple of hours and then started for Fort Omaha, some four miles out. There I found most of the Poncas ill with malarial fever. I saw despair in every face. In one tent a little sick child moaned piteously; in another a woman was wailing heartbreakingly as Indians wail for their dead.

Standing Bear, however, did not feel it would be proper for him to tell me their story for my paper until he should have his formal hearing before General Crook, but as soon as I tried on him some of the Soldier Lodge signs, he called a council to smoke the pipe of peace with me.

When I stepped from the lodge, the sun was almost setting. I had not eaten since breakfast. Jamming my notebook into my pocket, I set off cityward—to get every Omaha church I could reach that evening to appeal to the Secretary of the Interior to cancel his order. Almost service time—I began to run. By pelting back and forth from church to church with speeches to the congregations and pleas to the ministers I succeeded in lining up all the chief Omaha churches in an urgent appeal to Washington to let the sick, weary Poncas stay on the Omaha reservation.

I certainly enjoyed my good, square meal at eleven that night before I began to write up my records. Well after dawn I tumbled thankfully into bed.

At ten o'clock that morning I reached General Crook's office for the Ponca hearing. Against the groups of smartly uniformed officers and shabby Indians in white man's dress Standing Bear stood out vividly in his full chief's regalia. To him that red blanket trimmed with broad blue stripes, that wide beaded belt, and that necklace of bear's claws formed the only proper attire whenever he was to speak officially for his people.

Called upon for the facts, he told us through an interpreter the whole story of their removal to the territory.

"I had found the white way was a good way," he concluded. "I had often wished I could tell the Great Father how grateful I was to him for showing me and my people this new way. I always obeyed every order that was sent me. I never committed a crime in my life. Yet here we are—prisoners."

He sat down somberly, turning his calm, sorrowful, roughed old face toward General Crook.

An army officer beside me burst out:

"It's a downright shame!"

Then the general asked Standing Bear to tell why he and the rest had fled from the territory. The old chief answered with deep feeling:

"At last I had only one son left; then he sickened. When he was dying he asked me to promise him one thing. He was my only son now; what could I do but promise?

"He begged me to take him, when he was dead, back to our old burying ground by the Swift Running Water, the Niobrara. I promised. When he died, I and those with me put his body into a box and then in a wagon, and we started north."

He described to us this nearly incredible journey through very cold weather with almost no money and no interpreter. Because they kept well westward out of the way of soldiers, they passed among only very poor white settlers. "But these," he assured us, "when they saw us starving, helped us all they could."

Finally the Omaha chief, Iron Eye, and his daughter Bright Eyes had come to meet them and offer them a home with the Omahas who would give them land. And Iron Eye had prom-

ised that, when warmer weather came, he would go to the Niobrara with the Poncas to bury the dead boy.

"So we went with the Omahas," Standing Bear explained.
"Many of us were sick, but as soon as warmer weather came,
all who were well began to sow wheat. I myself was sowing in
the field when your soldiers came and made me a prisoner."

Then he begged the soldiers not to send them back south.
"I could earn my own living here," he insisted. "Above all, if
we must be sent back, first let me go and bury my boy. Let me
keep my promise to him."

He told us how the prairies were always beautiful to the
young, but hard for the old, and how he had persuaded his
tribe to build homes for their old age.

"I thought God intended us to live, but I was mistaken. God
intends to give the country to the white people, and we are to
die. It may be well; it may be well. I do not protest. But let our
bones be mingled together in the earth where our forefathers
lie, and on which we lived so many years and were happy."

With sad finality he wrapped his blanket around him and
sat down. General Crook answered slowly:

"I am a soldier and must obey orders, but I will do all I can
to have the orders commanding me to return you to the Indian
Territory countermanded."

An officer murmured to me, "Such orders as these always
come through the influence of civilians. The Army is in no way
responsible for this."

By the time I had written up this Ponca material, sent it
out broadcast, and done my work for the *Herald* it was again
three in the morning. But I settled down to sleep contentedly,
knowing that next day the whole country would read and discuss the Poncas' story.

Next day the newspapers everywhere came out strongly pro-
Indian, but the Secretary of the Interior sent no answer what-

ever to the appeal of the Omaha churches. Clearly I was in for another fight on the very same principle which had carried me to Bleeding Kansas in 1856, namely: that before the law all men are equal. Therefore in spite of my double night tasks for the *Herald,* I stole my forenoons from sleep to spend them in a law library. I had to devise a case and a method which could release these abused Poncas—and then could recast our nation's whole Indian policy.

At last I found the key to this need in the Fourteenth Amendment to the Constitution, adopted only eleven years earlier and still comparatively untested. It defined the right of any *person* in the United States to his life, liberty, and property unless these were removed by due processes of law. I felt sure that it gave these Indians as *persons* a right to call upon the courts to defend them. Yet how, without funds, could we obtain a writ before the Poncas were shipped away? I went finally to a brilliant young Omaha lawyer, John L. Webster, and asked him to handle the case without a fee. After a night for thought he told me:

"You've raised a constitutional question of vast importance. The principles to which you're appealing underlie all personal liberty."

He then asked me to get some older lawyer to act as counsel and appear in court. For this help I turned to A. J. Poppleton, the chief attorney of the Union Pacific Railroad. We had to work fast and secretly, for at any moment the Poncas might be ordered south. We had some anxious days before our messenger found Judge Dundy, who must hear the case and who was somewhere in the wilds on a bear hunt. Meanwhile General Crook, constantly dreading interference from Washington, was the most anxious person I ever saw to have a writ served on him.

The morning of April 30, 1879, the courtroom held a crowd

of clergy, finely dressed men and women, and deeply interested lawyers. General Crook appeared in the elaborate full-
dress uniform which he almost never wore, attended by an
equally ornate staff. Standing Bear came in his formal regalia,
followed by his leading men in their hopelessly tattered clothes.

By the first night Standing Bear, who of course had not understood a word of the hearing, was intensely anxious. After
many searching questions he commented to me, "No man can
talk for another as well as he can for himself."

Then he begged me to ask Judge Dundy to let him speak
in court. When I carried this message to the judge, that good
friend of mine queried with a smile, "Was Standing Bear ever
admitted to the Bar?"

Yet I knew—and told others—that the old chief would have
the chance to plead his own cause. Next day the courtroom
was jammed. When the attorneys had ended their arguments,
Judge Dundy announced that he would hand down his decision later. Apparently a perfect silence followed. All eyes were
fixed on the sad, mild, yet strong face of Standing Bear, who sat
in front of the judge. And only the two or three persons nearest the bench heard an interesting bit of routine.

For the marshal came close to Judge Dundy, who murmured
to him, "Court is adjourned."

The marshal, carefully facing front, proclaimed even more
softly, "Hear ye! Hear ye! The Honorable District Court of
the United States is now adjourned."

Then Judge Dundy told Standing Bear that he might speak;
and neither the chief nor the audience dreamed that the court
session already was officially over. An excellent interpreter
stood ready to translate sentence by sentence.

Standing Bear rose. Half facing the audience, he stretched
his right hand out before him, holding it still so long that the

audience grew tense. At last, looking up at the judge, he spoke quietly.

"That hand is not the color of yours, but if I pierce it, I shall feel pain. If you pierce your hand, you also feel pain. The blood that will flow from mine will be of the same color as yours. I am a man. The same God made us both."

Half facing the audience again, he let his gaze drift far out through a window. His tone grew tense.

"I seem to stand on the bank of a river. My wife and little girl are beside me. In front the river is wide and impassable, and behind are perpendicular cliffs. No man of my race ever stood there before. There is no tradition to guide me."

Then he described how a flood began to rise around them and how, looking despairingly at the great cliffs, he saw a steep, stony way leading upward. Grasping his child's hand, while his wife followed, he led the way up the sharp rocks while the waters still rose behind them. Finally he saw a rift in the rocks and felt the prairie breeze strike his cheek.

"I turn to my wife and child with a shout that we are saved. We will return to the Swift Running Water that pours down between the green islands. There are the graves of my fathers. There again we will pitch our tepee and build our fires.

"But a man bars the passage. He is a thousand times more powerful than I. Behind him I see soldiers as numerous as the leaves of the trees. They will obey that man's orders. I too must obey his orders. If he says that I cannot pass, I cannot. The long struggle will have been in vain. My wife and child and I must return and sink beneath the flood. We are weak and faint and sick. I cannot fight."

He paused with bowed head. Then, gazing up into Judge Dundy's face with an indescribable look of pathos and suffering, he said in a low, intense tone:

"You are that man."

No one who merely reads the speech can possibly imagine its effect on people who knew of the Poncas' sufferings when they heard it spoken by the sad old chief in his brilliant robes. I saw tears on Judge Dundy's face. General Crook sat leaning forward, covering his eyes with his hand. Except for women's sobs there was absolute silence for a moment, then the whole room rose at once with a great shout. Among the first to reach Standing Bear was General Crook. The entire audience came crowding after him to shake the chief's hand.

Over a week later Judge Dundy handed down a decision so vital in Indian annals that I still am amazed to realize that it has been ignored by historians. For he decided that "an Indian is a *person* within the laws of the United States." Therefore any Indian had the right to appeal to the court for relief.

He also decided that General Crook was detaining the Poncas illegally and that they could not lawfully be deported to the Indian Territory by force. Because in leaving the tribal territory land they had renounced their allegiance to the tribe, they now had acquired the same legal rights *as any foreigner* who might come here, and therefore in the same way they could ask the court to protect them.

The first step in freeing all Indians everywhere from the selfish and arbitrary domination of the Indian Ring and of Washington officialdom had been taken.

At once Standing Bear insisted on giving to each of us three who had fought for him—to Mr. Poppleton, to Mr. Webster, and to me—one of his few and loved treasures. To me, whom he called his brother with the promise: "You shall never want as long as we have anything. While there is one Ponca living you will never be without a friend," he gave a beautiful pair of beaded buckskin leggings. To Mr. Webster he presented the tomahawk he would never need to use again. And Mr. Poppleton's gift was a headdress, or war bonnet, the tribe's most ancient relic, probably at least three hundred years old, which had been worn only on their most sacred occasions. Standing Bear had refused large offers for it, but now, with tears in his eyes, he gave this "holy thing," which was all he had left to give, to the white man whose skill had saved him and his people.

Then almost at once he ran into fresh risk. Our lawyers had warned him: "If you set foot now on any Indian reservation, you can be arrested as an intruder." But some government attorneys came afterward and told him that he now could go straight back to his old home perfectly safely. So early one morning he unsuspiciously, without a word to any of us, made a beeline for the Niobrara. I heard about it that night and decided it would be the proper duty of his new "brother" to head him off.

Knowing that Iron Eye had two fast horses at the Omaha Agency, I hurried up there with a young Indian to borrow them. At four in the morning we started for Niobrara City, and by riding a hundred and twenty miles in eighteen hours we caught up with Standing Bear late that night where he was waiting to cross the dangerous river at dawn. We brought him back to set up a camp with his people at a safe distance outside the Omaha reservation boundaries. Here he went straight at the hard problem of providing for the whole band by setting his men to chopping wood for the townsfolk. But I admit that both parties to the bargain badly needed an interpreter.

22.

The Real Fight Begins

Though we had set Standing Bear and his band free to live where and as they chose, the rest of the Poncas were still stranded down in the dreaded territory. And there were threats that the ax would fall next on the Omahas, an equally peaceful, prosperous tribe, the Poncas' own friends and kindred, as a reprisal for their help to the runaways. The only way to save these and other worried northern tribes lay through the courts with Judge Dundy's decision to pave the way.

General Crook, Mr. Webster, and I talked long and often about which move to make next. We could see a hard struggle stretching out ahead, but we firmly believed that by winning it we should free every Indian in the country from ever again dreading that the whims of anyone in Washington could willfully control his person or his belongings or could hinder his liberty to live his own life reasonably. And we cared not a rap whether our campaign would land heavily on the toes of the red-tape Washington men, or those of the strong, ruthless Indian Ring, or those of the political bosses. We were anxious only about how to raise several thousand dollars quickly.

I sighed at hearing that this must be my role, but I already had put my hand to the plow. Now I resigned my comfortable post as assistant editor of the *Herald* and began to collect all sorts of written proofs about our cause. When I finally went

East, I had in hand official documents to support every statement and every charge I should make.

Also, with the Omaha Committee's approval, I sent Iron Eye
(Joseph La Flesche), the Omaha chief, and his daughter Bright
Eyes (Susette La Flesche) down to the Indian Territory to visit
the girl's beloved uncle, White Swan (Frank La Flesche). Each
of these three Indians had both an Indian home name and a
formal white man's name because the two men were sons of a
French trader who about 1817 had married an Omaha woman.
These sons, though reared as Indians, were exceptionally able
and ambitious. Iron Eye had married an Omaha woman, so
that Bright Eyes and his other children were one-fourth
French, three-fourths Omaha.

Bright Eyes, now twenty-five years old, was rated by the
Omahas and the Poncas as clever and dependable, with an
eager instinct for learning white people's customs. After six ex-
ceptional years in the Presbyterian Mission School at their
agency she had been given two years at a fine private school in
Elizabeth, New Jersey, where she had won high praise for her
brilliance, her willingness to work hard, and "her pleasant, winning ways." Back home again, she had been given charge of
the agency school—but only after two hard years of waiting and
at half the pay the white teachers had received.

She had followed every word about our Ponca struggle in my
Herald articles and editorials, and finally had written me a lot
of valuable facts from her own knowledge or from letters she
had received from her Ponca kinsfolk in the territory. Now that
we wanted reliable messengers to carry our good news to the
stranded Poncas and bring back word just how things stood
there, this girl and her father seemed the best choice.

Our two scouts found scarcely any roads or paths, temporary
tents, only six little houses for the whole tribe of Indians—and a

handsome residence for the agent which "somehow looked strangely out of place among the tents and graves."

The Poncas there had known nothing of what we had achieved for Standing Bear. All their mail, both in and out, was opened and often was suppressed. Now at last through our two safe messengers White Eagle, the head chief, sent me a long, touching letter. Here is his message to the lawyers who had saved the refugee band:

"We had thought there was none to take pity on us. I thank you in the name of my tribe for what you have done for Standing Bear, and I ask you to go still further in your kindness and help us to regain our land. I want to save the remainder of my people, and I look to you for help."

Those words at last gave us clear, written authority to act for the stranded Poncas as well as for those who had escaped.

Late in June 1879 I started East alone to fight the Poncas' enemies. Nearly five years had passed since I had taken that route to raise money for the grasshopper sufferers. Warned by what had happened then, I could easily guess what would lie ahead of me now.

In Chicago I gave reporters the facts which would bring the Ponca problem into the limelight, and I spoke at a large, finely sponsored public meeting which promptly contributed about $600 to the cause. But I knew better than to handle one cent of that money. The reliable Chicago men who collected it forwarded it straight to the Omaha Congregational clergyman who was the treasurer of the Omaha Ponca Committee. I was donating my time without any salary, but as I clearly could not live on air, this Omaha group paid my actual expenses on the trip.

As an introduction I carried with me a printed page of warm personal endorsements of me and of the Ponca cause from the governor of Nebraska, General Crook, the Episcopal bishop, and the leading Nebraska clergy. These were reinforced by extracts from Omaha newspapers. Important as these earnest statements from local authorities who knew the facts proved to be in winning me a hearing from strangers, they had even greater worth for me personally. For with these, when the Indian Ring and the Washington officials planted all sorts of slams at me in leading newspapers everywhere—including downright implications of personal dishonesty in my handling of funds which actually never were in my hands or my control for a single moment—I could comfort my naturally proud spirit. I found the greatest inspiration of all in the kindly comments of my recent fellow-workers, the Omaha journalists. These men who knew my faults and failings as completely as my virtues had wished me Godspeed in a worthy cause of which they understood every detail—and the memory of their words helped me through many hard moments.

From Chicago I hurried on to Boston, only to find one important person after another out of town. But a loyal letter from my wife, whose sympathies were strongly with this work, brought me fresh courage. Just as fearlessly as she had ridden the wild horse or braved the shootings in our gospel tent, she now was facing this new venture which might wreck our own fortunes for good and all. In my next attempt I reached the influential editor of the Boston *Advertiser,* who promised me his paper's backing. Then Edward Everett Hale broke the Boston ice for me by an emphatic *Advertiser* editorial.

On July 30 I spoke to a special meeting of the directors of the Society for Propagating the Gospel among the Indians and Others of North America—all that! My plain statement of facts resulted in the birth of a Ponca committee of five leading Bostonians who promptly planned a big public gathering. Though this was set in August, an interested crowd of folk came up from their summer homes to attend. The chief speaker was to be Wendell Phillips, then sixty-seven years old. In my newspaper work I once had met him briefly; now he sent me word that I must give the opening talk so that he could hear what I had to say before he made his own appeal.

Reaching the hall early, I sat in a corner of the platform with Mr. Williams of the committee, head of a lecture bureau, who pointed out each notable to me. Poets, historians, scientists, lecturers—in they walked until I got thoroughly frightened; yet all the while some quirk in my brain made me wonder what old Two Bears would have thought of them. The mayor of Boston opened the meeting; and there at the far side of the platform sat Wendell Phillips, the famous abolitionist orator, frankly waiting to hear my speech.

By the time I got on my feet I was trembling so badly I could hardly walk. For fully a moment I stood where I had been told to stand—silent, the world a blank. My shaking hand could not hold my manuscript and my bunch of proofs. Luckily the thud with which these fell brought back my senses. Instead of retrieving them I kicked them aside and began impromptu:

"I take it this audience doesn't wish me to read from those official documents. They're at the service of any person present. What you wish is to hear some salient facts upon which you can form a judgment. If any statement seems doubtful, you all know where to find the government documents to solve the doubt. I make no assault upon any individual. I assault a system. If the angel Gabriel were President of the United States, and he should select his cabinet from the courts of heaven, neither he nor his cabinet could prevent the wrongs against which I protest—so long as the present system is in force."

Then I gave details about the system's evils, and proposed the only feasible remedies, namely: to allot lands to the Indians "in severalty" (which meant the individual ownership of a plot of land by each Indian instead of the general ownership of a tract by the whole tribe) and also to bring the Indians *as persons* under the protection of the courts. While the audience was applauding at the close of my speech, Phillips hastily rose, crossed the platform, and whispered in my ear, "Don't go away after the meeting until I have an opportunity to speak to you."

His address was a masterpiece. When he was done, nearly all those present came forward to shake hands with me, and pledged themselves to do everything they could to better the Indian system. But Phillips merely waited in the background until they had gone. Then he came up and, saying, "Come take dinner with me," led me to a modest little restaurant on a side street. There he sat down opposite me and looked me straight in the face without a word for so long that I grew embarrassed. At last he remarked:

"I don't know what to say to you."

I answered, laughing, "I wish you would say something."

He laughed too, and then went on:

"I suppose Boston would not say you were an orator according to its standards, but you influenced that audience in a way I could not. I never saw a Boston audience act in just that way before. But here's something to keep in mind. You remember what they all said to you when they came forward to shake hands. The sentiment seemed to be that all that needed to be done to change this vile Indian system was to present the matter in a few cities and at Washington as you did today. But don't let those remarks deceive you in the least.

"I want you to go on with this work. You have the facts and a peculiar way of presenting them that takes hold of the hearts of people when they hear you. I have been delivering lectures on the Indians for a great many years, but I have never produced any effect. I made my fight for one race—the Negroes— and I feel that you are called to make the fight for the Indian race. But don't be deceived by the enthusiasm of that audience. I know the Indian Ring. Your hair will be gray before the first law is passed that does away with the present system. Men of national reputation will attack you. You will have to endure and suffer and drink the cup of bitterness. But go on. You may call upon me at any time to render any service that is possible."

His prophecies came true, but it really took only four years to turn my thick black hair gray at forty-three in that terrible fight with the Indian Ring.

23.

Sympathy for the Indians

When I got back to Omaha on September 6, I walked straight into a new problem, namely: that the Omaha Committee, urged on by a noted Boston lecturer who had been visiting there, wanted me to take Bright Eyes East to plead for the cause. Bishop Clarkson, too, was pushing this plan. Already he had persuaded Bright Eyes to speak with Standing Bear in a large Omaha church.

When the day came, a big audience jumped to its feet with cheers, clapping, and waving handkerchiefs to welcome the Indian girl. There stood the little figure, trembling, and gazing at the crowd with eyes which afterwards thrilled many audiences. They were wonderful eyes. They could smile, command, flash, plead, mourn, and play all sorts of tricks with anyone they lingered on.

Bright Eyes waited there a full moment, plainly frightened almost out of her senses, like a bird in a net, but hers was a graceful, appealing fright that never lost its dignity. Finally she spoke in a rich voice which carried clearly to the crowded church steps. Here are a few of the notes I took:

"Why should I be asked to speak? I am but an Indian girl, brought up among the Indians. I love my people; I have been educated and they have not. I have told them that they must learn the arts of the whites and adopt their customs; but how can they, when the government sends the soldiers to drive them about over the face of the earth?

"The soldiers drive Standing Bear and his wife and children from the land that belonged to him and his fathers before him—at the point of the bayonet; and on the way his daughter dies from the hardships of the journey. The Christian ladies of Milford, Nebraska, come to the Indian camp, pray for the dying girl, and give her Christian burial. Oh, the perplexities of this thing they call civilization! Part of the white people murder my girl companion and another part tenderly bury her, while her old father stands over her grave and says: 'My heart breaks.'"

Her slight figure swayed to and fro; she clutched the pulpit for support. Women on the platform hurried to lead her away. Bright Eyes had broken down in her very first speech, but her breakdown had thrilled the audience like an electric shock. Women cried, men shouted, and some swore—there in church, with the bishop on the platform. And one leading Omaha citizen yelled:

"If I were Standing Bear, I would let the courts go hang. I'd take my tomahawk and scalping knife and follow the trail of the Secretary of the Interior. Then I'd settle the thing right there!"

Now I already had signed a contract for my campaign with Mr. Williams of the Boston lecture bureau, and I had fully expected to take Standing Bear East with me to speak—all the more because the Secretary of the Interior had lately issued a press statement that the old chief was "morose, sullen, and indolent." I knew that no one could see the kindly old man and believe such nonsense, but I must admit that I did not favor adding Bright Eyes to our party, if only because of the added cost. Bright Eyes herself, always shy and shrinking, refused even to consider it, and her father disapproved utterly.

Suddenly we all learned that a bill to remove the Omaha

tribe to the territory actually had been introduced in Congress. By a trick clause in a treaty—a clause which Iron Eye insisted had not been interpreted for him before he signed it—this tribe was completely under the control of Congress. They could be removed whether consenting or not. Under such an alarming dread Iron Eye yielded—partly.

"Bright Eyes may go East to lecture," he conceded, "if her brother Woodworker goes with her."

Woodworker, or Frank La Flesche, was then nineteen, a splendid, thoughtful young Indian.

In mid-October we headed East. It had been agreed by all those in charge that Woodworker, according to his habit, should dress in civilized style, and that, except for leaving his hair long, Standing Bear should do the same at all times when he was not making a public appearance to speak for his people. Bright Eyes, as usual, would dress like any American lady of the day. She commonly wore some plain dark dress with a white lace scarf at her throat.

A sudden change of plan halted us in Pittsburgh, but here a telegram from Mr. Williams, handed to me on the lecture platform, ordered us to board the first train for Boston.

There we found that, thanks to the mayor, we were to be the city's guests for a week at a hotel where that very morning the mayor, the city council, and many prominent folk would hold a big reception for us at which we each should have to speak briefly. And that evening a great public reception would be given for us by the city. Amazed and delighted, we almost dared to hope that we should win the dreaded fight very easily. That afternoon of October 29 we laughed at everything, especially at Standing Bear's many puns.

Suddenly about five o'clock Mr. Williams walked in, looking ghastly. I could see the effort with which he told me: "I have

some very bad news. You and Standing Bear must prepare yourselves for heavy blows."

I noticed that he held some telegrams.

"These followed you from Chicago round by Pittsburgh," he
faltered. "They're three days old now."

Finally he told us that my dear wife, suddenly taken ill with
peritonitis, had died inside of twenty-four hours; and Standing
Bear's brother, Big Snake, had been foully murdered at the Indian Territory reservation by orders of the agent.

Prostrated, I went to my room and flung myself on my bed.

Presently Standing Bear came to me, knelt by the bed, and
evidently prayed in silence for some minutes. Then, with tears
pouring down his cheeks, he laid his hand on my head and
began to pray aloud in his own tongue. Soon Frank La Flesche
joined us, and the old chief spoke to me through him. I remember some of his argument, and Frank remembered more, which
he wrote down afterwards.

"My friend," Standing Bear told me, "you have lost the one
you love most. I knew her too. She was beautiful and good. Your
heart is very sad. A wife is closer to a man than a brother. We
both suffer, but remember those others who suffer and die in
that strange land. Don't go back home. Don't stop trying to
help my poor people. They have no one to help them but you.
Many husbands have seen their wives die, down in that hot
country. They have no missionary to tell them of the good words
God has spoken to those who have trouble. You can read God's
book, and kind people will say words to comfort you. You suffer
greatly but they suffer more. Promise me that you will not for-
sake them."

What could I do but take his hand and promise?

Meanwhile other telegrams told us that my wife had been
buried that day and that Mr. Webster had placed my two little

girls, eleven and nine years old, in a private school under Bishop Clarkson's supervision.

The Boston Indian Committee, feeling that the ground had dropped from under their feet, faced the problem of that huge civic reception which was due to begin almost at once. Sorry though they were for us both, they all felt that the Ponca cause was a greater matter than our private griefs, so they told us that we must appear at the meeting and must even each of us speak a few words. One committee member argued: "A soldier on the fighting line, if his brother falls or his wife dies, still must keep his place in the battle."

But I felt I could not face that ordeal.

Then Standing Bear reminded me that he had not given up under all his own terrible losses of his children.

"I am older than you," he went on, "and I have suffered more. Now my brother is dead. He did not die of disease, but was cruelly murdered. All these things I bear. Your wife was dear to me. I know how sore your heart is, but do go to the meeting and say one word for those who suffer and die with no one to pity. If you can do that, it will make your burdens lighter, not heavier."

I went to the reception, but the only thing I remember about it is that next day all the Boston papers printed long accounts of it. My mind was not at the meeting—it was living over, moment by moment, eighteen hard, brave, wonderful years that now were done.

Big Snake, known to the Poncas as the "peacemaker," was a large, kind, gentle man. His one crime was his close tie to this brother, who now had come East to fight for his tribe. No one even tried to punish the murderer, and the Department of the Interior merely issued a statement that "Standing Bear's brother, Big Snake, a bad man" had been "shot accidentally."

But a Senate committee later heard a different story from one of the department's own inspectors and from an eyewitness.

Over a year afterward Senator Dawes declared forcefully in the Senate that this murder had taught the Indians who still were helpless in the territory that, if any Indian dared to resist, he risked his own life and the lives of any relatives who were within the rulers' reach. In fact Big Snake's wanton murder influenced every subsequent decision and act of the territory Poncas.

Boston now was really stirred up. Endless people stopped me on the streets to shake hands. Many unknown folk, including cranks, had to be shunted away from our hotel, but one day Mr. Williams eagerly brought me a Mrs. Jackson, a stranger to him, who had asked for a talk with me. Like him, I recognized at once her extraordinary intelligence. Though close to fifty she was somehow fascinating with swiftly changing expressions. After I had checked over and praised an article about the Poncas which she said she would publish in the New York *Independent* over her "usual signature of H. H.," I realized that she was a popular writer of essays and poems, though I never before had heard her full name of Helen Hunt Jackson.

Bright Eyes and Standing Bear quickly became devoted to her. She wrote up the Ponca cause for newspapers and magazines and even traveled with us. She threw every ounce of her own strong influence into the scale in dealing with members of Congress, senators, editors, and writers. I strongly doubt if we could ever have won without her help.

Soon I turned over to her my whole mass of records. She spent months in studying and classifying them, and finally in 1881 used many of them in her own book on the Indian problem, *A Century of Dishonor*, where they formed the Ponca chapter and part of the Appendix.

Before long the Boston Committee took over the complete

charge of our group, handled all funds, decided where we should stay, and when and where we should lecture, gave us our allowance for personal expenses, and provided its own agent to travel with us.

From then on the campaign stiffened. Our side grew more aggressive, and our Washington foes more alert. Our group of three lectured steadily around Boston and all over New England to huge audiences. Besides big public daytime receptions for us we were guests of honor at private dinners, luncheons, and "at homes."

Bright Eyes had wished to appear only under her formal name of Susette La Flesche, but from the first the papers caught up her little home name instead—perhaps because it suited her so vividly. Finally she realized that the quaint label had taken such a hold on the public fancy that it definitely helped our cause. Unfortunately the shy girl of the plains found it a terrific ordeal to stand each day for two or three hours patiently shaking hands with strangers. Usually our agent had to stay close by her to warn the apparently never-ending line: "Please don't squeeze her hand. Shake it gently." Twice even in those early months Bright Eyes fainted at the task and had to be carried from the room, yet whenever I urged her to stick to the lecture platform and leave out the social side, she argued earnestly:

"When the people come and hear us talk, they go away and forget, but if they come to a reception and I shake hands with them, they will remember longer and will do what they can to save us. If we cannot get the protection of the law, we shall be driven from our reservation, and then what will become of my father and mother and my sisters?"

In fact her heaviest load was her own belief that she, the "educated Indian," must win new friends for all Indians. She must meet wisely each attack of our foes—and there were many

attacks—and must foresee and forestall every new threat to the
Omahas. Worse still, as in the case of Big Snake, her family, her
tribe, and even her race now would be in worse danger than
ever simply because she herself was making the men in power
so bitterly angry. Therefore, while there was a breath in her
body, she must not shirk for a single day or miss even one
vital move.

I myself thought the most interesting dinner reception was
the one Mr. Houghton, the publisher, gave at his Cambridge
home to let Mr. Longfellow, then in his early seventies, greet
Bright Eyes. I was amazed to see how many literary folk turned
out to watch the Omaha chief's daughter meet the poet who, a
quarter of a century before, had given the world a new idea of
an Indian maiden.

A traffic snarl made us late, and we had to weave through
lines of carriages drawn up for blocks around. Mr. Longfellow
had been eagerly watching for us at the window. When we
started on foot up the long front walk, we saw him fling the
door open and stand waiting, while his friends crowded into
the wide hall behind him.

At the steps I dropped back. Bright Eyes went on alone. Mr.
Longfellow came forward, took her hand between both of his,
studied her intently without a word, and then said earnestly:
"*This* is Minnehaha."

Still holding her hand, he led her through the smiling nota-
bles to the quietest corner of the room. They sat and talked
there for a long time. Afterward Mr. Longfellow told me: "I've
been a student of the English language all my life, and I would
give all I possess if I could speak it with the simplicity, fluency,
and force used by that Indian girl."

One of Bright Eyes' most illuminative sayings became

widely quoted both here and in England; more than a thousand sermons and lectures were based on it.

"The people who first owned this soil appeal to you," she told the keen-minded traders of the Boston Merchants' Exchange. "They ask for liberty—and law is liberty."

"How did you get at that idea?" I inquired one day. "What made you say, 'law is liberty'?"

She was sitting by a window; she pointed to the people who were passing up and down the busy Boston street.

"I see it here," she explained. "I see all people coming and going as they like; they can go to Europe if they wish. That is being free; and it is because they have law to take care of them that they can go."

For Bright Eyes, a "ward of the government," knew that at any moment she might be arrested for being absent from her tribal reservation without cause. So the chief appeal for her in this cultured city with its beautifully dressed crowds was that the citizens who hurried past us were free as she and her people were not.

On December 2 our Boston backers held a noontime public meeting in Faneuil Hall because it had been the "cradle of liberty." No woman, they told us, had ever before made a public speech there.

Three days later we reached New York, where hundreds had to be turned away from our huge meetings. The famous cartoonist, Thomas Nast, lined up for us. One day Standing Bear saw on a newsstand and recognized one of Nast's large, clever portraits of our friend the Secretary. Unable to ask the price, he gave the newsboy a quarter, took the paper, and returned to the hotel. There he borrowed a pair of shears from the barber, and cut out that skinny, elongated cartoon, neatly following the figure's outline as a clever child would cut out a paper doll. He then asked me to put it in my scrapbook, where it remains

to this day. He often would open the book, look at that cartoon
—and laugh.

Early in February we steadily spoke to or else met in receptions huge Philadelphia throngs—until on the tenth we went to
Washington to appear before the Senate Investigating Committee's almost daily sessions. Even then we often were sent to
lecture in various Pennsylvania towns.

As we entered a large Carlisle church, the presiding officer
told me they had arranged a little surprise for me. Suddenly
I heard, floating out, the strains of a duet which I had written
years before for my own little newsboy church. The Presbyterian Church in Omaha had taken it up, and the choirmaster of a
large Philadelphia church had heard it there and had copied
it. He often used it in Philadelphia, and for this Carlisle occasion he had volunteered to come and furnish the music. I certainly heard that duet with all the pleasure he had hoped to
give me.

In Washington, Bright Eyes' name now was being bandied
about so hotly and with such sarcastic comments from the
Secretary himself that Senator Hoar of Massachusetts one day
delivered a long eulogy of her in the Senate. I was told this was
the first time any woman had been given that honor.

Naturally this unsought advertising made still more people
eager to meet the amazing Indian girl and to entertain her in
their homes. They never stopped to think how they were drain-
ing her energy, for in public she seemed a smiling, happy young
lady who carried her cares lightly. If those cordial folk could
have seen her in the reaction after a reception, lying motionless
on a couch, cold as death, they would gladly have shielded her.
But to all my protests she made only her old answer:

"The lives of my father, mother, brothers, and sisters, and of
thousands of other Indians depend upon the success of this agi-

tation. Everything else has failed for a hundred years. It is better for me to die than that all the Indians should be exterminated."

For months we went on shuttling back and forth between our Philadelphia appointments and the Senate committee hearings. Early in March, White Eagle and another Ponca chief were called to Washington from the territory, but our Indians, including their own fellow-chief Standing Bear, were not allowed to see them.

White Eagle testified firmly, "Better go back to the old reservation and have not so good houses and live in them and have health in them than to have good houses and fine things down in the Indian Territory and be sick all the time and die. All the people want to go back."

But the Department of the Interior still saw things differently.

By early April, when we went to lecture in Baltimore, we all felt pretty battered. Though we did not know it, a noted Boston philanthropist, Mrs. Hemenway, chanced to be on that train and studied us silently. From Baltimore she not only telegraphed the Boston Committee that we all were so utterly worn out that we must be allowed a few days' rest, but she sent with her message the money to give us ten days at Old Point Comfort.

Very soon after that blessed rest we all went back home to recuperate, for our agent wrote the Boston Committee that even a few more lectures and receptions just then would surely end in Bright Eyes' death.

To our amazement we found Omaha penetrated by an element we had never known there before, and we were told that this state of affairs had been going on there for three months.

A substance filled the air and stopped up the nose, eyes, and ears of every man, woman, and child. It stained the sun and filled all open spaces to the height of hundreds of feet. Every few minutes minor whirlwinds of it swept along the streets, and while those discomforts went surging by, everyone hurried into shelter. To keep the substance out of the houses, all windows were closed, all blinds shut, all window shades pulled down. The taste of it flavored every particle of food. The substance was dust.

Nebraska by that time had been settled for a little over twenty-five years, but only in the most recent epoch had large tracts of the virgin prairie soil been laid bare to the ever-blowing prairie winds. And now six long and weary months had just passed without rain enough to wet the ground.

When I stepped from the train, I walked straight toward a typical major dust crisis. All day, I was told, the wind had blown nearly a gale. For moments together the almost solid banks of dust had gone dashing along the streets, hiding everything more than ten or fifteen feet away. At six o'clock there had come a strange calm, followed by a new, ominous rumbling. This unfamiliar noise, coming apparently from the south, was the very first thing I noticed as I walked along the station platform. So I glanced far off southward and saw a dense black mass rise up as if the prairies had been ground into fine powder and then spouted out by volcanic force. The mass moved up toward Omaha with terrifying velocity. It hid the sun, and then almost total darkness closed down upon the city. The wind, as official records proved afterward, was blowing forty miles an hour. I took hasty refuge in the hotel—really appalled, because in all my previous years up and down the plains I had never seen even the mildest form of such a spectacle.

There in the hotel lobby I found a Boston lady whom I had met on the train. Ghastly white and with eyes of blank horror, she stood facing the window and clutching the back of a chair.

Then we felt the moving mass strike the side of the hotel like a wave of the sea. Dust piled up inside the closed window on the sill. It sifted into the air of the room through countless invisible crevices in the walls and doors.

A porter lighted the gas, but the Eastern lady, unnoticing, still stood facing the blank, black window, rigid with hysterical fear. At last she turned toward me with evident effort and asked me through stiff lips:

"What *is* this?"

Feeling that I must do something to lessen the moment's tension for her, I took refuge in a pun as excruciating as those which Standing Bear had been loosing on us at intervals all these months.

"Prices out here are subject to violent fluctuations," I informed her. "This is only a sudden but general 'rise in real estate.'"

But under my joke I knew there lay a fundamental truth: in this era of transition even the soil was passing from the plains with the buffalo and the roving tribes. The unchanging grass-grown days were gone forever.

24.

I Visit the Indian Territory

Of course our weakest point lay in our being cut off from the territory Poncas and in their not knowing what we were doing and planning, so Mr. Webster and the Omaha and Boston committees all urged me to go down there in person and interview the chiefs. We found that by statute it was a crime for any white man except a government employee to enter a reservation, but we also found that a first offender would merely be forcibly removed, though for a second visit he would be fined and imprisoned.

I left Omaha on Monday, June 14, 1880; soon Henry Fontanelle, son of a noted Omaha chief, joined me to interpret for me. At noon of June 15 we reached Arkansas City, Kansas, the nearest railroad station to the Ponca reserve, which lay on the northern border of all the tribal lands, just where Ponca City and White Eagle, Oklahoma, stand today. I hired some good horses, and we went straight to the Ponca reserve, stopping at the first Indian house an hour before sunset. I wore no disguise whatever. Messengers soon collected fifteen or twenty Ponca men.

"Many chiefs," these told us, "have gone with White Eagle to visit the Cheyennes, about two hundred miles to the southwest. The Cheyennes have invited them again and again, but until now the agent has always refused to give the passes they had to have."

They also warned me that orders had come from Washington directing the agent to arrest any member of the Omaha Committee or anyone they might send to the Poncas. I decided my best chance to see the other chiefs was to go to meet them— and quickly. I knew that no agency horses could overtake ours— the only way to capture us out there, where no telegraph line ran toward the Cheyennes. Our council ended late. Poison Hunter offered us his tent, close by, for a brief sleep, and we were glad to use it, but I did not learn for over a year what came out of that bit of hospitality toward us.

Early next morning Fontanelle drove openly to the agency and purchased supplies; because agent Whiting himself had gone away for several days Fontanelle was not hindered or even questioned. Soon after ten o'clock, June 16, we started toward the Cheyennes, pushing our horses at top speed. By noon we passed outside the Ponca reserve. To Fontanelle's disgust from the first I had insisted on our going wholly unarmed, so of course that afternoon we saw three antelope and a small flock of turkeys. "I'm just as furious as you are," I told him, "and as hungry for good fresh game. Still, I vowed when I left Missouri in 1873 never to carry arms again, and I consider that promise too precious to break."

Down through the present state of Oklahoma we went, mostly over red sandy soil with brick-dust-colored streams which seldom were fit to drink. After two days of intense suffering from heat and thirst we reached a cattle ranch on June 18 and restocked our supplies. After that we often met bands from various tribes; my knowledge of the sign language let me ask them the right route across that desolate country. At last we found the Ponca chiefs' actual trail, which led us on June 19 to the Cimarron River. As we sat studying the wide, dangerous crossing, we noticed a large band of Indians on the far bank. They were the returning Poncas, led by White Eagle.

225

The Cheyennes had given them liberal presents of ponies, blankets, and trinkets, and had divided with them all their scanty stock of food, but this was not enough to feed the Poncas properly the whole way home. I drove one of their wagons about three miles to a trader's store and bought several sacks of flour, and some salt pork, coffee, and sugar. These White Eagle divided among the band, who eagerly built campfires. I found solid satisfaction in watching those Indians eat one good meal.

In the council afterward I soon gave up the effort to explain judges, appeals, and test cases offhand to those inexperienced minds, and I spoke instead of the general council in Washington. "Surely this will decide," I argued, "that the Poncas' land on the Niobrara belongs to your tribe, so that you will return there—if only you yourselves don't sign any papers in the meantime that will give up your proper title to it." They began to answer by addressing me formally, not as "Friend," but as "Great Father," the Indian title for the President. When I protested strongly, they asserted:

"The President sent Standing Bear to the Indian Territory and he ran away. The President had him arrested and made a prisoner. You took Standing Bear away from the President and made him free. You are a greater man than the President, and therefore we address you by the most honorable name that we have."

A year later the Sioux followed the same logic to the same conclusion—as did other Indians for several years.

All June 20 Fontanelle and I traveled on with the Poncas, faring tolerably well until we reached the region where Texas cattle trails crossed. There the cattle had stood in all the water holes and streams. A young Ponca rode ten miles off the traveled route, trying to get me a jug of clean water. What he brought was not fit to drink, but I made very strong coffee with it. Now that I had temporarily joined White Eagle's band, he felt so responsible for my safety that he kept sentries far ahead to warn us if they saw any police approaching. Long before dawn, June 21, he woke me apologetically to tell me: "A runner has just brought word that a white man with a lot of Ponca police is camping only ten miles ahead. Some of them will surely reach here before daybreak."

Even at that hour it was so hot that I felt no energy. Fontanelle told me: "I'd rather go on with the Indians than strike out across country. They won't arrest me, because I'm an Indian. But you've got to make a wild dash for the Kansas line, and get out of these regions which the Indian agents rule, and go back safe to those governed by law." So I started north with an Indian guide—across the cattle trails, with all the water so vile with manure that the horses refused it. All day and far into the night we pushed on, as fast as we could force our half-dead beasts along. Still not a drop of decent water. At midnight we lariated the horses, which nibbled a little at the grass and then lay down.

With sunrise we started on; by noon we reached a spring of clear water—and, refreshed, pushed on to the state line. But now I realized that the bad water of the preceding days already had made me really ill. By nightfall I could not mount without help—could not even sit erect in my saddle, but lay forward limply on my horse's neck. At last I thankfully reached Caldwell, Kansas, and sent the horses back to Arkansas City, where I had hired them. I asked at a half-fledged hotel for a room. The woman proprietor led me to it, remarking that she was going to send for a doctor. I felt too ill to contradict her. Soon a young doctor turned up, wrote a prescription, and departed. Back came the woman, saying, "Yer must leave at once."

"Why?" I questioned.

"Waal," she answered reluctantly, "that doctor says it ain't possible for yer to live, an' I ain't got no time ter wait on yer, an' if yer die on me here, yer'll hurt my business fer weeks."

The next events are a total blank. I woke at last to find myself in bed in a nice room in a private house, with a lady sitting looking at me. On a handy table stood a lot of bottles.

"Have you been giving me that stuff?" I asked.

"The doctor left it for you, but I couldn't make you swallow it —or anything else."

"Throw it all out of the window," I ordered firmly.

She rose at once and tossed out the whole batch.

"I'm not going to die yet," I told her. "If you'll follow my directions, I'll be out in a week. Get some fresh milk; boil it at least five minutes; season it with pepper and salt. Give me a cupful, as hot as I can swallow it, every hour—and two grains of quinine every two hours for twenty-four hours. Don't wake me for the milk, but wake me every time for the quinine dose."

I was back in Arkansas City by the twenty-fifth, and Fontanelle promptly rejoined me.

"On the morning of the twenty-first," he reported, "while you were making your dash to Caldwell, I was arrested. They were simply scouring the Ponca reserve to find you."

And late on Saturday, June 26, a Ponca Indian who eked out his one or two English words with the sign language came to tell me that the agent was heading for Arkansas City with a large part of his force.

To avoid trouble, on Sunday morning I hired a horse and jogged over to see a Frenchman fairly nearby whom the Poncas considered a good friend of theirs. After dining with him I rode into the territory. I was planning to stop at a ranch northwest of the Nez Percés' encampment which lay due west from the Ponca reserve. I wanted to meet Chief Joseph, who with his band had been sent there after they had been deprived of their Idaho land. That act directly violated the terms of Joseph's surrender to General Miles. I knew that the general was vehemently protesting about this breach of faith. "The ranch you want lays about fifteen miles inside the state line," the livery-man had told me, but I soon found that most of my way followed merely a faint Indian trail.

Late that afternoon, as the route led me across a small stream, my horse plunged toward a pool of water a few feet above the ford—and sank up to his body in a quicksand. After a brief struggle he gave up completely, and would not even respond to sharp blows of my whip. My only tool was a medium-sized pocket knife, but with this I was able to cut the two poles needed to make a "plainsman's windlass." With this and two hours' hard work I got that horse winched out. Sundown found me out on the broad prairie on a trail too faint to follow through the short grass until daylight came again.

To make matters worse, one of the fearful storms of that region came sweeping over the shelterless plain with terrific thunder and almost continuous flares of lightning. I took off the saddle and sat on it with my back turned to the wind; the horse pressed close to me, his rump toward the storm, and stood motionless for hours until the worst of it was over. At midnight it stopped raining. I was still so weak after my illness and my starvation diet that I stretched out exhausted on the wet grass with my saddle for a pillow and my horse lariated to the saddle horn.

The next moment, it seemed, I was roused by feeling that saddle jerked from under my head. The pony began running about me in a circle, threatening to dash away. As I twisted a noose around his nose to hold him, my ear caught a strange, dull thudding and a sharp clatter. The horse was right; we were squarely in the path of a rush of thousands of Texas longhorns the storm had scared into a stampede.   •

I grabbed up the saddle, lariat rope, and bridle and somehow tossed all of them and myself helter-skelter across the horse's back and urged him on to go anywhere away from there. In no time I heard a steady roar of hoofs and clash of horns—but they were well behind us. A cowboy dashed past, proving that we had reached the outskirts of the danger track. Soon I dismounted, saddled my horse, and rode on till I was ready to drop off from weariness. Then I lay down again in the wet grass to wait for daylight. When at last I mounted for good and rode to the top of a little rise ahead, there lay the ranch itself, less than a third of a mile away. To reach it I had traveled thirty-eight miles instead of the liveryman's promised fifteen. I was glad to rest there all of Monday, June 28.

I learned that fifteen thousand Texas steers had stampeded that night and had left a trail of churned mud nearly half a mile wide. If my horse had not warned me in time, I should have been ground down into the mire and found there later, battered beyond recognition.

Next morning I went on to Chief Joseph's camp, but he had gone out on the reserve. I ate my dinner at the employees' house and talked with the interpreter, an ordained Indian minister, who sent a messenger after Joseph. About four o'clock, while I sat waiting on the porch, an armed Nez Percé Indian rode up and told me through the interpreter: "I've been ordered to arrest you. A white man will be here in a few minutes."

The white man came next—and blurted out roughly, "You're the man I want. Stay right where you are until further orders or you'll get badly hurt." Then he rode off, leaving the armed Indian to guard me.

"Now I'm completely in the agent's power," I thought. "The little monarch who rules here is an *absolute* monarch."

I wrote out a telegram to Mr. Webster. Then I turned to the interpreter. "Here's ten dollars," I suggested, "if you'll send word to the ranch that I've been arrested, and will tell the ranchman to go over into Kansas and send this telegram." But the interpreter would not even take that piece of paper from my hand. "I can't," he faltered. "The Indian guard is watching us. He might report it and get me into trouble." Such was the general state of mind just then on many an Indian reserve.

Later the white man came back, bringing three other heavily armed white men. "Mount your horse," he ordered me, "and go with them to the Ponca reserve." That was about fifteen miles away. Other white men who had been out searching for me joined the group as we rode along.

At the Ponca agent's headquarters I was ordered to sit on a porch, with an armed man on each side of me. Then a dapper little clerk came out of the house and called me various insulting names, including sneak, thief, and liar. Soon the mighty agent himself arrived and took his turn at calling me the same things. Only he added, "You ought to be hanged!"

It was all so petty that at first I felt actually amused. But finally he asserted, "You're busy with a lot of murderers and thieves, trying to stir up trouble among the Indians so that you can profit by an Indian outbreak. You want to start a war in which thousands of white women and children will be murdered and scalped."

Just why this came as the last straw I don't know, but the surge of fury it sent through me must have shown in my face, for the two guards swung their rifles into position and two more guards stepped up behind the agent. All this made me so angry that I thought five or six bullet holes through me would feel good. I rose deliberately, walked over to the agent, put my nose within an inch of his, and told him:

"You're a dirty coward. Any man who will abuse an unarmed prisoner is a coward."

He turned slowly and walked away; half an hour later he came back a different man. Apparently he had decided that I was merely the innocent tool of the villainous Omaha lawyers, whom he denounced roundly.

Later, as his supper guest, I shared a bounteous feast, and I spent the evening in his parlor telling the ladies of his family amusing Indian incidents which seemed to interest them. About eleven o'clock I was led to a second-floor bedroom where a straw bed with a quilt was laid on the floor. Armed men searched me for weapons. By orders from Washington a guard was stationed at the door to look in often during the night, but for this detail the agent himself actually apologized to me.

Next morning, after all the ladies had shaken hands with me heartily, I was asked to mount my horse and ride over to the Kansas line with an escort of several mounted Indian police and the armed white police chief and his assistant in a spring wagon. They all paid little attention to me, spreading out at will. Once, when a dip in the prairie hid me from the spring wagon far ahead, an Indian, pointing to a densely timbered creek, told me in English: "You go!" and seemed amazed when I shook my head. In a mixture of English, Ponca, and the sign language he argued that if I, his good friend, fled, he would obey the bad, mean agent's orders to shoot—by just firing into the air.

All of us halted at the reservation border. I rode across into Kansas. Then the police chief warned me, by the agent's orders:

"If you ever come back into either the Ponca or the Nez Percé reserve, you will be treated a good deal more roughly."

In Arkansas City I learned that the agent's information about my second venture into the territory had come from the Poncas' trusted Frenchman.

Meanwhile the Washington Indian Bureau had released to the press a letter written by the agent after my earlier visit.

"I am credibly informed," he had reported, "that Mr. Tibbles went into the Ponca camp disguised as an Indian squaw with a blanket around his shoulders. . . . Poison Hunter and his wife are the only Indians whom he induced to leave as yet. I arrested Mr. Tibbles' interpreter and had a long talk with him in which he acknowledged that the course pursued by Mr. Tibbles was not an honorable one, and went away feeling very different from what he did when he came."

The suggested picture of me with my goodly height and heavy whiskers masquerading from terror in squaw's dress quite tickled the fancy of those who had heard me speak for the Poncas. And Henry Fontanelle's reputed meek repentance made his friends eager to hear his account of that interview.

After two days of threats and insults from surly ruffians in Arkansas City I telegraphed to Mr. Webster:

"State line towns live on Indian patronage and are controlled by Indian agents. My life is threatened in Arkansas City. If I stay, I must arm. More Poncas left yesterday. I want advice."

Mr. Webster's answer to me was: "Come home."

On July 8 Henry Fontanelle made a long affidavit which completely endorsed my own written report to the Omaha Committee as to the Poncas' despair, their housing conditions, and their longing for their old home.

In short, by much discomfort and some risk, we two, sent by the Poncas' legal advisers, had learned truths which their friends needed to know, and had given them advice which we could not have conveyed to their isolated band in any other way.

It is hard not to include here the various dramatic stages of the new campaign we began in Boston that autumn of 1880. Assertion and counterassertion, move and countermove filled the pages of the newspapers and the Congressional records. But all that really belongs here is a summary of the climax.

The President, confused and worried by the many quirks and turns of the problem, finally appointed a splendid Ponca Commission of his own, which included both Brigadier General Crook and Brigadier General Miles, to visit the actual ground of both the old and the new tracts, and to bring him back the whole truth. Their report amply justified every step we had taken to save the tribe. Better still, it led to a bill which Congress passed on March 3, 1881, in the very last hours of its session, which let each individual Ponca choose the land he preferred, either in the territory tract or on the Niobrara. It also reimbursed the Poncas for their losses, and provided appropriations for houses, schoolhouses, and teachers' pay.

Practically two years had gone by since the dawn when General Crook and I had walked together out of the Omaha *Herald* building, pledged to give the Poncas back their land. From the start even the Department of the Interior admitted that an error had been made and that the Poncas had been cruelly treated, yet from the first to the very last moments it had fought with incredible stubbornness against the simple, obvious idea of undoing that wrong, so far as it ever could be undone, in the way the Poncas wished.

By using the courts, the press, the aroused public opinion of a nation, the eloquence of statesmen, clergy, Indians, philanthropists, and businessmen we at last had beaten down that obstinate, reasonless resistance. The outcome had justified us, and we not only had reinstated the Poncas, but we had established the rights of all Indians to turn to the law for protection. Also we had weakened the power of a horde of minor but absolute monarchs over a helpless race.

The toll I myself had paid had been still heavier than I had foreseen. I had been the one white man chosen as a target for the attacks. Weakened in health; lonesome for my wife and comrade who had died and been buried before I even knew she was ill; anxious about my little girls, who now wandered wretchedly back and forth from boarding schools to one relative's home after another; almost penniless, with my good position gone and my reputation smeared by shrewd, ruthless, lying innuendoes which I knew would never be wholly cleared from people's minds while I lived—or even, perhaps, afterward—I was a good example of the cost of trying to help the helpless.

Because Mrs. Jackson had insisted so strongly that she did not know enough about Indian ways to write a popular book of fiction to help the cause, I now considered meeting that need myself. So I rushed through a novel, *Hidden Power,* which appeared in June 1881. It frankly was propaganda against the system: *A Secret History of the Indian Ring.* Though carefully not drawn from actual incidents, it was based on happenings quite possible under existing conditions. Of the many kindly reviews it received the most comforting at that time to its anxious author was the following from the Boston *Transcript:*

Notwithstanding all the venomous things which have been said of that gentleman by the anti-Indian press, his honesty has never yet been successfully impeached, nor his statements proved unfounded. His book can hardly be praised for literary excellence; yet despite that fact, it cannot help making a strong impression.

25.

Guests of the Ponca Tribe

While we were in Boston in 1879, a lady told me that after studying ethnology for years in books and museums she now wished to visit Indian tribes in their own lodges, living as they lived and observing their daily customs herself—especially the women's and children's ways.

"Did you ever camp out?" I asked.

"No, never."

I found it hard to take her plan seriously. She, a thorough product of city life, was evidently nearing her forties. I could not imagine her leaving all her home comforts to go out to the far frontier and live among the Indians in an Indian lodge. Still, she was so earnest that I reluctantly agreed to take her someday with our group for the trip she wished. But I gave her fair warning:

"You can't stand such a trip. You'll have to sleep on the cold ground. The food will be strange to you. You'll meet storms on the open prairie and be wet to the skin. Burning sun and wind will blister your face and hands. Long days of traveling will exhaust you. You'll have no privacy night or day. I'm sure you never can endure it."

"Yes, I can!" she insisted.

Circumstances kept her from joining us in 1880, but on September 1, 1881, she arrived in Omaha with letters of high praise from the Secretary of War, the Secretary of the Interior, the Postmaster General, and many scientific men. So Bright Eyes and I assembled a camp outfit and we all set out. Unfortunately the rain poured down all the first two days, but by the third night we reached the Omahas. We visited Bright Eyes' sister, and there all the leading men and their wives came to call on us.

First of all Bright Eyes' father, Iron Eye, arrived with his wife. Of medium height, with a clean-cut, intelligent face, he was neatly dressed in civilized style. He had lost one leg and, in spite of an excellent modern substitute, limped slightly, but still rode horseback magnificently. He and the later guests kept Bright Eyes interpreting all day long for the ethnologist until she was nearly exhausted.

Iron Eye told us: "Other people once lived here, who made the pottery I've often plowed up. After them came savage folk who ate human flesh and stole little children to cook and eat them. They had large bodies and immense heads. Once when I was young, and out hunting near where Fort Randall is now, I found a burying ground of those people and I dug up many skulls. These were all very long and flattened at the sides."

The women callers brought our ethnologist gifts—wooden bowls, horn spoons, sinews for thread, bits of buckskin and porcupine quills for trimmings.

In each group the talk soon turned and returned to the problem of titles to their lands. These Omahas knew well that only such titles could save them from extermination.

When night fell, a campfire was made and we all gathered around it. The ethnologist and Bright Eyes shared a buffalo robe. The rest, including a number of intelligent Indians who belonged to what was known among them as the "citizen party," i.e., the group eager to be given citizenship, stood or sat upon the grass. And the first topic mentioned around that fire of the redskins of the plains was the outlook for our wounded

President Garfield, who was then in his ninth week of fighting for his life. They did not approve of the treatment he was receiving.

"The doctors," asserted Iron Eye, "will finish Guiteau's work."

"If they had sent him out to us," said Kaga Amba, a chief who had just returned from Washington, "we should have cured him."

"I know an Indian who was shot in the back, and the ball went almost through him, and he got well," Wajapa, one of the leading men, volunteered. "Sticking that tube into the President every day is what is killing him."

"Too many doctors will kill any man," Kaga Amba agreed.

Iron Eye chimed in again:

"If a man lives until the fourth day after he has received a dangerous wound, we think he is sure to get well, and we call that fourth day by a special name which means 'the walking day,' because an Indian doctor makes his patient get up then and walk at least a step or two."

"If a person is shot in the leg or arm," Kaga Amba commented, "the white doctors always want to cut it off. There was Enumaha, who was shot in the arm up here above the elbow. We took out a long piece of the bone. When we reached camp, the white doctor wanted to cut that arm off. When her relatives wouldn't let him, he said she was sure to die. But she didn't die. She's alive and well, and she can cut wood—and yet there's a place in her arm where there's no bone at all."

Each visitor then took his turn in telling a story about how the Indians had healed some desperate wound. And then the talk swung back again to "land titles."

Next morning I persuaded the two women campers to leave at the reservation about half of their "absolutely necessary" baggage, and we set out in a light spring wagon drawn by a pair of Indian ponies. Wajapa, whom I had asked to join us, rode our third pony. We drove northward across the Winne-

238

bago reserve and the Santee Sioux Agency—through a steady series of rainstorms, broken whiffletrees, muddy roads, balky spells of a pony, thunderstorms during our night camping, and winds which burned our ethnologist's face to a blister. But that city-bred lady stood everything without one complaint.

To her great delight Wajapa therefore gave her an Indian name from his own tribe and family—the eagle family. The word described the sweep of the eagle when high in the air. After Bright Eyes had made several faulty attempts to translate it by some one English word, I hinted that "Highflyer" might do, but that suggestion did not please our ethnologist at all.

Our next goal was that recent bone of contention, the Ponca settlement just north of the Niobrara, on land which a boundary change not long afterward took from Dakota and added to Nebraska. When we reached the river we pitched our tent near what they called the lower ford. There the stream is divided by islands into a narrow, terribly swift current and a broad stretch of shallows and quicksands. An hour later I happened to look upstream toward the upper and safer ford, and there, crossing and hurrying down the bank on our side in wagons, on horses and oxen, or afoot, in a variety of gay colors which made a beautiful sight against the brown prairie and the river, came the whole Ponca tribe, men, women and children, led by Standing Bear, a joyously happy throng. I was amazed at a proceeding so contrary to all Indian custom.

They insisted that we must cross the river and eat with them. Wajapa volunteered to look after our camp, so our Highflyer, Bright Eyes, and I climbed into Standing Bear's wagon. At the ford he turned his team down into the treacherous stream. On they plunged through the quicksands, sometimes down, sometimes on their feet, while the tribe trailed along after us. Suddenly our wheels sank deep; water, cold as ice, rushed over the top of the wagon box, around our feet and up nearly to our knees. Standing Bear stood up, roared out something very like Ponca war whoops, and lashed the horses with his whip. They, poor brutes, reared and plunged. First their forefeet and then their hind feet were caught in the sands. At last with a terrific struggle they surged ahead onto firm footing—and we could stop and let the water drain out of the wagon bed.

Once safely across, Standing Bear took us to his tent to dinner, as his house was still unfinished. Now our ethnologist had a good chance to realize a guest's first duty in reaching an Indian village. No matter what time of the day or night one arrives, he must eat before anything at all can be said or done. We ate. Then, in a huge shed which Bear Head had constructed in front of his house, the whole tribe assembled to hear me explain to them the "final settlement" of their affairs at Washington. At present their most serious complaint was that white men were stealing from their lands all the wood which meant fuel and building timber for the tribe.

When this council broke up, the sun was sinking low in the west. Tazhebute, one of the habeas corpus case Poncas, who knew the Sioux language, had agreed to go on with us to visit the Lower Brûlé Sioux. Now he took us in his wagon to the lower ford and then brought us over the first channel, the swift deep one, in a boat, leaving us to make our way across a long narrow island and be fetched across the shallower channel by Wajapa in another boat we had seen there that morning. But now Wajapa stood helpless on the high bank, shouting that a white man had taken that boat away.

So there we three stood shivering in the early evening chill, our chance of retreat gone with Tazhebute, and ahead, between us and our camp, the ugly stretch of quicksand swept by rapid though rather shallow water. Just as we were feeling utterly at a loss Tazhebute suddenly spoke behind us. He had had a "hunch" that something might go wrong, and had come back to see us safely and surely across. Now Wajapa came wading over, and both Indians insisted that the best solution would be for one of them to transport our Highflyer on his back. So tall Tazhebute crouched down, she put her arms around his neck, and away he splashed through the water, lugging that Boston-born lady-ethnologist back to her belongings. Wajapa kept close behind them, ready to help. I took off my shoes and offered my back for Bright Eyes to mount.

When we had gone hardly thirty feet, Bright Eyes began calling in the Omaha language to Wajapa across my head at the top of her lungs. He dashed ahead, straight through the quicksand and water, hard as he could tear. Then she shouted in the Ponca tongue to Tazhebute: *"Te unaha! Te unaha!"*

Looking up at the bank, I saw that our camp truly was on fire. I speeded up. Bright Eyes was slender, but I learned then that any woman grows heavy to carry when one is running through three feet of water over a quicksand bottom. By the time I dropped her on the shore, I was pretty well winded, but still I had to dash up the steep bank and fight the fire with a saddle blanket.

Tazhebute and Wajapa, working like steam engines, soon put out the flames. Though we had carefully camped on a mown and cleared spot, the short dry stubble had burned so furiously that in five minutes the blaze had destroyed some thirty dollars' worth of our belongings. Each of us had lost something valuable. After Tazhebute left, Wajapa disappeared for several hours.

As it happened, the fire had merely come as the last straw of a long, unusually hard trip. Also, the pony Wajapa had ridden from the Omahas had been so badly gored by a cow at the Santee Agency that we had been forced to leave it there, while Wajapa followed us afoot. That morning, as I had expected, Standing Bear had agreed to lend us a horse for the rest of the trip, but this plan had infuriated Wajapa.

"Standing Bear's no true Indian at all," he had growled to me privately. "You could hunt through all the traditions of all the tribes in the world and not hear of a single case where a traveler who had lost a horse by accident and then came to an Indian friend and told him his trouble wasn't given a horse by that Indian. Don't accept his loan. I can walk every step of the way without any fatigue."

Though I had tried my best to explain that our arrangement was wholly proper by the white men's ways to which Standing Bear had grown accustomed, Wajapa, I knew, had been only partly pacified. Now, right on top of everything else, had landed this fire—while he alone was in charge of our camp. So Wajapa vanished. After considerable hunting I found him sitting on a bank in the dark, staring straight ahead of him, motionless as a rock. I turned back to camp, for I knew the symptoms. Wajapa had the "dumps."

Wajapa dressed in civilized clothes, and really abhorred the paint, feathers, blankets, and dances which so recently had formed a large part of Indian life. He prided himself on having discarded every Indian custom and superstition, and asserted that, for the sake of his children, he had turned his back on the past once for all. He owned a large, well-kept farm with a small farmhouse which he himself had built. Nevertheless, unknown to him, many of the ancient ways still clung to him—especially this strange mood which plainsmen called the "dumps."

As I hurried back to the others, I recalled another Indian who had traveled with me a few seasons before—an educated man in civilized dress, who spoke perfect English. We had been making a long, hard trip through barren cattle country where the only water was so befouled that even the horses refused it. Late one afternoon, after we had been without water in the blazing sun for nearly two days and almost as long without food, we reached a little hole in a bank of red sand rock where we had been told there was always water trickling out of the bank into a tiny basin. We found the water pure and good, but the basin was too high for the horses to reach, and it held less than a bucketful. Without water the horses could not go on.

Then and there my Indian gave up, wrapped his blanket around him, sat down on the grass and would not stir. He had made up his mind to die right on that spot.

There wasn't much life left in me, either, but after I had spoken several times without getting a word out of him, I went back to the little basin to study things out. Across the top of the bank above lay a big cottonwood log. I climbed up, examined it, and decided that if I could roll it down to make a base, I could build up enough brush and stones around it to let a horse stand high enough to drink out of the little rock basin.

I hunted everywhere till I found a pole for a lever. Even so, though the big log lay loose on the ground, I could not budge it. I went back to my Indian and found him singing his death song:

> *"Where shall I go to live forever?*
> *Where shall I go to live forever?"*

On and on, over and over. I told him, loud and clear, that I could water our horses if he would help. He just went on crooning. I realized that he was fast getting into the self-hypnotized state in which Indians do not feel even a knife thrust. Then I got mad and said rude things. He paid no heed. I stated unpleasant facts about an old quarrel between his family and the head chief of his tribe. No result. I told him how low, mean, and despicable he and all his relations were. He just crooned on.

So back I went to the spring. At last I found a longer lever and tumbled the old log down the bank. Then in no time I filled in around it with loose earth and stones so that it would hold a horse. I led one thirsty beast up there and paddled in the tiny pool with my hand. He rushed at the water. That small basin filled so slowly and held so little that it took quite a while to satisfy both horses, but finally I led them away, over to my crooning friend. I wanted to walk them right on top of him, so as to rouse him, but they shied around him. I lariated them in some good grass close by, and they fell to eating eagerly.

I came back and contemplated that Indian. He still sat motionless, but he had stopped crooning. By this time I was so tired and weak myself that I was fast getting to the state where I, too, didn't care whether I lived or died. Suddenly I remembered that, as we were starting out, an Indian woman had given me a small package. I pulled it out of my pocket and found it was a favorite Indian delicacy—dried meat and dried wild fruits pounded up together—about as rich as an English plum pudding. Sitting down close to that half-starved Indian, I began to eat it; surely the odor of it would bring him back to existence. It did not take the slightest effect. At last I leaned over and, putting my mouth within an inch of his ear, yelled with all my might:

"The horses have been watered!"

Slowly he turned his head toward me. His eyes had a strange look. After a moment he said, "Hah?"

Though until now he had always spoken only perfect English to me, "Hah?" was Indian for "What?"

"Come and eat!" I replied.

That speech was an inspiration, and I ought to have remembered earlier that those are the words to which an Indian responds instantly. This man rose slowly to his feet, shook himself as a dog does after a roll in the grass, and reached out his hand for the little package of primitive plum pudding. His dumps were over. But here on the Niobrara I could well let Wajapa manage his own recovery.

The Poncas continued to overwhelm me with attentions and

with all sorts of problems to be solved. White Shirt wanted to go to the Indian Territory to fetch his old mother and an aunt. Members of other separated families were eager to send for their relatives. Hour after hour I listened and gave the best advice I could contrive. One case really saddened me. On my 1880 Indian Territory trip I had accepted Poison Hunter's offer of his tent for a brief rest one night. Later the agent had announced to the press that I had induced Poison Hunter and his wife to leave the agency. What had really happened was that as soon as that same agent learned that Poison Hunter had sheltered me, he threatened to arrest him and treat him as the previous agent had treated Big Snake. Therefore Poison Hunter and his wife had fled in the night with only two ponies and had hurried through to the refuge of the old reservation in only ten days. Now, more than a year later, he still was very feeble from the strain and fatigue of that trip.

"I had to leave behind me everything I had in the world," he told me, "my wagon, my harness, my cow, and all my own little treasures. Now that we are to be allowed to stay here, do you think I could get some of my own things back?"

So at last I had heard the pathetic outcome of that episode, begun so harmlessly hundreds of miles away.

Oddly enough our popularity actually forced us to cut our stay near the Poncas rather short. As I have said before, when an Indian—any Indian—comes, night or day, starving or heavily fed, to any other Indian's house or tent, it would be an insult if the host did not place food before him at once—and an equal insult if the guest did not eat all he could and carry away the rest. Even a white man must submit to this tradition far enough to invite all who are around his tent at a mealtime to "come and eat." With about a hundred and fifty Poncas eager to entertain us and be entertained by us, we soon decided it was wise and necessary to move onward.

Tazhebute came to join us with a good Indian tent and a still greater treasure in his wagon. Those tents have no equal for camping purposes. They shed the rain well, and in cold weather one can build a fire right in the center of them, with the smoke rising cleanly up out of the top, where the flaps are set to suit the way of the wind. So we felt very grateful to Tazhebute for this and for his other and still better contribution —something without which any Indian camping party is bound to suffer discomforts. For his even greater treasure was an energetic, good-natured, hard-working Indian woman, his own wife. On any long, hard trip such a woman is worth five men. She pitches the tent, cooks, washes up, drives a team on the march, or rides horseback, driving the extra ponies, and does a thousand other things quicker and more deftly than any man. Also she is less likely than any man to have the "dumps."

This woman was a little heroine. In our six weeks of camping and eating together, no suffering from fatigue, cold, or hunger ever caused her to vary from her respectful, modest manner or destroyed her lighthearted good humor. Whether she was sitting out dreary hours in a tent on which the rain or snow or sleet beat down, or whether in her thin calico dress she was sticking the heavy tent poles into the ground after a long day's march, while the cold wind whistled around her, she was always smilingly ready to reply with a respectful answer. By Indian etiquette we never heard her personal name. We all called her "Gaha," an honorable title akin to "Grandmother," which pleased her exceedingly.

While we packed, Standing Bear brought me the horse he had promised to lend me, one trained for wagon work as well as riding. Off we set, with Tazhebute and his wife leading the way in his own wagon with Standing Bear, who would leave us at the upper ford. I bade the Poncas good-by, mounted the borrowed horse, and rode after the wagon. Bright Eyes and the ethnologist sat waiting in the buggy for Wajapa, who stood a little apart, gazing off into the distance, a motionless statue. I felt anxious. Would he climb into the buggy and follow me, as agreed, or would he start back on foot for the Omaha reservation? Who could tell? I decided that my best course was to ride along, not turning my head to left or right, and leave him standing and the two women in the buggy waiting. For several minutes I rode and wondered before a turn in the road granted me one swift, imperceptible glance rearward. Far back I could see Wajapa just climbing into the buggy.

At the ford Standing Bear was waiting to shake hands with everyone but Wajapa, whom he somehow did not see.

26.

On Our Way

After we had followed the south bank of the Niobrara a little way along a terrible road, we halted for the night, thankfully leaving all details of camping in the experienced hands of our Indians.

And here let me advise anyone who plans such a trip as ours with a party of Indians never to interfere with their mode of doing things. Practically always there is some good traditional reason for every act. Again, no matter how small the group of Indians is, it always is fully under the control of one leader—a *nudunaga*, such as I myself had been for a very brief time in my young days with Two Bears and Meepee and Sunshine. This leader selects the camping places, gives the orders for halting and moving on, and, though commonly doing none of the actual work of the camp, always receives the first food cooked by any of the others, each of whom has his own assigned position and duties. The *nudunaga* also receives all gifts made to the group and then distributes them to the rest.

In our tent that first night out we took our respective places in the most convenient order. By long-established custom, for all the rest of our trip we occupied exactly those same relative places. Such had been the habit of every person in all the plains tribes in their roving days, so that on even the darkest night the head chief could silently lay his hand on any person in the whole tribe without risking a mistake.

All night long it rained—in a country where autumn rain was literally unknown. All the next day it rained. And all of many days afterward. To use some of the time to advantage, practical Gaha brought into the tent armfuls of green sticks, ranging from some as small as a man's little finger up to others an inch thick and four feet long. She had cut them from a certain kind of dogwood which, Tazhebute explained, could not be found up where the Sioux lived.

Gaha with her butcher knife swiftly stripped off the outer bark. Then Tazhebute with a similar knife pulled off the inner bark. He next slit an end of one of the larger stripped sticks down into three splints, each a foot long. By weaving a small withe in and out through these he contrived a three-pronged fork on which he could lay the bark to dry over the fire. Later he would shred the dried bark up fine, ready for mixing with tobacco on a basis of three parts of bark to one of clear tobacco, the genuinely favorite smoke of those great smokers, the Indians.

Meanwhile we all sat in the tent while the ethnologist joyfully absorbed the stories and legends told us by Tazhebute, who, as Wajapa explained to us, was the greatest of the three Ponca medicine men. Incidentally Tazhebute blamed us for the bad weather because we had tossed some odds and ends of salt into the fire, and by so doing had made the Rabbit angry. So now Tazhebute began to invoke the Rabbit in order to propitiate him, but Wajapa promptly made fun of the whole performance, with the result that Tazhebute stopped short in the middle of his prayer. For Tazhebute, a man of gentle soul, set small value on his own wisdom. His belief in the old traditions was slowly giving way, though the new light was only just beginning to dawn for him. So he at once deferred to Wajapa's greater knowledge, judgment, and assertiveness. Yet I suspect that silently he still considered the Rabbit's attitude as more important than Wajapa wanted to admit. One fine thing I appreciated in Tazhebute was that he was able to give in without sulking. In all that tedious trip he never once had the "dumps."

One of the stories told around our fire particularly interested me because I had known the hero of it in my long-ago year among the Indians. I remembered him as a tall man with very long hair and exceptionally clear-cut, intelligent features. Now at last I heard his story.

When he was a boy and his tribe was at war with a tribe to the west, he had set his heart on going with a certain raiding party to steal the enemies' horses. And then its leader told him: "No; you're far too young to go."

That night the boy stole one of the best horses in his own camp and took the trail after the raiding party. Unluckily for him its leaders soon followed the usual technique of hiding the trail so thàt, in case of disaster, the enemy could not trace it back to its source. But the boy, though he lost all signs of the rest, pushed straight ahead until on the fourth day he suddenly found himself right inside of the hostile camp. And the same instant he saw hìs foes they saw him. He thought quickly. If he should try to escape, he would surely be killed. Deciding to brazen it out, he rode squarely into the middle of the camp.

The enemy, bewildered, asked him the routine questions put to all strangers: "Where are you going? What do you want?"

Instead of answering he dropped off his horse, fell into spasms, frothed at the mouth, cut himself with his knife, ran arrows through his arms, and began to prophesy that a fearful calamity was soon to fall upon this camp.

"You have neglected the holy tents!" he told them. "You have desecrated the peace pipe and have brought down on yourselves the displeasure of the Great Mysterious One!"

"But what can we do about it?" his frightened hearers asked him.

"You must hold at once a sacred feast and dance. You must

set up your sacred post and bring your horses around it. You must fetch out your holy white buffalo robe and pile presents on it. If you fail to do this, a fearful disease will come. You all will fall before it like autumn leaves before the wind."

"And if we do all that you say, what then?" they asked him.

"When all your presents are gathered there, and while you still are dancing around the sacred post, you must send out twelve old men, one from each band, dressed in rags, with their bodies painted black and their faces plastered with white clay. They must carry in their hands the sacred peace pipe. Whomsoever they meet first they must invite into this camp to receive all the presents that are on the robe. When these visitors leave, the disease will leave with them. Then you all must move away at once to the far western edge of your own land and live there for four years."

All this, announced by the boy's foaming mouth, and emphasized by his frantic gestures, while blood poured from his many self-inflicted wounds, got onto his hearers' nerves so badly that one of the women fell down in a fit. The boy saw her fall.

"Behold!" he shrieked. "You disbelieve the words of truth. The vengeance has come! The terrible disease is here!"

At once he sat down, pulled his blanket over his head, and began the funeral wail.

A few of the leaders advised killing him at once, but the mass of the tribe, crazy with fear, rushed around to put through the ceremonies the boy had demanded. The twelve old men were rigged out just as dramatically as he had specified, and were started on their way—only they insisted that the boy must go with them. Reverently carrying the peace pipe before them, they began their search for the visitors who should bear away the curse.

Naturally they soon ran across the raiding party who, bewildered enough at seeing this strange peace delegation, became almost panic-stricken when they saw the boy whom they had left at home riding here, honored, in the midst of the twelve old men. Cheeks blanched. Bodies trembled with fear.

But the boy explained firmly:

"The Great Bear took me up in his arms and carried me through the clouds to bring a message to this people. Do as these old men tell you, or I will pronounce a great curse upon you, and you all shall die."

And his own friends and kin, who could not imagine any other way to explain the boy's turning up there in such fashion, sincerely swallowed his story entire, and meekly followed him and his ragged old band into the hostile camp.

A feast was held which lasted all night long. In the morning the raiding party were given two hundred horses, which carried on their backs nearly all the available wealth of the whole tribe. And the unfortunate enemies all hastened away to spend four long years beside the western boundary of their land.

So back home rode the runaway boy in a halo of mystery and glory. He not only was bringing back riches but, without losing a man, he had driven away his own tribe's foes on terms which ensured four years of peace with them. That boy's career now was marked out for him. He became a medicine man—one who was greatly feared and very resourceful in dealing with every problem which arose. Such was the mature man as I myself had known him.

To all intents ours was an Indian camp, with all of such a camp's normal life except the dancing. This, too, we should have had at times except for the constant vigilance of Wajapa, who would have none of it. If Tazhebute in a gleeful mood even started humming a dance tune and took a step or two, Wajapa instantly clamped down on him with sarcasm which promptly ended that impulse—to the ethnologist's hardly concealed fury.

One new fact, which we realized as we heard our Indians discuss the trip, was that not only every stream but every prominent hill, strange tree, large rock, unusual land formation, and body of timber had its individual name. Therefore, when Wajapa returned from the trip and named to Iron Eye the details of our route, that old chief sat down and made a perfect map of the country we had traversed with our route marked on it by all these natural features he knew well by sight or hearsay.

And speaking of landscape marks, although I have been as intimate a friend of several tribes as any white man can well hope to be, and although these Indians, expressing confidence in me, have treated me like one of themselves, there still are matters which not one of them has ever been willing to explain to me adequately. And one such matter is the meaning of the round piles of stone which top many hills. Some of these, eight to ten feet high, must have required hard work to build; most of them are from a foot and a half to three feet high. Even my most intimate friends would not give me any real information about these structures, although whenever I pressed them hard they supplied me with all sorts of plausible explanations. The piles were guideposts, or they indicated an Indian's claim to those bits of land, or they were memorial markers for notable events which had happened there, et cetera. But because these reasons were altogether too varied, I knew perfectly well that probably not one of them was the true one.

Once I even saw an Indian in the act of building a pile.

"What are you doing it for?" I asked him.

"Just for fun," he answered.

But it was on an extra-hot August day, and he was lugging the stones up a long, steep hill. Perhaps he could see fun in it, but I failed to.

There in our tent I now asked Wajapa and Tazhebute what such stone piles meant, but none of their answers proved satisfactory.

Now and again on this trip I found traces of another Indian habit which, though I have lived beside or among Indians a goodly part of my life, is a thing I cannot account for. I refer to the speed with which the Indians spread news among their own people. However, I felt better about my own bewilderment when General Crook himself told me:

"Although I have used every means to learn how the Indians send messages hundreds of miles in a few hours, my efforts have brought no result. I'm sure it was not done by helio-graphing with their small mirrors, or by sending up smoke signals by day, or by fire signals at night. Yet I know for certain that their messages actually traveled vast distances almost instantly.

"Take this instance," he went on. "I was in camp many miles away from [the Little Bighorn] where Custer was defeated [on June 25, 1876, and where the slaughter of his troops went on from two o'clock until sunset]. About four o'clock in the afternoon on the day of the battle I noticed the strange conduct of my Indian scouts. They were quartered in a tent not far from mine. A dreadful gloom seemed to settle down on all of them, all at once. I knew that certainly something very distressing had happened, but none of them made any report to me, as they surely would have done if they had had news of any hostile advance upon our own position. We all know, of course, that individual Indians will get the 'dumps' and turn profoundly melancholy for a day, but that whole campful of Indians seemed to be in a state of despair.

"Toward night I grew so anxious that I sent for one of those scouts and asked him what the matter was. It was a long time before I could get anything out of him. At last he told me that Custer and all his men had been killed that day by a Sioux chief who had a bad reputation among the Indians. I tried every device I could think of then to induce that scout to tell me how he had got the information. The only reply he would make was that they got it 'in the Indian way.'"

It took us a week to travel the hundred and fifty miles from the mouth of the river up to Fort Niobrara, near where Valentine, Nebraska, stands today. For much of the way we dragged slowly along through deep sand, often spending days without seeing a house or any living thing except insects and a few birds.

We knew, however, that we had nothing to dread from any Indian. The Omahas had sent runners ahead of us to the Poncas, and the Poncas in turn to the Rosebud Agency. From there more runners had gone to the tribes to the north and east with the most impressive formalities. I heard that No Flesh, a favorite Sioux orator, already had visited many of the bands to tell them not only that I had taken Standing Bear away from the President and set him free, but also that I had always been a friend of the Indians and once had actually forced a con-tractor to return to No Flesh's own tribe the price of fifteen hundred cattle which that contractor falsely claimed that he had furnished them. Therefore, argued No Flesh, the Sioux were bound to pay me the highest honors they could confer.

At Fort Niobrara we rested a couple of days as the comman-dant's guests; and when we left, he detailed his chief scout, Thigh, a large, personable man, who was very reserved and quiet, to attend us over the nearly forty miles north to the Rose-bud Agency. But right then we ran into one of the difficulties which so often befall those who must make practical arrange-ments by means of an interpreter. Through a Negro who was the official interpreter Thigh had heard the commandant's or-ders to go with us whenever we should start. Unluckily this Ne-gro had added wholly of his own accord that, seeing that one of our wagons was being repaired, he did not believe we should start until the next day. So when early in the afternoon, with the wagon duly repaired, we all waited, drawn up in line, to be escorted as ordered, there was no Thigh on hand to do it.

By the time he had been routed out and asked by the disgusted commandant questions which Bright Eyes translated into the Ponca tongue for Tazhebute, who then repeated them in the Sioux language to Thigh, it was far too late for the latter to get his wife and his outfit ready for a start that day. So we set off northward alone, prepared to camp by the Minichaduza River until Thigh and his wife could overtake us.

Late that afternoon it began to rain. By the time we made camp at dusk everything was dismal and irritating to the nerves. Evidently, too, a real tempest was brewing. The ethnologist, who had bought a lining for the tent, proposed slipping it in under the tent poles. While we were discussing how best to do this, Wajapa made some remark which led the lady to comment impulsively: "You speak to us as if we were children."

I saw Wajapa's face change. When I looked up from my task a moment later he was gone.

Outside the tent the rain now beat down in torrents. The wind, unhindered for hundreds of miles, came howling across the prairie. The sky hung inky black. Once I slipped out of the tent for a moment to look around and listen from the shelter of a wagon. A lightning flash lit up the world—and there, some fifty yards from the tent and near our huddled herd of horses, stood Wajapa in the dumps, motionless as a rock, taking the full lashing of the storm. Two hours later he came into the tent, wet to the skin, sat a few minutes by the fire, and then without a word wrapped himself in a buffalo robe. In three minutes he was asleep.

Under all these circumstances I was thankful that I already had met one pressing problem of that day more tactfully than the Highflyer had met hers, but, unlike her, I had known the

Indian mind from long personal experience. In my own problem I had promptly realized that I was facing that unalterable thing, a "notion." For one of the most baffling traits in almost any Indian is the fact that if he "takes a notion" into his head to do or not to do a certain thing, no matter how absurd that thing may be, no one can reason him out of it. Or he may make some utterly ridiculous or false statement. Then you can talk to him endlessly, explaining and proving in detail its complete absurdity—and still he will say it right over again, just as calmly as if you had never volunteered a word against it.

Strangely enough, I have not found that educating an Indian can change him at all in this respect. On any subject in which he feels no especial concern he will argue as logically as anyone, but once let him make a personal issue of any matter and "take a notion" to act thus or so about it, then it is time to stop arguing with him, for protest is useless. So well do the white men who understand the Indians realize this trait that, once a "notion" is clearly indicated, if they can assert actual authority, they use it; otherwise, letting the Indian go his own way, they merely fall back on subterfuges to try to lessen any harm that is done.

To my mind "moods," including the "dumps," and "notions" have been two of the greatest obstacles in the way of Indian advancement. And one must frankly admit that there is likely to be in any Indian a twist which at times causes him to act like a spoiled child. One day he is an orator, a reformer, a pioneer looking toward a better life; the next day he has the "dumps" or is acting on a "notion" utterly without reason.

Though education really greatly modifies the "dumps," I have never known a full-blood Indian, however well educated, who was not subject, often without any adequate cause, to periods of melancholy moodiness. But mercifully these do not last long. For example, before night closed down on the next day of our trip, Wajapa had again become friendly toward the Highflyer, and they were playing games, cracking jokes, and having a thoroughly jolly time together.

That day my own problem in the "notion" line had happened because the kindly commandant had given me five rations of thoroughly dried shelled corn for our journey. Familiar with this feed, I had shown Wajapa exactly how much of it was a proper meal for a horse. But Wajapa had "taken a notion" that such a small amount would not be enough. Therefore he had fed to each of our five horses in one big helping its full supply for five feedings.

His act was so plainly a "notion" that I could waste no time in arguing it. As soon as I discovered what he had done, I hastily invented a task for him elsewhere, and then secretly managed to smuggle away from my own team two thirds of what he had given them. The three other horses all were foundered—a troublesome handicap for us all the rest of that journey.

Throughout that first night and all the next day the rain poured down, while the thermometer dropped about a degree an hour. At noon Thigh and his wife reached us, chilled through, and then we all simply waited around our fire for the storm to end. Most of the afternoon the three Indian men sat talking together, with Tazhebute interpreting between Thigh and Wajapa. And what did they talk about? Well, first, like Civil War veterans of the North and South when they met in later years, they discussed their own old wars—between Poncas, Omahas, and Sioux, and fought their battles over again. Then Wajapa, with his face alight, made a long, earnest speech on the whole Indian question, giving an amazingly comprehensive view of it along with a simple statement of how it could be solved through agriculture and land titles and citizenship.

"I know that I myself can never really become like a white

man," he concluded emphatically. "It wasn't for my own good that I cut off my hair, laid aside my Indian clothes, and put on white man's dress. I did it for my children, for they can and must become like the whites. If they don't, they'll die of misery and want."

Thigh quite agreed with him. Twelve months ago he had decided to break his relation to his band and his tribe and become independent. Since then he had refused to receive anything from the government except what he actually earned as a scout —and he intended never again to receive a cent from an agent's hands. But he warned Wajapa:

"When we reach the Rosebud Agency, you'll do well to keep such ideas to yourself. They'd make you very unpopular with those Rosebud Indians."

And now that I have duly recorded poor Wajapa's two racial weaknesses of "dumps" and "notions," I wish in all fairness to pay a sincere tribute to his individual nobility and honesty.

Already on our trip a group of educated white men and women had visited our tent one day in a jolly mood. Someone noticed that Wajapa was sitting beside an unused camp stove which would be a fine substitute for an Indian drum. So the women guests, both young and old, joined hands in a big circle, ready to dance, and urged Wajapa to beat time for them on this improvised instrument. Wajapa refused—and kept on refusing. I felt rather provoked at this stubborn disregard for our guests' wishes; so later I asked him why he had not been more obliging. He answered firmly, "I told you all that I had turned my back on those Indian ways—and I have done it once for all."

Again, in facing this trip ahead among the Brûlé Sioux, he knew that most of them disapproved of forsaking the old habits and customs and of breaking up the tribal tradition. He understood clearly that most of them felt that any Indian who put off his blanket and breechcloth and put on a coat, trousers, and a hat was to be regarded and treated as a traitor to his own race. By going to those Sioux in his present clothing Wajapa would probably meet coldness and suspicion. He well knew that a tangible reward too was at stake. If for just those few days of our Sioux visit he should dress in his native style, he would be welcomed as a visiting Indian in good standing and therefore automatically would be given horses and other valuable gifts. But in his white man's clothes he would be given absolutely nothing. Yet Wajapa firmly rode northward dressed as I was dressed, and by his face I knew that he was impelled, not by a "notion," but by a principle.

For no smile or appeal of pretty girls and friendly guests, no certain prospect of valuable gifts, and no dread of being ostracized by his own race could induce this man to vary by one hairbreadth from the course of conduct he had laid out for himself as his duty to the coming generations. A full-blood Indian, he showed now, as he often did in the later years when I knew him still better, such nobleness, firmness, courage, conscientiousness, and honesty as I have seldom found in even the best specimens of our own cultured white Christians.

Ugh! How cold it was the next morning! The wind, blowing sharply keen from the north, came through our clothing as water flows through a sieve. We waited till eight o'clock before starting, then for five hours we faced that piercing blast as we drove straight against it over a treeless plain. At one o'clock we halted under the shelter of a little bank near a lake. Gaha stuck a tent pole into the ground and made a three-cornered windbreak out of the tent cloth. Then, as there was not a scrap of wood within miles of us, the Indians fetched sticks which they purposely had brought in their wagons for such moments, and we made a fire. Chilled as we all were to the very marrow of our bones, we found that a quart of hot coffee apiece did not more than warm us through. So as soon as possible we pressed on to accomplish somehow the two hours more of icy riding which would bring us to the Rosebud Agency.

Just before we had left Omaha, General Crook remarked to me:

"A man may live his whole life among Indians and yet know nothing about them."

I, for one, could bear witness to that. Also I knew that it truly was harder to win admission to the best circles of Indian society on terms of absolute equality and true friendship than it then was to gain the entree into the most exclusive set in Boston. With the Indians, if you failed in some minor observance, you suddenly fell under suspicion and found yourself an "outsider" again. Therefore, because we all knew that customs varied somewhat with the different tribes, we began to feel seriously anxious about how to conduct ourselves and what to say when we should make our first formal appearance among these strangers.

When, early in our trip, I had consulted Standing Bear about all this, he had answered:

"As for you, you need only tell them that you are the man who helped the Indians and that you've come to pipe-dance them, but for the Highflyer it will be harder."

I soon realized how true this was when I overheard Wajapa, who already had spent several days almost constantly in our company on our way up from the Omaha reserve and who himself had given our ethnologist her highly complimentary Indian name, nevertheless telling the Poncas with obvious sincerity:

"She has come to see the Indians. She seems to be a very nice woman, but I haven't known her long enough to say for certain."

27.

Pipe-Dancing the Sioux

We knew that, when Indians paid one of their frequent visits of a few days to a friendly tribe, they were always given valuable presents on leaving—horses, blankets, robes, or some other worthy gifts. Therefore, a ceremonial visit was a matter of serious importance; from the point of view of the visited tribe it was a costly luxury. That was why tribes usually were visited in this ceremonious way only by invitation, after which elaborate preparations were made. Every tent a visitor entered, as well as its contents, was considered that visitor's property for as long as he stayed there.

Because the actual presentation ceremony, elaborately spread over four days and the greater part of four nights, always included a dance, white men named the process "pipe-dancing," a poor rendering of the Indian word for it. As a matter of fact, no Indian ever merely "visited" in our sense of the word "visit"; he always went to "pipe-dance," that is, both to visit and to receive presents. Moreover every outsider, on entering a camp, was always asked why he had come. His entire reception and entertainment hung on the word he used in reply. This basing of the procedure of days or even weeks upon the use of only one word was simply one of a hundred instances in which any visitor had to follow Indian etiquette with infinite delicacy. Tazhebute decided it was wisest to say that we had come to "pipe-dance."

When the Rosebud buildings, of which the near ones were mostly small log houses thickly surrounded by tents, at last lifted themselves into sight across the prairie, Thigh drove ahead with the other Indians. I, who was driving Bright Eyes and the ethnologist, fell to the rear. As Gaha passed us, I noticed that she had painted nearly the whole of both sides of her face red, and also her hair parting. Tazhebute now wore a blanket; his parting, too, showed red paint, but Wajapa had made no change at all.

Somewhat short of the settlement a tall, impressive-looking Indian who was wrapped in a blue blanket stood awaiting us. Thigh, as merely our temporary guide, here turned aside, and Tazhebute as our leader and interpreter went forward to meet this official greeter.

"Where are you going?" the Sioux chief asked in the conventional form which corresponds to our "How do you do?"

"We have come to pipe-dance the Brûlés," Tazhebute answered, and briefly summarized who each of us was.

"It makes my heart glad that you all have come," warmly responded the chief, who, Tazhebute soon told me, was Ausapi, one of the more important Sioux leaders.

Ausapi then led us to a very large tent which could hold a hundred people. We alighted and tossed our belongings out onto the ground. As Indian women led our horses away, Ausapi drew back the flap of the tent, saying:

"This is your house."

The place was empty except for a huge fire which was roaring and crackling in the center. We stood in a circle around it, holding out our icy hands toward the blaze. Less than ten minutes later Ausapi returned to say: "Come and eat."

"My son-in-law," he explained, "lives in a house a little farther off and lives like a white man, with a table and white men's dishes, but I thought you might be hungry, and therefore I had something cooked for you quick at my own home. After this, though, you can eat at my son-in-law's, as it will be pleasanter for you there."

He led us a few steps to his own little log hut. Rude bedsteads were built around three sides of it; a cookstove stood on the fourth side; there was a vacant space in the middle, where blankets were spread for us. As soon as we sat down on them, each of us was served with two or three pounds of boiled jerked beef, three or four very large biscuits, which a Sioux woman had asked a white woman's help in making for the white visitors, and a whole pint of very strong, very black coffee.

The Highflyer looked with horror upon the immense pile of food which etiquette demanded that she should eat, though we had dined heartily out on the prairie only two hours before. She turned an appealing glance toward Bright Eyes, who could offer no help. But Gaha, noticing the look, said in a low tone in the Omaha language, which she was certain that none of our hosts understood, "Tell the white woman that she need not try to eat all of the meat. She can put into my dish any of it she doesn't want."

This was a genuine kindness, and Bright Eyes and I also took advantage of it.

After the meal we went back to the tent and began to get ready for the night. The ground was exceptionally rough and hard, and there seemed little prospect of comfortable sleep, but just as we had decided that we must make the best of it, Ausapi and a few others came in with great armfuls of hay. Ausapi explained that he knew that white people were not used to sleeping on the ground, and therefore had feared it would be very difficult for us. Then he went and fetched his wife and daughters for a formal call on us. Now that we had eaten, Indian convention at last let us talk to our hosts.

Ausapi told me he was glad I had come, and that he had been expecting me for some days.

"We have had great trouble here lately," he went on, "because Spotted Tail was murdered, but now everything is at peace."

"He was a great man," the chief's wife chimed in, "just like a father to us all."

After a few words more Ausapi left us, to return almost at once and tell us that our supper was waiting for us at his son-in-law's house. On leaving our tent I noticed that all our belongings—lariats, saddles, blankets, and cooking utensils—still lay where we had dropped them off the wagon.

"Is it safe," I asked Ausapi, "to leave all those things lying there while we're away?"

He looked at me as if grieved and answered:

"There's not a white man within a day's journey except the agent and his employees, and they never come over here."

Though only an hour had sped since we had eaten, we could not avoid the fact that we must eat again. Gaha again went with us to help us out. The same articles of food were served to us at the son-in-law's and in enormous quantities.

Back in our tent at last we found that fresh wood had been piled on the radiant fire; and there were four chairs in the tent. Ausapi, realizing that it was hard for white people to sit on the ground, had borrowed these for us. But we were hardly seated in them when a big, handsome Indian arrived to shake hands with us and to add: "Come and eat."

We looked at each other. It was so impossible for me to eat or drink another mouthful that I heartily regretted that I had ever come pipe-dancing. I suspect my face wore the same look I saw that the ethnologist and Bright Eyes were wearing. But a truehearted gentleman had seen that look too; Tazhebute leaned toward me with a kindly air.

"You need not go," he reassured me. "I will try and arrange the matter."

Knowing the stern demands of Indian etiquette, which had been based on the former vast distances between tribes and the meat hunger of a primitive people, I did not see how he could settle it without the insult of a refusal, but eat again now I could not. I decided to trust it to him. We three watched him talk with all the Indians present for a few minutes; they smiled frequently. Then he, Wajapa, and Gaha went away with our latest would-be host. Afterward Tazhebute told me that he had explained to this Indian that a white man could not eat more than three times a day without getting sick, and that Bright Eyes, too, through associating with the white people had acquired this absurd failing. But the rest of our party would gladly accept all additional invitations for us. Tazhebute, however, also took the wise precaution of explaining that infirmity of ours to Ausapi, who promised that after this first day he would arrange matters so that we ourselves need not eat more than three times a day during our visit, on condition that Wajapa, Tazhebute, and Gaha would act as our recognized substitutes at any meals beyond those basic three. This method of settling the problem was perfectly satisfactory even to our own Indians. Throughout that same afternoon and evening they continued to perform faithfully. In all they must have eaten no less than six or seven hearty meals during that time without one grumble, unless one so interprets Gaha's comment after the final feast. She came in rather heavily, sat down by the fire, put her hand close up under her chin, and remarked, "I am full clear up to here with coffee and meat."

More than this, whenever the three Indians came back to the tent from a feast, Gaha walked behind the rest carrying a large quantity of meat. Beef cut into thin pieces, sun-dried, and then boiled slightly will keep long and well. By the time our visit ended, Gaha had packed away into our wagons a really large amount of such dinner gleanings.

Meanwhile on that first evening White Thunder and a number of other chiefs called on us and gave us a right royal welcome. A half-breed came also, an agency employee, to interpret for the ethnologist. She began to use him in questioning Ausapi about agency affairs, but she found the chief very reticent. Finally the half-breed began to talk to her on his own account, his words almost tumbling over each other. His statement that they had only part of a sawmill there, at which nothing was done and no Indian could get any lumber sawed, while the agent's own nineteen-year-old boy, small for his age, drew a salary of fifty dollars a month as the miller, caused the ethnologist to express great indignation. She took out her notebook to record the facts, but as soon as she began to write, the half-breed grew so frightened that he would talk no more and soon left the tent.

Then I began to worry. We knew nothing about that half-breed. He might go straight to the agent and, repeating every impulsive word the Highflyer had said, add to these a great deal she had not said at all. It was only a year since I had had my own troubles and had faced genuine risks in the Indian Territory reserves. Now we were completely in this agent's power. He had large, obedient government forces under him. There was no law but his in that entire great tract of land, and no judge to issue a writ of habeas corpus if the agent should deem it proper to arrest us and hold us. True, my friend the Secretary of the Interior's power was over, but I was personally responsible for the safety of these two women and of our group of Indians.

So I earnestly begged the Highflyer not to talk publicly about anything except the scientific angle of her work. She must repress any other remarks until we all had left this reservation well behind us. But she would not heed my warnings. She was sure that no agent would dare to arrest her, though I told her that I had seen judges, lawyers, authors, and scientists make the same mistake out here on the plains—to their cost.

The next morning we breakfasted with Ausapi's son-in-law in white-man fashion. We sat in chairs at the table, had dishes, knives, forks, and spoons, and were served steak, biscuit, coffee, and even butter. Ausapi, who had escorted us there, waited for us in an adjoining room. Once I saw him go out for a few minutes. As we left the house, he suggested:

"I think you all had better go up and see the agent." After a moment he added, "He has invited you there."

"Here's trouble," I told myself, "even sooner than I was expecting."

"What does he want of us?" I asked Ausapi.

"He's sent for you. Perhaps he wants you to take breakfast with him."

The Rosebud Agency is set on high, barren sand hills. In those days there was no timber within seven or eight miles. All the hay used there had to be hauled from ten to twenty-five miles. Every article of merchandise or food consumed there was brought in wagons from the Missouri River, ninety miles away—except the live cattle which were issued to the Indians.

The agency buildings—storehouses, agent's and employees' buildings, shops, etc.—stood on one of the high sandy hills, surrounded by a stockade in which every entrance was always kept closed with a spring lock. Spotted Tail had been the only Indian ever allowed inside of that stockade. Any other chief, even, who wished to talk with the agent had to stand outside the enclosure and talk through an opening in the upper part of a door. Yet the stockade would have been little defense against a genuine Indian attack.

Soon our whole party with Ausapi went to visit the agent. At a locked stockade gate we came to a standstill. Before long a hard-faced Indian, armed to the teeth and wearing a police badge, came out, looked us over, and passed on, while Gaha shrank up close to me for protection. Then a white man came along. When we told him our errand, he unlocked the gate and let us walk in, directing us to the office.

But our Boston scientist scorned the office. She insisted on calling at the agent's house; walking up to its door, she knocked for admission. Meanwhile an interpreter had come to the office door and was motioning vigorously for us to go over there.

"Not a bit of it," quoth our Bostonian dame to me. "The house is the proper place for the agent to receive a lady."

But no one answered her knock, the interpreter kept on waving, and Ausapi showed increasing uneasiness. Finally he told me:

"I'm afraid we'll all get into trouble if the white woman will not go to the agent's office."

When Bright Eyes had interpreted this to the ethnologist, she turned away from the house and started with the rest of us for the office. Once there, she led the way in and introduced herself to the agent, a small, dark man with long hair which hung straight down over his shoulders; then she presented the rest of the party. He shook hands with each one except me. Whether he skipped me merely by accident I cannot say. The ethnologist thereupon calmly introduced me to him all over again. This time he shook hands with me, remarking, "I've heard of you." His tone implied that what he had heard had not been very good.

The Highflyer then spoke casually about the weather, and the agent commented:

"I regulate everything here except the weather."

This, I knew, was a favorite remark of agents, a ready-made device for asserting their supreme authority. The Highflyer, however, failed to take in its full significance and merely made some light and pleasant reply. Then she handed the man her letters of introduction from her powerful government friends in Washington. He read them—in fact studied them intently—and finally told her with a total change of manner: "This is a satisfactory account of your appearance here."

At the last he even gave our Bostonian lady a key to one of the stockade gates.

When the whole affair was safely over, Tazhebute told me that Ausapi had not let him tell us that the agent's order for us to appear before him had been distinctly peremptory. After we had left the stockade behind us, Ausapi volunteered thoughtfully: "I'm one of the chiefs of this tribe, and I've been here ever since this agency was located, but today is the first time I've ever put my foot on the floor of the agent's office."

That night and each of our remaining nights at the Rosebud Agency, the ethnologist, Bright Eyes, and I spent in the parsonage as guests of the missionary's daughter, though we all passed our daytime hours among the Indians. Good beds were too great a luxury for us to resist after the many long nights we already had spent sleeping on the cold, hard ground. But even for our days, now that these were growing very cold, Ausapi decided that the big tent was no longer suitable. So he asked his son-in-law, his daughter, and their three children to move out of their nice home and give us the use of it for all of our activities except sleeping.

Meanwhile our own faithful Indians did duty for us at various formal feasts. From one of these Tazhebute came to me looking deeply troubled. He had heard that men from Washington were again stirring up unrest in some of the other agencies because they wanted each Sioux to vote his consent to letting the Poncas have the Niobrara land. The Sioux, who felt sure that this matter had been settled for the whole tribe by their own chiefs during a recent trip to Washington, were threatening to refuse to have anything more to do with it. But I knew that the agreement itself actually called for a two-thirds majority vote of consent by the whole Sioux nation, who must vote individually and not merely by an agreement of their representative chiefs. In other words, here was another clash between the white and the Indian viewpoint.

To the white men who had made that agreement a vote had seemed the normal solution. To the Sioux a vote of the individual tribesmen was something incomprehensible. There was not even any word in their language to convey the idea. Their natural reaction, therefore, was that here were new men turning up simply to start trouble; the Sioux tribe was being "picked on," and that was all there was to it.

Councils were held among the chiefs, runners hurried to and fro among the dozen or so tribes which made up the Sioux nation, and between the bands which made up the tribes. Of all this stir the white staff of the Rosebud Agency, aloof behind their stockade, and ignorant of the Sioux language, did not dream.

When White Thunder and some of his leading men came to talk the problem over with me, I read him the actual clause in the agreement which demanded a vote, and I tried to make him understand that, when he himself had signed that agreement in Washington, he had consented to have a vote taken. But he could not see it. Meanwhile our Ponca Indian, Tazhebute, was sick with dread for fear the Sioux, by refusing to vote, would keep the Poncas from getting back their land—a state of affairs which would again render him and his homeless and landless.

I turned to and tried by every possible argument to persuade those Sioux to sign. At last one of the principal men in the tribe, who was present while I was having still another long argument with White Thunder, told me forcefully:

"I want nothing to do with the agents or their interpreters or with what they tell us to do. But you are our friend; you have

271

come to visit us as one Indian visits another—the first time a white man ever did such a thing here. And we all know Bright Eyes and what she has done. I think we had better listen to you."

Then he shook hands with me and strode from the room. Thereupon a fresh council was held, with Tazhebute and Wajapa both present. On the basis of my assurance that the procedure would not harm their interests, the chiefs agreed to let all the Indians sign the papers. Runners at once carried this news to Red Cloud's Indians—and at that agency, too, all the Sioux began to sign. Before long every Sioux had voted. And, except for the readers of this book, no one will ever know just how it happened that late in 1881, for the first time and without friction, the whole Sioux nation actually voted as individuals, to give their assent to that important agreement.

28.

We Look Before and After

In all, about sixty-seven hundred Indians were encamped in or close to the Rosebud Agency, chiefly on land which for many miles around simply could not be farmed by any methods they could use. Nearly all of the Indians who were herded there lived in uncomfortable canvas tents, poor substitutes for the old shelters of weather-tight buffalo hide. A few of the more ambitious men were building themselves log huts, but for the most part, with all their old activities and occupations gone, the various bands lived in idleness, merely going from tent to tent to eat and dance. The almost constant beating of at least one drum gave the key to festivities always going on somewhere. There was no school of any kind.

"The agent pays no attention to schools," one chief told me. "He doesn't care anything about them."

Over twenty years earlier I had met this same group of Sioux far to the west. I had admired them as a healthy, hardy race. Now I found them actually diseased by this new, unnatural way of life. I saw many of them covered with running sores, others with scrofula. Often men in their early prime dropped dead in their tracks from stoppage of the circulation. This was caused by the thickened blood caused by excessive meat-eating without the counteracting exercise to which Indian bodies had been used for centuries. Also, the old vegetable additions to their meat diet were gone, the *wabruga* and the *nuskeda,* as well as the various health-giving roots and native plants and wild fruits familiar to a roving race which often had been forced to depend wholly on these when meat was lacking. Civilization as yet had offered these Indians nothing to take the place of those former vital foods. Many of the women here could not bear children after their twenty-fifth year; then they at once grew old and withered.

In short I found the whole tribe deteriorated mentally, morally, and physically. And indeed, merely to stand on one of the barren, treeless hills and look across that dreary, useless country which stretched away for miles in every direction, dotted here and there with a few tents or little log huts, and lying in a silence broken only by some distant drumbeat, would bring to any sensitive soul a sense of complete desolation and degradation. And the Indians are a sensitive race.

Some of the chiefs I had known earlier were still alive; one of them rode in over the prairie to see me.

"Twenty years ago," he asserted, "I thought I had a future before me. Now I have none. When I look forward, I look into blackness. See these Indians around here. They're worse off than they were before they came to the agency 'to learn the ways of white men.' Who teaches them those ways? There's no future for these people—nothing but extermination. Where are the schools the government promised us fifteen years ago? Where are the promised houses? I look all around, and I see none.

"In place of our old lodges, which used to shed the rain in summer and kept out the cold in winter, I see those miserable cloth tents which do neither. Look at these Indians! Look at me! Have we anything to hope for? Won't we all be dead soon? Wouldn't it be better to revolt and be shot down than to die off slowly in this way?

"That man there," he pointed to Ausapi, "is a chief. He has a very hard place to fill. Once I was a chief; I also was head soldier in this tribe; but when, try hard as I could to help my people, I found I could do nothing for them, I threw both those honors away. I said, 'Let someone else take my place.'

"The men in Washington are always sending for the chiefs to go there. Each time they go, our lands get smaller. Now we have nothing left but this land; and little by little the government will take even this away. Soon the Indian will have no spot on earth to call his own. Then the government will say, 'What are the Indians doing here? This land doesn't belong to them. Kill them and get them out of the way.' That will be the end of our race."

He had spoken all this with deep intensity, accompanying it with vigorous, dramatic, graceful gestures which would stir anyone's heart to sympathy, and which perhaps often had stirred Indian hearts to dream of war. What could I answer? I could only tell him:

"I'm certain that already the East feels differently about the whole Indian problem. I feel sure the years just ahead will be far kinder to the Indians than these recent ones have been."

"I know all that you've been trying to do," he answered. "You tried to help the Indians, and the white people put you in jail for doing it. There's no help for us."

"But I was in jail only one night and day," I argued, "and the agent who arrested me has been dismissed. Truly the Indians' friends now are stronger than their enemies."

But, ignoring my answer, he went on:

"When I was a young man, and Spotted Tail was young, he was very ambitious. When he wanted to make war, I held him back and led him to follow a very different course. I went with him on his dreadful winter march to bring in the hostile bands. We all came near dying, but we prevented a great war. For that service the government promised to build me a house. Where is that house?"

I could give him no answer.

275

A day or two after we reached the agency Young Spotted Tail, who had become a chief after his father's death on August 6, sent us an invitation to visit his band. Kindly Old Spot and equally kindly Crow Dog, who killed him, both had been helpless instruments and victims of the meddling gossip which so often magnifies a simple but sincere misunderstanding into a deadly feud and then forces the reluctant foes to "shoot it out" on sight. The two chiefs, after months of careful mutual avoidance, at last accidentally met face to face—and Crow Dog shot first. For this he was fined so heavily under Indian law that, as time was to prove, he and his whole band were poverty-stricken for years.

With my warm remembrances of Old Spot, and my deep admiration for the way he had "bluffed" the Indian Commissioner at General Crook's request, I was truly eager to meet his son. All of us except Gaha, who was busy with some task, went over to Young Spotted Tail's tent, where one of his two wives entertained us until he came in. Rather above medium height and about thirty years old, he had a graceful manner and a very intelligent expression. I was especially struck by his modesty about his own success in being made a chief so young. Already his familiar name in the tribe was the "Boy Chief."

When we all had talked only a few minutes, another chief came in and invited us and our host to hurry at once to a feast. We could not well refuse. A huge quantity of jerked beef was laid before each of us. We did our best with it, but here we had no Gaha either to help us eat it or to carry the uneaten remainder home for us. Gaha, we now remembered too late, always had brought with her something to carry the surplus home in. We had nothing but our hands, yet if we left any remnants, we should seem to insult our kindly entertainer. In fact the Indians even had a special name for all that remnant food. If an Indian ever came back from a feed or a feast without lugging away something, the folks at home would ask him:

"Where is your——?" But I cannot possibly supply that missing word because it is one of those nasal, double-diphthong things which no sound in the English alphabet could indicate at all.

We sat and looked at the heaped-up food which still lay before each of us five guests.

"We can't possibly walk away carrying all that in our hands," I announced in despair. "Let's leave it there and just tell them we have different customs."

The ethnologist heartily agreed, but our own Indians would not hear of this solution. Tazhebute said that, if we could get hold of a stick somehow, he would sharpen it, and then could spear the meat onto it. We all had talked frankly about the problem in our various languages, which we did not think any Sioux present could understand, but just as Wajapa was starting out to find a stick, our host's wife smilingly brought us a large tin pan to meet our need.

We then went back to the Boy Chief's reception tent, where he at once presented me with a large peace pipe. While I was still examining the beautiful porcupine-quill work on it, I saw with horror that another feast was being spread before us. Yet it had not been fifteen minutes since the Boy Chief himself had finished the previous feast with us. And our kind Gaha still was elsewhere. I looked at the new pile of meat in front of me— and then at Tazhebute, and I scowled. But he only laughed and laughed and laughed, and considered it a good joke on the white half of our group.

A few years earlier Old Spot, at General Crook's request, had made the terrible winter trip to which his friend, the old chief, had referred in his intense speech to me. Unselfishly and capably he had brought in a big band of angry Indians and had prevented vicious bloodshed. So the government, just as General Crook had promised in advance, had built the old chief a fine two-story frame house with a porch, folding doors, wide halls, and excellent finish throughout—a really valuable house. Ever since the old chief's death it had stood deserted. In fact one of the Sioux women had remarked to Bright Eyes:

"I don't see why Spotted Tail's ghost stays around that house so long and keeps all his relations feeling unhappy. They all had loved him and had been kind to him."

For this one night in honor of our visit the Boy Chief had ordered the place reopened and warmed. He led us there when we had finished our meal. Having assembled all his leaders in one of the large rooms, he asked me to address them. Tazhebute, in telling me of the plan, had warned me not to suggest citizenship to this audience because it was bitterly opposed to the idea; so I spoke warily. But when Wajapa's turn to speak came, to my amazement he launched out into all his own advanced views on the Indian question and on the necessity for citizenship and land titles, and for court decisions in settling all difficulties. The usual polite "Hows!" of approval were pretty feeble, except for one enthusiastic old fellow, who, the moment that council was over, promptly made a special feast for his own particular friends to meet Wajapa.

After Wajapa's talk I told the Indians that by white men's customs wise women often were invited to speak at public meetings. We had such a woman in our group. If they would like to hear her, she would be happy to say a few words. There was a full chorus of eager "Hows!" So our Highflyer made a very neat speech to everyone's satisfaction.

The Boy Chief then showed me the official papers which had made Old Spot, in return for his valiant services, the head chief of the whole Sioux nation and also a colonel in the U. S. Army on full pay.

Just as the council ended, the ethnologist confided to the Boy Chief that she was longing to see one of the formal Indian dances. He promptly ordered his band to hold one at once for her to watch. Now, as all those who were working with me to save the Indian race were convinced that dances were among the greatest obstacles to its progress, I personally felt pretty unwilling to countenance one of these by being present, but I found myself in for it without a loophole left. So as soon as we heard the drum, I escorted my two charges over to the huge tent, forty or fifty feet in diameter, where the dance would be held. On our way we had to cross two brooks, one bridged by a shaky pole, the other with steppingstones made of old camp kettles set in upside down.

A large pine-stick fire lighted the tent, where forty or fifty men sat on the ground in a big circle well back against the canvas, waiting to take part. The place of especial honor had been left vacant for us. I led the way to it, followed by the Highflyer and Bright Eyes. A moment later, at a loud drumbeat, all the warriors sprang up with a single bound and began to dance. A few of them wore fantastic leggings and buckskin shirts with beadwork or porcupine-quill ornaments, but the men who were really "in full dress" sported only a breechclout, and their bodies were painted in all sorts of colors applied in the typical Indian straight-lined designs. All the dancers were covered with small bells which were buckled around their legs and waists and hung over their shoulders.

Six or seven drummers now were beating time on two drums, and two women were singing in high voices. The dancing men took up the song. The rhythm varied frequently but it was always tense and stirring. To and fro the dancers swung in time to the beating drums and the singing voices; they shook their bodies until the flesh seemed about to fly from their bones; they dashed back and forth, and around or past each other; they stooped far over; they bent from side to side; and they jingled their thousand bells—all this for ten minutes without a break. Then the music stopped and the dancers, covered with sweat, sat down to rest in their big circle along the tent edge. Soon the loud drumbeat crashed again and they sprang up as before. And so over and over for fully an hour.

Once when I looked past the whirling, painted dancers toward the front of the tent, which had been thrown open wide to let a great crowd of gaily dressed Indians, lighted up by the big fire inside the tent, look on, I saw the Boy Chief standing wrapped in a dark blanket, motionless as a rock. His quiet smile seemed to say: "Let the boys have a good time."

Meanwhile I had seen eight or ten large camp kettles full of soup lugged in, and I had noticed that, according to the old familiar custom at dances, each dancer had brought with him a bowl and a spoon. I could foresee that very soon we should be called upon to eat prodigiously for the third time in about four hours, so I grew more anxious with every flying moment. I kept urging the ethnologist to leave, but she sat there as if entranced. After each round she would beg me, "Let's stay for just one more. I want to study this thing."

At last I managed to get her onto her feet and homeward bound, but even when we were outside of the tent, she lingered longingly to look back at the mazy whirl of those gaudy, almost naked dancers. Gaha, who had turned up outside among the watchers, was greatly amused at the ethnologist's interest. Afterward she never tired of telling how by my orders she finally had literally to pull the white woman away. Later we heard that the dancers had been greatly disappointed at our leaving so abruptly, because they had planned to close the performance by giving each of us presents. But I for one was well content to lose even the rarest gifts rather than to have to eat again.

One day the old Indian who had spoken so forcefully to me about the white people's program for exterminating his race led us across the prairie for some half-dozen miles on a ride. As we topped a hill we saw nearly a mile ahead a cluster of five tents. Around one of these I noticed a crowd of people, as well as eighty or a hundred more not far off, who were approaching it in an informal procession. The old Indian halted till we caught up with him, and then told us: "There's been a death in that tent. If you'd like to go, I'll take you there to see the funeral ceremonies."

Of course the ethnologist could not be denied that chance. We found the tent opened nearly to the top, and its sides thrown back so as to display its whole interior. Outside the tent, on three sides of it, forked poles a dozen feet high were planted in the ground with other poles resting in the forks as cross poles. On these poles hung all the dead man's property in blankets, clothing, robes, and any other articles which could be made to hang on poles. Near or under them were placed the cooking utensils, wagon, harness, and other property.

We saw the official mourners, about fifty men, form an arc which faced the tent about twenty-five yards from it. We watched the dead man's two wives wander about, wailing and weeping. Then his horse was led in front of the tent and was shot. His dog was driven across from the tent toward the end of the mourners' arc, from which two shots were fired at him. He, poor thing, went limping and howling away until, quite a distance off, up the side of a hill, he lay down and died. One of the wives then went after him and dragged his body down to the tent. Silence closed down.

Then a man came to the front of the tent and announced solemnly:

"This man is a forerunner for us into the unknown country, and we have sent with him his dog and his horse. Receive him kindly, for he is provided for his long journey."

Thereupon the official mourners sang a low, sweet, exceedingly beautiful chant. After they had repeated it three times, the two wives, beginning at one end of the arc, placed their hands upon the head of each mourner in turn, just as a bishop goes along a confirmation line. Then the dead man was laid out straight and his face was painted. Next came the giving away of all the articles which had been exposed to view. Even the tent was stripped of its every content, so that the family were left with only the tent poles and tent cloth. In other words this family not only had lost its husband and father, but in his funeral ceremonies it had lost everything else, so that his whole household became desolate paupers.

With this case in mind the reader perhaps can understand better why the white men who truly understood Indian ways always have insisted that the race could not make any permanent advancement and especially could not accumulate any property until its old customs and habits which still persisted from the happy-go-lucky days of nomad life should be changed. But any Indian tradition has always proved hard to change. Any man among them who would not give away much or all of his property whenever a death occurred in his family would be regarded by the rest of his tribe with the same horror we should feel at a man who would throw his own child's dead body out of the door and refuse to bury it. Clearly the impulse toward this necessary change could not be given by any act of Congress or Indian Bureau order. Such interference would merely rouse the Indians to resentful and superstitious fury. The change could come only by a slow process of Christian instruction and general education. No government organization as yet had even attempted it; to achieve it would call for infinite patience, endurance, and faith.

As we rode hastily away from that scattering of all of a bereft family's resources, I recalled how in my early days with the Indians of the plains such giving had seemed to me an odd but not a tragic event, simply because all food and possessions had been so freely gained or so easily replaced, thanks to the vast buffalo herds and to the chances offered by intertribal warfare. But life now was no longer fluid. When acquisition had become so hard, dispersal clearly ought to be cut down as soon as possible to correspond. I recalled now that in recent years various leading Indians had apologized to me for their poverty by merely saying, as a complete explanation, that recently there had been a death in the family. But it had taken the actual sight of this economically outrageous funeral on the desolate prairie to bring the existing situation home to me in all its bearings. And I realized that Tazhebute, and the old chief, and, most of all, Wajapa were drinking in all our comments on it with the deepest interest.

During our visit to the Sioux I was told that several of the young folk had been students at Carlisle or Hampton, but in not one instance could I see that these youngsters differed at all from the other Indians. If I spoke English to them, they did not answer me or indicate in any way that they understood me. This, of course, was a perfectly natural result where the children had had to return from their schools to households in which everything was prescribed by custom. They had been expected to keep silent until maturity gave them the right to speak. They had had to seek the exact places prescribed for them in the tents, sleep on the ground, and eat with their fingers, and that without benefit of soap or towel. They had had no knives, forks, or dishes. Therefore, day by day the acquired teachings and habits of their school days were bound to slip away from them.

On some of the reservations, however, where boarding schools existed right in the midst of the tribe's daily life, so that the visiting parents could see how the new way functioned, the results were far more lasting.

"If only," I commented to the ethnologist, "the schools like Hampton and Carlisle could take over children who already

had been taught for four or five years at home, and who therefore were far enough advanced to appreciate what they learned
there, what a great gain that would be for the whole race. Then
the brighter scholars from the reservations could be sent there
to finish an education which already was firmly founded, and
would return home only when old enough and capable enough
to make their influence felt."

For in Bright Eyes the ethnologist and I had right before us
an excellent example of what Eastern school training could
achieve when it had been built upon the honest basis of earlier
mission-school teaching at home. But I sighed when I realized
how many well-meaning Eastern theorists were seriously expecting that after a scant two years the fledgling boys and girls,
who were being abruptly transplanted from the reservations to
a great Eastern school, where they must learn new ways in a
foreign tongue, would, when back in the tents, be able to exert
an uplifting influence on their own tradition-bound world.

One case at Rosebud Agency struck me as a very large order
to be expected of a twelve-year-old girl by her own devoted
father, a Sioux chief named Cook. When, at his invitation, we
went to eat with him, we were surprised to find him dressed
in a neat suit of black made in white-man fashion. The meal,
though served on the ground, was spread on a tablecloth; to
our delight and relief it consisted of light bread, stewed toma-
toes, roast beef, plum pie, coffee, and a pitcher of milk. He
had hired a white woman to bake the bread for him, and in
the other items he had tried to have his household conform as
closely as they could to white people's ways. For he himself
knew those ways. His little daughter, his only child, was at
either Carlisle or Hampton; I forget which. The previous summer he had gone to see her and had stayed there for two
months.

"I liked the white people's ways so much," he explained,

"that I wanted to stay among them all the time. I learned a great deal about them and I bought this suit of clothes. Before my daughter comes back, I'm going to build me a house. She's been at school a year now, and she'll be home next summer. Then I'll fix up everything in the house just as she wants it. I'll buy bedsteads, chairs, and a stove. And I'm going to live like a white man."

Think what duties were awaiting that little girl with her two scant years of schooling, with no one to turn to for advice or instruction, and with no further chance even to learn by observing white ways in that agency, where the stockade hid from Indian eyes all that the white people did. Cook, too, who lately had given away all his property because a relative had died, was surely going to have his hands full to acquire a house within the time he had set himself. For in that timberless land house materials were hard to obtain. Near Cook's own tent, for example, I saw a feeble old man, scantily clad, hard at work putting up a log house for himself. He shivered as he toiled there in the piercing wind from the north. The small logs he worked with were six to eight feet long.

"I've been busy on this house all summer," he told me. "I haven't any ponies or wagon, so I've had to bring each log seven or eight miles on my own back."

Before very long I had felt for several days that trouble was brewing somewhere. Though the ethnologist begged for more time there, our own Indians had grown restlessly eager to leave. One afternoon White Thunder asked me to come and see him that evening. I already had called on him in his big log house, and he had proudly shown me his bedstead and his stove, but now I found him wrathful and sullen. After we had sat for a long time without a word, he began angrily:

"You had better start home early in the morning. There's

going to be trouble at this agency. You came here to visit us as a friend, and I don't want you to be blamed for it."

Something in his manner jarred on me, so I did not answer, but sat looking just as sullen as he did. Soon he turned and pointed to two very small parcels which lay on the bed.

"I went over to the agency this morning to draw my rations, and there's what they gave me to last my family a week."

I examined the two packages; in one there were three lumps of sugar, each about the size of a hen's egg, in the other considerably less than a pint of coffee.

"Now," growled White Thunder, still very angry, "the government owes us our rations. We sold the Black Hills to the whites, and they made a great deal of money out of the bargain because there was a lot of gold and silver in those hills. Now I want to go on drawing my promised pay for them. I will not be treated in this way. Tomorrow morning I'm going to take these packages and show them to the agent, and then throw them either at his head or out of the window!"

If that happened, trouble certainly would come—and quickly. So I tried to talk him out of it. I suggested that business might have fallen behind because the President had been busy; or else high water caused by the very wet weather might have tied up the trains which brought supplies.

"No!" he answered scornfully. "The storehouses are full of goods. I asked the clerk why he had given me those small packages, and he just pointed to a list written on a piece of paper that hung on the wall, and said the agent had ordered those amounts issued and that that was all he knew about it. If there's any good reason, why doesn't he tell it to us?"

I felt pretty downhearted. Any revolt started during or soon after our visit certainly would be blamed on us, and might hamper all our future work for the Indians. I decided to put the matter frankly up to White Thunder on that basis.

"Suppose you do just what you've said," I told him, "and make trouble. All the tribe's rations will be stopped at once—and winter is beginning. There is no game. What will you do? And now look at what it will mean to me. I've tried to help the Indians. If you make trouble while I'm here or just after I leave, I shall be held responsible for it all. Then I'll never be able to help any Indians again. It would be much wiser for you to wait and let me present this matter to your friends in the East and get it all straightened out properly."

Gradually, to my relief, he gave up the idea of creating trouble, and when I left him, he appeared in a much better humor. But after that incident it was useless to urge Wajapa and Tazhebute to stay at Rosebud. They offered me no less than seventy good reasons why we should start the very next day. And we did.

As a matter of fact, however, our plans for leaving very soon had been pretty well drawn up already. It was late in the season and a blizzard might strike us at any time, tying us up either here at Rosebud or out on the trail. Also a few days earlier Tazhebute had told me secretly that a runner had arrived from Sitting Bull. This man had asked to see me, unknown to the agent or to any other white person. So Tazhebute had led me way out through the evening dusk to Cook's modest tent. There I had found Cook himself, White Thunder, another chief who was a member of the Soldier Lodge, and Sitting Bull's Indian messenger.

He told me then that Sitting Bull had heard I was planning to visit the Yankton Sioux, just across the Missouri from Fort Randall, where he was held as a prisoner, a little above where the northern Nebraska boundary now meets the great river. He asked me please to visit him. Moreover he added that he was a prisoner, with everything he had owned taken from him by the soldiers, so that he could not make any of the gifts proper for a visitor to expect, but he hoped that nevertheless I would have pity on him, remember his condition, and come anyway.

It is easy to guess what I answered, but at once I found myself in a corresponding dilemma about Sitting Bull's messenger. I knew that the bearer of such an invitation should always be given presents, but what had I that was worth his taking? What should I do? And Bright Eyes, my adviser on etiquette, was not there to consult! I often have thought that Indians have intuitive skill in reading one's mind. Right in the midst of my uncertainty White Thunder told me quietly:

"Don't be troubled about presents for the messenger. I've attended to that."

So at last we said good-by to the Rosebud Agency. The Sioux women had packed up everything for us, including, as I have said, enough food, thanks to Gaha and to the many feasts where we had been honored guests, to last us all for a long time. For our first day's journey we had an escort of five warriors.

However, it was a long and cruel trip, with real danger throughout a great deal of it. Our route led us a hundred and forty miles through uninhabited country. We were a week on the way, for once we were snowed in for two days. The rains had ruined the grass, and we had no corn except a little we had been able to buy before we left the agency. Therefore our teams grew very weak and had to travel slowly. Twice we had to camp without wood. We were sincerely thankful when this difficult section of our journey lay behind us.

29.

Sitting Bull Welcomes Us

On reaching Fort Randall at last late one afternoon we pitched our tent a little northwest of the main buildings and all went down together to report ourselves to the commanding officer. And there for the first time our Highflyer deserted us and took up her quarters in the fort. Sitting Bull's camp, we heard, was out on the prairie half a mile to the west. Its tents were drawn up in a great circle which had sentries stationed fairly close around it.

Certain formalities had to be complied with before I could be allowed to call there, so throughout the next day I stayed in camp, while a number of Yankton Indians came over from their reserve just across the Missouri River to call on me. Sitting Bull's own interpreter, whom he had picked up somewhere in Canada, also called, quite uninvited. Although the army officers at this fort already had told me what a firm friend of the tribe this white man was, and how he was trying with all his power to help these Indians, I did not take to the man at all. When I made this comment to Tazhebute, he told me that the visiting Yanktons all had told him that this interpreter was a very bad man. Then we dropped the subject.

By this time the sun was sinking low, the brass band was playing beautifully, and all the soldiers' quarters were astir. So we all left our tent and went out to watch the dress parade. This lasted until dusk.

As we left the fort again, we met Sitting Bull himself, with his head soldier and two others of his band. We had been told that he and a few of his head men were allowed the freedom of the fort on parole. Discarding all formalities, he came at once to greet us. Of course in talking to him I was handicapped by the need for speaking through Bright Eyes to Tazhebute, who translated Sitting Bull's answers into Ponca for her to turn them into English for me. It was slow work.

The old chief's main desire now was to tell me that he was in great trouble. Unfortunately the reason was not fit for a woman even to hear, much less to interpret. And Tazhebute, when Sitting Bull had talked with him for a few moments, bore out that statement. Sitting Bull insisted that all he could say here and now was that he wanted that special interpreter of his sent away and a new one appointed. I promised to find some man who could interpret directly from Sioux to English for us and to arrange for a thorough talk on the subject. Sitting Bull then went off to his camp.

I at once reported his request for a talk to the commanding officer, and he promptly gave an order which would let both Bright Eyes and me visit the chief whenever we wished. That night I found an English-speaking Yankton Sioux, so the next morning I achieved a really satisfactory talk with the much-described and much-discussed Indian leader.

First of all he asked me how much time I could spend with him. When I had told him, he said with relief that then today he need talk only of this one problem. While he had been in Canada a white man who could speak the Dakota language had come to him, claiming that he had been sent by the President to invite Sitting Bull to come back. If the chief would consent, he would be given a reservation, horses, cattle, wagons, plows, and rations for thirty years. This white man also asserted that he himself was a friend of the man-with-a-star-on-his-shoulder, and that therefore all these promises would surely be carried out.

Therefore Sitting Bull had come back to the United States and had surrendered to the man-with-a-star-on-his-shoulder; and Sitting Bull's band was the very last band of American Indians who had surrendered. He was very emphatic in stating to me his claim of being the very last Indian of all the Indians in the world to give up his gun. He wanted me to be absolutely certain to remember that fact: that he, Sitting Bull himself, was the very last Indian anywhere to give up his gun. So, in memory of our friendly talk, I here record that statement.

This same white man had been with him and his band ever since then as their only interpreter, assuming absolute authority over the camp, and treating some of the best men shamefully. In his very first week he had demanded a young girl as his wife; Sitting Bull had made the girl's father consent. After the man had lived with this girl awhile, he demanded the wife of one of Sitting Bull's best men. He threatened that if he did not get her, he would put their whole band on a steamboat the next day and would take them all down to the Indian Territory.

"I was helpless," the chief assured me. "We were unarmed and surrounded by soldiers. I did not know how much power this white man really had, so, with the advice of my leading men, I told the Indian that he must give up his wife. He went sorrowfully back to his tent, kissed her, and told her that she must go to the white man. That man has done many other things that were very bad. I do not know white men's ways and customs, but I am sure that the officers do not know what is going on in my camp. I can't endure it any longer. I want him sent away, and I want a good man for interpreter."

He gave me further details about the man's doings; they were far too vile to record here. I went straight to the commanding officer with the story. He listened in stern silence, angry because he had been led to believe that this particular interpreter was a lifelong friend of the Indians. He promised to have the matter investigated at once. When the other officers heard the story, they grew equally disgusted and furious.

That night the weather grew still colder; the next day Sitting Bull's camp was moved to a more sheltered location. One evening, after his band was well settled in the new camp, Bright Eyes and I went down there to call. It was then that he told me his history—that he was not a warrior but a priest, or medicine man. God had often spoken to him in visions and dreams, and had told him that he was to live as an Indian and not adopt the white ways. But now the buffalo were gone, and therefore he thought God wished him to live in some other way.

"All I ever wanted," explained Sitting Bull, "was to be left alone on the land God had given the Indians."

He did not want the white people to support him, and he had urged his warriors to defend their lands against white men's aggressions. Finally he had gone to Canada, hoping to live there in the Indian way, but he did not find there the life he wished. He had to return here or starve. Now he had agreed to live on a reservation, adopt white men's ways, and raise such crops as he could. As soon as the President should give him a reservation, he would live there, obeying all the President's orders. He would keep his word to the Government. I felt touched when he asked me to arrange to have his daughter sent to school.

Before we left, he took from the folds of his blanket a photograph of himself, which he presented to Bright Eyes, saying:

"My daughter, when we are relieved from this imprisonment and have our own reservation, come and see me again. Then I shall be prepared to make you the presents which your work for the Indians and your rank demand."

He took a pencil and, asking for the photograph again, wrote his name on the bottom of it—to my great surprise. But the Yankton interpreter promptly explained that, although the chief did not know how to write, he had asked someone to write the name "Sitting Bull" for him and then had copied it so many times that he now could write it readily, although he did not know one letter of it from another.

We had planned to cross the Missouri the next morning and return to the Omahas through the Yankton Agency, but here at Fort Randall the only ferry was a small, low-sided flatboat. Unfortunately the wind now blew almost a gale for several days. Once we persuaded the boatman to try the trip, but soon so much spray came dashing over the sides that he insisted on putting back. Reluctantly we gave up the Yankton visit and started down the west bank of the river. The Yanktons were so disappointed that two of them, on the night when we camped opposite their agency, actually swam the Missouri to shake hands with me, although thin ice was forming on the water. But our faces were turned homeward now and nothing must delay us. Another trip to the East lay ahead, and more hard fighting in behalf of all these kindly Indian folk was awaiting Bright Eyes and me. And Highflyer, our ethnologist, had gained a new name, several notebooks of material, and a store of strange memories she would never forget.

30.

Our Long Fight Ends

When President Garfield appointed a new Secretary with a new Indian Bureau staff, our bitterest struggles ended. We saw the ideals we had fought for gaining ground steadily. On August 7, 1882, less than a year after the Omahas had talked over their title worries so anxiously with us and our ethnologist, an act was passed which gave the Omaha tribe permanent individual allotments of their lands with all their existing rights recognized.

From that day on Bright Eyes realized that her hardest strain was over. She must help her race, but her own dear people and their kin, the Poncas, were safe. So she lectured with less effort and very few collapses, though she always actually suffered from timidity when she faced an audience. I too could carry on the fight more impersonally, now that Congress and the courts had proved it was so completely justified. But I can well leave to the historian's more technical handling the details of the campaigns which gradually settled all the current Indian problems.

It is enough to say here that after we had lectured everywhere together and appeared together constantly before Congressional committees for three seasons in all—1879–80, 1880–81, 1881–82—Bright Eyes and I were married on June 29, 1882, in the picturesque old stone Presbyterian Mission, which stood on the Missouri bank in the Omaha Reservation. At first we settled in my former Omaha home with my two young daughters; later we all moved up near the Omaha Agency and Bright Eyes' people. All through the 1882–83 season we two lectured together all over the East; after that we each came and went according to the needs of the Indian situation—though with each year Bright Eyes clung more and more eagerly to home life.

Some of the Boston Committee asked me to try my hand at drafting a severalty bill which would express my ideas. I turned my attempt over to a committee member, Professor J. B. Thayer, head of the department of constitutional law at Harvard. He made a few technical changes and then sent it on to Washington. There, because of politics and other reasons, a few more points were altered. But in the long run that rough draft of mine became the backbone of the famous Dawes Severalty Act of 1887. This was the final step in ending the Indian Ring's control over Indian life and property.

Whenever we went East, especially to Boston, we were welcomed by the friendly writer group. Whittier, Lowell, Holmes, Miss Alcott, and Edward Everett Hale all could be counted upon as firm friends. Dr. Hale gave many luncheons and dinners at his home so that Bright Eyes could meet noted writers and artists. By this time she herself was writing Indian stories and articles for *St. Nicholas* and other magazines and was growing deeply interested in painting.

Then all in a moment we would turn our backs on the prosperous, kindly East and go back West, practically penniless, to our quarter section of Nebraska prairie—a homestead claim—with, at first, only a tiny sod house to shelter us. Here, because prices were cruelly manipulated against all the Western farmers, we had to burn for fuel the corn we had raised hopefully —the corn for which people in the nation's cities were starving. But we never were sorry that we had fought for the Poncas and the Omahas—and had won. And we never doubted that we should win the still-wider battle to free the whole Indian race.

In 1884 we felt wildly happy when Helen Hunt Jackson's Indian novel, *Ramona,* took the whole country by storm. In March 1881, just after the Ponca victory, she had told Bright Eyes a very sad farewell, following their two winters of warm comradeship. Bright Eyes then was planning to go back to her work on the reservation among her own people. To ease the parting, Mrs. Jackson had promised then and there to write one more book in the hope of rousing the American people to end the Indians' wrongs. "And if that doesn't succeed," she promised, "I'll find some other way to help them."

Soon she had made a plan to go with us—just as the ethnologist went afterward—on a trip through the northern tribes, but just then Senator Hoar was able to get her a government appointment as commissioner to the mission Indians of California. Out of that experience she wrote *Ramona.* And *Ramona's* success won new readers for the *Century of Dishonor.* So our whole nation, for the first time, became genuinely aware that there was a lot to be said on the Indians' side.

When the news of Mrs. Jackson's death came to us in August 1885, Bright Eyes shut herself into her room and wept all day long. For weeks afterward she mourned the loss of this closest of her intimate friends, who had given herself so wholeheartedly to save an unhappy race.

Slowly the Dawes Act was traveling along toward its inevitable passage by Congress. Our help would no longer be needed in the same way. I remember one final triumphant meeting with the Boston Indian Citizenship Committee, after which we started westward, stopping over a few days in New York. There Major Pond, the famous lecture-bureau manager, asked us to lecture in England for a year. We hesitated a long time, but finally signed the contract and, after many further delays, sailed in May 1886.

The agent Major Pond sent with us was a former theatrical manager. When he found himself directing a couple of lecturers on ethnology and the American Indian, he felt so utterly out of his element that he dropped us flat to take charge of a London theater instead. This left us feeling stranded. Finally an Englishman made us an acceptable offer and kept us lecturing in England for him five times a week for a whole year.

I remember that I took over with me about four hundred introductory letters, all sent me to use on this trip by judges, congressmen, ministers, and especially by literary folk in Boston who had English friends. For instance, James Russell Lowell gave us a letter to Rev. Dr. Frazier, then the head of the Presbyterian Church in England, asking him to let his congregation hear us.

At first Dr. Frazier was appalled at the thought of letting Bright Eyes speak there, because women should keep silence in the churches, but that was before he talked with her. Then he arranged an evening service to meet the legal minimum of a hymn of one stanza, a scripture lesson of two verses, another one-stanza hymn, a three-minute sermon, and a brief prayer. With only eight minutes spent, he had me give my talk and then introduced "the Princess Bright Eyes from America."

The moment my wife had finished speaking, Lady Ellen, the sister of the Duke of Argyle, came forward to kiss her on both cheeks. Immediately the well-trained congregation hastened to do the proper thing likewise. Contrary to Dr. Frazier's predictions, as great a crowd pressed around Bright Eyes then as ever had flocked around her in America. As this was the church attended by the Scottish nobility during the London season, I heard Dr. Frazier roll off his tongue the titles of dukes, lords, baronets, and their wives as he presented them to Bright Eyes. Consequently we got long write-ups in the chief London papers next day, which fixed our status. Lecture engagements came easily after that.

Lady Ellen became very fond of Bright Eyes and urged us to visit her in Scotland, but by the time our tour took us north, she had been ordered to the South of France for her health.

Bright Eyes was far too democratic to like being introduced as a princess. Her own earnest efforts to win self-government for her people made the notion actually repulsive to her. In fact, when our lecture agent turned up joyously with a lot of publicity notices featuring her as "Princess Bright Eyes," she refused ever to speak again unless they all were destroyed. Her one concession was to be described as the daughter of a head chief in an Indian tribe.

She hated, too, to accept the deference paid to royalty, until I explained that we must conform to the customs of the country we visited, just as I, when among the Indians, had fallen in with their ways. After that argument she did not rebel if, when the nobility entertained her, they treated her as though she were of royal blood—rising when she entered the room, and standing until she was seated. For their unchanging English customs insisted on carrying on the tradition begun with the welcome of Princess Pocahontas two hundred and seventy years before.

Lady Henry Somerset, the English temperance leader, took a deep interest in Bright Eyes and asked her again and again to lecture on temperance at least once. When she finally yielded, Lady Somerset hired one of the large London theaters for the occasion. I heard that the audience, almost wholly of titled persons, behaved exactly as unusually as Dr. Frazier's congregation had done. This was the only lecture Bright Eyes ever gave anywhere on any subject except the past, present, or future of her own race.

In our whole English and Scottish year we spent very few

days in lodgings or hotels. Almost always we were guests in private homes—visiting sometimes the nobility, and sometimes the middle class; three or four times we stayed with working folk. In all, we found as wonderful chances for studying actual English life as we had given our ethnologist for studying Indian ways.

When that amazing year was over, we went back to our little farm on our homestead claim at Bancroft, Nebraska. Here I had the fun of demonstrating that the local scientists did not know their grasshoppers. Another raid of the pests began, not so bad as the 1874 plague, but still serious enough to cause real distress. The scientists were fighting it on the theory that the insects ate and traveled only by day and spent their nights quietly and harmlessly in the fields. My experience had taught me differently, but as usual everyone laughed at my statements. My proof was simple. I took a big kite, coated it with tar, and sent it soaring far aloft into the dark. When I pulled it down, there, stuck fast in the tar, were hundreds of grasshoppers which my kite had met up aloft there on the wing.

Instinctively I had picked up my free-lance newspaper work again, and before long we realized that my chief interest in life and best outlook for earning a living lay there and not in farming. So in June 1888 I leased the farm to a tenant, sold him all my stock and implements, and went contentedly to rejoin the Omaha *World-Herald's* editorial staff.

31.

Trouble at Pine Ridge

Late in 1890 a novel situation developed at the Pine Ridge Agency in South Dakota, just above the northwestern Nebraska border. The Sioux there were still under the tension of having lost their old ways without having received any adequate substitute. There had not been time to apply the Dawes Severalty Act provisions to the Pine Ridge problems, but unfortunately certain government officials had conceived the brilliant notion that if they cut down the tribe's rations, they would force these Indians to raise crops. What Washington brains failed to grasp was that crops could not be raised on that particular type of land by any method except those for which this tribe had no equipment.

Just then a rumor swept across the plains that a messiah was coming, so that all the white intruders would leave the land. Then the buffalo would come back—and the old happy hunts and independent life. Of course Bright Eyes, as the daughter of the Omahas' head chief, promptly heard from her own people some of the earliest reports to reach civilization. Both of us, rightly estimating the movement as just a religious craze of the sort we had often seen run through large groups of white people, refused to worry at the news. We could not think of it as preluding any Sioux outbreak. Nevertheless, because of our Indian affiliations, we both were sent to the Pine Ridge Agency, a potential trouble center, as special "war correspondents" for the Omaha *World-Herald* and the Chicago *Express*.

We found there an amazing state of affairs. Though there had
been no outbreak of any kind, the place was jammed with "war
correspondents" who were expected to produce thrilling "war
news." Hanging around the hotel day after day, they constantly
dispatched new inflammatory stories made out of whole cloth.
Burning arrows were being fired into the agency buildings;
the Indians were perpetrating horrors in every direction—according to those writers. Yet in that peaceful agency the Sioux
crowded the trader's store, the children went to school, the congregations worshiped as usual, and rations were distributed
methodically.

Bright Eyes and I chose to stay in an Indian household, where
we could hear facts instead of fiction. Here the Sioux men all
called on us and kept us informed of every event in the tribe
and the whole Sioux nation. They confirmed our theory that,
except for that sudden craze for ghost-dancing in ghost shirts,
all was peaceful. Four of our friends had actually made a long
journey up into the mountains to see and talk with the messiah,
and he had given them instructions about the new dance.

"It's a peace dance," they insisted. "No one is allowed even
to carry a weapon of war nearer than half a mile to the place
where the dance is held."

Besides the gang of loafing correspondents, there was just
one thing wrong in that agency—and that was the unusual mass-
ing of Army troops there under Brigadier General Brooke. The
9th Cavalry under Colonel Henry came and went. South of the
peaceful agency was camped the 7th Cavalry under Colonel
Forsyth. Right in the heart of its buildings were a regiment of
infantry under General Wheaton and a battery of three-inch
rifles, one Gatling and some Hotchkiss guns under Captain Ca-
pron, and one company of Cheyenne scouts under Lieutenant
Taylor. Many of the officers, including Major Whitside, Major
Butler, and General Wheaton, were old acquaintances of mine.

They and their fellow-officers discussed the whole problem frankly with me, trusting in my discretion. Many an evening Bright Eyes and I entertained them as guests in our Indian lodgings, and learned that they agreed with us in not anticipating any trouble. The only officer who treated me curtly—as in truth he treated almost everyone—was General Brooke, so I kept out of his path.

The Indians' explanation of why these soldiers were there was that the brand-new agent had been a coward and a fool who had brought this trouble on them. When some Indians had started the new religious dance not far away, this agent had sent his Indian police to break it up and arrest the leaders. The police came back to report that their little force could not stop the dancing because there were hundreds of Indians on the scene.

"Just let them dance it out," the police advised. "They'll get tired of it. Nothing will come of it."

In fact, as they knew, many of the dancers, some almost starving, had gathered there near the agency, hoping to be fed. The new, nervous, inexperienced agent promptly lost his head. Leaving his wife and family unprotected from the imagined perils, he tore over to Rushville, Nebraska, the nearest railroad station, and sent frantic messages to the government and to Army headquarters that there was a general uprising among the Sioux. Then he waited there till the troops came to guard him in returning to the agency.

So the harm was done. When those large bodies of troops turned up out of the blue, the white civilians along the reservation border left their homes and fled to the railroad; many of the even more frightened Indians fled toward the Bad Lands for refuge. They were especially upset because they knew that no Indian had stolen or destroyed any property or killed anyone at all, yet here were troops and more troops. The groups of

Christian Indians, however, merely laughed at the craze; and Chief American Horse's large band, just south of the agency, considered that the problem was no affair of theirs.

Messages constantly came and went between the agency Indians and those who had fled foodless to the Bad Lands. Life-saving supplies were smuggled out there. Every day some Indian brought me the latest tidings from the refugees. Soon I heard that Crow Dog, whom I had known ever since I met him at Rosebud on our Sioux trip of 1881 and who was a fellow-member of the Soldier Lodge, had just reached the Bad Lands with his band. The military authorities, hearing this news, sent him an earnest invitation to come in to the agency. I at once sent him a special message to come to Pine Ridge, with my personal promise that no harm should befall him. Soon he and his band came to camp north of the agency near old Chief Red Cloud's house. Next day he came to see me. He was a sinewy, well-built man of medium height with large brown eyes and a well-shaped head.

Crow Dog said readily that he was no believer in the messiah craze, which was all foolishness. He had merely gone to the Bad Lands because he knew that hundreds of soldiers had come to Pine Ridge and that others were bound toward Rosebud.

"I know," he told me, "that a lot of my own tribe hate me because I killed Spotted Tail." (He had told me the whole of that pathetic outcome of misunderstandings when I met him in 1881.) "If there should be trouble, all the blame would be put on me and my band. I'm afraid we'd all be killed."

We spent day after day together, then for a day or two I did not see him. When he came again, he looked troubled and perplexed. He said he wanted to see me alone; and so we went to a hill, halfway between the agency and the camp of the 7th Cavalry, and sat down.

"Even here in Pine Ridge I'm afraid of trouble," he began, "for eight or ten men who've joined my band lately are very bad. They won't obey either me or the head soldier. They care nothing for the holy things. They ought to be hanged or else sent off somewhere and kept as prisoners as long as they live.

"They always keep their packs tied up," he added, "and at night they sleep beside their horses—ready to mount in a minute. I don't know what day or night they may kill somebody— and then I'll be held responsible. Won't you ask the general to send a squad of soldiers to my camp to arrest those bad men? They can be taken any time, and my own head soldier and police will help."

As soon as he had gone, I hunted up General Wheaton and told him what the old chief wished.

"You should inform General Brooke at once," Wheaton commented.

"Sorry," I replied, "but General Brooke has been so uncivil to me that I don't want to go near him. Won't you please inform the general yourself?"

After some more useless argument he asked me:

"Will you take General Brooke a letter from me?"

"Of course," I agreed.

He wrote a letter which I promptly carried to headquarters, where I faced in turn all the formalities the general loved— sent in a card, was passed from one orderly to another, sat through a long wait. At last I presented the letter. General Brooke read it.

"Who are you?" he asked me, "and how do you come to be in communication with Crow Dog?"

I explained. Then he told me: "That is all." I retired.

When I reported back to General Wheaton, he looked ruffled and asked me to come back in a couple of hours. As I neared his quarters again, I met General Brooke, who for the first time addressed me courteously.

304

"What do you think would happen," he asked, "if I sent a squad of soldiers over to arrest those men?"

"Nothing would," I assured him, "if you and Crow Dog arranged the time for the soldiers to appear."

He shook his head gravely. "It's my opinion," he asserted, "that it would precipitate a fight then and there."

General Wheaton was deeply disappointed at this outcome, but of course by army tradition could not criticize his superior openly. Later on we learned what resulted directly from General Brooke's refusal.

Meanwhile Bright Eyes and I were having our own problems. Our newspapers had grown indignant with us for not turning in anything interesting about this "great Indian war" all around us. Other dailies had whole columns of thrilling stuff, but our readers, finding no exciting "news from the front," flung their papers down in disgust. Because we absolutely refused to manufacture tales about a "war" which simply did not exist, we soon were sharply ordered home as complete failures. Only a personal appeal to the various powers from General Miles, the division commander who was with another line of troops some sixty miles north, made it possible for us to stay on at Pine Ridge, where we so greatly wanted to stay until we could see the whole problem solved—thinking that we might help somehow to bring about a peaceful solution.

We had troubles threatening us from another source, too. The railroad towns near the reservation, after hard years, were suddenly reaping a rich harvest by furnishing supplies for the Army and its followers. Hay had leaped from being a drug on the market to an army purchase at as high as $25 a ton. Both excitement hounds and refugees jammed hotels and lodging-houses; all local rates more than doubled. Saloons made fortunes; gamblers and other adventurers swarmed everywhere. All this prosperity depended on the correspondents' keeping

up a constant outflow of thrilling "war news." When the prof-
iteers heard that I was not playing their game at all—in fact,
was ruining their business by sending only matter-of-fact reports of the actual events—it grew dangerous for me to enter
those towns. They hated me as bitterly now for not creating
false news as the Nebraskans of 1874 had for not suppressing
unpleasant facts about the grasshopper famine. I decided that
the way of a truthful reporter was difficult.

One night at Rushville, where I had gone to telegraph in
my report, I was so hard-pressed that I had to put my hand
behind me as if reaching for my gun—to keep at bay a pack of
assailants who were loudly threatening me for hitting their
pocketbooks.

How long all these queer conditions might have lasted if no
new characters had come on the scene no one can tell, but just
then into the center of the stage came Big Foot and his band.
The official story of their coming has been told in Bureau of
Ethnology reports and in so many other easily accessible
sources that I need not repeat it here, but so far as I know the
Indian account of the affair has never been recorded. Here is
that story as the runners brought it to us day by day.

Long before this an Indian had told me that Big Foot was
already on the way to Pine Ridge, because the government
rations at Big Foot's station had been so reduced that he and
his band, who had lost all their summer's crops through hot
winds and drought, were actually starving. Therefore, he had
defied his own agent and was coming into Pine Ridge, where
he knew that the Indians were better supplied, so as to get
food for his women and children. In fact he was convinced
that their agent was stealing government supplies sent to them
and thus was causing their sufferings. The Indian messenger
absolutely denied that Big Foot intended to join any hostile
Indians or commit any depredations. He declared firmly that

the chief was coming straight to Pine Ridge, and was doing it solely to save the women and children from starvation. All the later Indian evidence I heard confirmed these facts.

I knew, next, that Major Whitside, who had seen long service on the plains and was a man of sound judgment, was sent out with the 1st Battalion of the 7th Cavalry to meet Big Foot and escort the whole band into the agency. I heard, too, that, when he received his orders, he remarked that it would have been much better if he had been allowed to go out alone on that errand, because just at this time the mere departure of any group of troops would stir up the Sioux in general and make everyone anxious. Also, the Indians had told me that all the refugees in the Bad Lands had decided that at last it was safe to return to Pine Ridge and had begun to straggle in. So, as I saw no slightest reason to expect any trouble, I did not go with the 1st Battalion.

After Major Whitside, guided by his Sioux scouts, had been out two or three days, he met Big Foot's band and agreed with them to come in with them to the agency. According to the Indians, though the military reports run differently, there was no trouble whatever about the matter because it was exactly what Big Foot had intended to do from the first. After a day's marching Whitside and Big Foot encamped their forces nearly together at Wounded Knee. This same night of December 28, I heard later, the last of the Bad Lands refugees had nearly reached the agency and had camped at the Catholic mission only five miles north of us.

Just at this crucial moment General Brooke somehow reached the conclusion that it would be a good thing to make a show of force, so he sent Colonel Forsyth late and secretly with four troops of cavalry, Lieutenant Taylor with his company of Cheyenne scouts, and also four pieces of light artillery all out to Wounded Knee to join Major Whitside. Apparently General Brooke himself had no really well-defined motive for this step. No officer at the agency was given any reason at all as to why Forsyth had been ordered out to reinforce Whitside; consequently everyone—whites and Indians alike—felt the gravest fears. The air was full of rumors of pending trouble, but no correspondent was told anything officially.

32.

The Battle of Wounded Knee

I for one had no idea where or why Forsyth's troops were being sent. I had been talking with some officers on a little rise of ground just south of General Brooke's headquarters when I saw a man on a jaded horse dash up, dismount, and rush into the general's office. A moment or two later two orderlies ran out, hastily mounted their horses, and started off at full speed, one to the 7th Cavalry's camp, the other to Taylor's Indian scouts. Each camp was about half a mile away.

It seemed only an instant until I heard the bugles sounding "boots and saddles." In just twenty-four minutes by my watch from the time those orderlies had run out, Taylor's scouts were in line in front of headquarters. Two minutes later the 2nd Battalion of the 7th Cavalry also were there with the mule pack train. They all stopped only a moment to get their orders, and then dashed away eastward. I concluded that trouble was brewing somewhere and I meant to reach that spot.

It took me a couple of hours to procure an Indian pony, which the man who rented him to me vowed was "one of the best travelers on the reservation," and also to lay in some suitable food to carry with me. Then I followed the track of the troops. Soon two Sioux I knew joined me, and together we trailed the soldiers through the dark. Some fifteen miles out they had left the main road and headed directly north over the prairie.

There on the open ground I met two soldiers leading pack mules, loaded with ammunition, back toward the agency. When I asked them why, they said that while stopping to fix the packsaddles they had lost the troops. That fresh trail of four hundred soldiers showed up so plainly that I simply laughed at those two deserters and made them face about and keep me and my two Sioux friends company, for I knew that if trouble really started, the cartridges would be badly needed. Soon we began to see Indian fire signals here and there. It was clear that their forces, too, were on the move somewhere and might be looking for trouble. For this reason the two Sioux at once anxiously started back toward the agency, but I urged the deserters on and pushed ahead with them as fast as we could make their mules travel.

The trail turned sharply east and then south. We overtook Forsyth's troops just as they halted on the north side of Major Whitside's camp. Every officer I talked with told me that there was not likely to be any trouble, so before long I followed the trail back a mile to an Indian house I had noticed. I found it deserted, and learned afterward that the Indian teacher and missionary who lived there had left everything early in the trouble to go into the agency. I stabled and fed my pony and crept in through a window for shelter from the cold. Though Indians of all kinds had been passing this place for weeks, nothing had been harmed or even touched, in spite of the newspaper accounts of wholesale depredations. I, the white man, was clearly the first intruder. In the morning I even found a lot of chickens running around the house—good food which scores of hungry Sioux must have seen and passed by. To pay for my night's sleep, I drew water from the well for the flock.

That Monday morning of December 29 I rode over to the encampment about eight o'clock. Colonel Forsyth, without thought of trouble, had drawn up his troops in a big hollow square around the Indian camp. On the south, just beyond a deep ravine with almost perpendicular banks, were Lieutenant Taylor and his Cheyenne scouts. A little to the northwest, on a low hill, were the four Hotchkiss guns with Captain Illsley in charge. When I rode near, he came over to talk with me. A young lieutenant, joining us, remarked to the captain:

"Isn't this rather a strange formation of troops, if there should be any trouble?"

I saw exactly what he meant: if any troop should try to shoot any Indian, it must fire straight in the direction of some other army group stationed in that enclosing square.

Captain Illsley laughed. "There's no possibility of trouble that I can see. Big Foot wants to go to the agency and we're a guard of honor to escort him in."

There was nothing for me to write up as news in that quarter. I rode on in front of the troops who were drawn up as the north side of the square. Here, inside of their line, I found the Indian men seated in a half circle in front of Colonel Forsyth, who was making a speech to them through an interpreter. I had been present at so many Indian councils that they had grown monotonous to me; this was just another of them. I noticed Indian men and women scattered all over the encampment, with a few white persons here and there among them. I saw Father Craft in his regulation priestly clothing. Captain Wallace, I observed, was far out in front of his company, trading and dickering with the Sioux for curios. He and the Indians around him seemed to be having a jolly time. No news for me there—or anywhere. For one thing, the soldiers so heavily outnumbered the Indian men that I saw no possible chance of any outbreak.

I sat on my pony for about an hour, watching everything, then, as I was anxious to dispatch my daily report, such as it was, I rode down the east side of the square, and finally along behind the Cheyenne scouts to pick up the trail back to the agency. It was a beautiful day. There was not a cloud in the sky, and the air was just cool enough to be bracing. As my pony slowly ambled along up the creek, there was absolute stillness everywhere. In about half an hour I turned out of the valley and, following the trail along a gulch, came out on the higher, rolling sand hills. Suddenly I heard a single shot from the direction of the troops—then three or four—a few more—and immediately a volley. At once came a general rattle of rifle firing. Then the Hotchkiss guns. I saw curls of smoke rise up through the still air. I could see Indians moving on the hills between me and the camp. What did it all mean?

Later I learned that the first volley had come from the troops on the north side of the square, and that its bullets had whizzed across straight through the thin line of Cheyenne scouts opposite. These promptly retired pell-mell eastward, to escape the fire of their own forces. I feel sure that Captain Wallace was struck down by one of these soldiers' bullets which raked the whole encampment fore and aft. A moment later the Hotchkiss guns, too, opened fire on the little central band of Indians— 106 men, all told, and 252 women and children. Every warrior, including Big Foot himself, who was ill in his tent with pneumonia, was killed or seriously wounded. Only 5 men and 51 women and children escaped and were brought later to Pine Ridge, but all of these except one little baby and one old grandmother were wounded. Several of them—including, I think, three of the men—died afterward at the agency from their injuries.

[The Smithsonian Institution Bureau of Ethnology's Fourteenth Report also gave the total Indian deaths as about 300. This estimate is nearly double the number stated by government sources and spokesmen.]

Afterward I learned, too, that the first shot of all—the cause of the whole trouble—was actually fired by one of those same bad Indians whom Crow Dog had vainly asked to have arrested and imprisoned for the common good. Several days after the battle General Miles himself told me that if General Brooke had arrested that group of Indians when General Wheaton asked him to, there would have been no massacre at Wounded Knee.

I was told, also, that though the active attack lasted perhaps twenty minutes, the firing continued for an hour or two, wherever a soldier saw a sign of life. Indian women and children fled into the ravine to the south, and some of them on up out of it across the prairie, but soldiers followed them and shot them down mercilessly. I heard that the first Indian to fall in the battle was the very medicine man who had taught this band that ghost shirts would make them immune to bullets. Many bucks and scores of little ten- and twelve-year-old boys later found dead on the battlefield were dressed in these shirts.

Much was written about how eagerly the 7th Cavalry seized this chance for vengeance on the Sioux for the Custer massacre of 1876, but except in name this was not the same regiment. Few of the officers, even, had served with Custer, and the men were mostly raw recruits from city slums, new to the plains. Desertions already had been frequent. Inexperienced, they acted without orders, especially in firing that first volley which precipitated the real disaster and which so greatly endangered the Cheyenne scouts.

Days afterward I talked with a newspaper correspondent who had been caught in the very midst of things when the firing began. He had crawled out through that rain of shot and shell on his hands and knees until he reached the army line—unwounded, but with wrecked nerves. But all these various facts came to me later. At the moment I could only listen and surmise. The boom of the Hotchkiss guns and rattle of the rifles, however, quickly satisfied me that hardly an Indian would be left alive. It must be a terrible fight. My job was to ride hard to the agency and send out the news. But because I had known definitely that not one single leading man among all the Sioux bands intended or wanted to fight, I had ridden way out here unarmed. And by now there might well be hostiles between me and the agency.

Soon I met a large wagon train loaded with army supplies which General Brooke had ordered out there. It had no soldiers with it as escort. The wagon master, like his drivers, as soon as he heard the roar of the guns had halted, bewildered. Now he ran to meet me.

"What shall I do?" he panted.

"Throw out sentries in every direction," I told him hastily, "so that you can see any suspicious group coming a long way off. Then push on toward the troops. If any hostiles turn up, you'll have ample time to park your train and prepare for an attack before they get to you."

I whipped my pony on. Though he was in good condition, that highly praised specimen was the laziest beast I ever had the misfortune to mount. I longed for my good old Colonel Titus of Kansas days. To keep this animal going at four miles an hour, I had to ply my whip constantly. Two Sioux on horseback overtook me; they were friendly and they knew me. First they warned me to turn back for fear of bad Indians ahead, but I refused, for I had to send out my dispatches at once. Then these Sioux, seeing the sort of pony I had, began to help me along by riding behind me and taking turns at lashing him on. After four or five miles they turned off southward, probably to join their families, but they made vigorous parting signs to me to "Go! Go! Go fast!"

Soon I again heard the clatter of hoofs behind me. Looking back, I saw three Indians, bareheaded and in war paint, overtaking me at full speed. Each carried a Winchester and led an extra pony. I told myself, "Well, a man has but one time to die anyhow," and rode on. They passed me singing war songs at the top of their voices, and only gave me one sharp glance. Two more parties rode right by me, bareheaded, in full paint, naked to their waists. Why did they spare me? I don't know, unless, being some of Crow Dog's "bad Indians," they all recognized me as having been often in their camp.

Within five or six miles of the agency I found the whole land dotted with Indians fleeing northward, some on ponies, some with children on travois, a few in light wagons carrying poles and tent coverings. All were pitifully frightened. Hurried though I was, I intercepted one party I knew—an Indian, his wife, and two children in a light wagon into which they had hastily thrown a tent cloth, poles, and a few cooking utensils. The Indian told me that he and the others had been ordered through signals by the head men to flee to the Bad Lands because the soldiers would kill them all, including the women and children, just as they were killing Big Foot's band.

"Go back home," I told him, "or else come to the agency. I'll see that none of you are harmed."

So he turned and drove in with me and pitched his tent near the little log house where we were staying.

Just east of the agency the road forked. One branch went past the cattle pens, where beef cattle were issued to the Indians; the other fork bent slightly southward. After a moment's indecision I chose the southward road. Exactly when, on the other route, I should have been passing the cattle pens, I heard shots from that direction. Later I learned that these shots were fired at the only civilian killed during the whole trouble.

On the outskirts of the buildings a lieutenant and two orderlies overtook me on fagged, sweating horses. The lieutenant hailed me sharply:

"How long have you been here?"

"Just arriving," I answered. He looked relieved. Colonel Forsyth had sent him to report the fight to General Brooke, and he wanted the honor of delivering the very first message as much as I wanted the honor of sending my own paper the very earliest press dispatches. Correspondents were not allowed to use the army wire at the agency; therefore, at once I started a brief account on its way to the telegraph at Rushville. So far as I know, my dispatch was the first to reach any newspaper in the United States. And at last I was free to take in what was happening at Pine Ridge.

33.

The Aftermath at Pine Ridge

I found a frightful panic starting at the agency. Women and children, white and Indian both, were rushing into a big group down among the buildings.

I noticed a Sioux warrior, who wore a ghost shirt, breechcloth, leggings, moccasins, and full war paint, riding slowly down the main road and shouting some announcement. I was watching several of the quartermaster's Indian wood choppers just when they first heard him; they all dropped their axes instantly and bolted. Then I saw that every other Indian within hearing was bolting too. They would not even stop to tell me what he said. Still calling the same words at the top of his lungs, he rode on down among the buildings and completely around the little band of soldiers who now were drawn up in an open space just south of the main buildings. None of the officers seemed to understand the crier, but as he was unarmed they did not molest him. He finished his circle around the main part of the agency. I felt that we ought to know what his message was.

Finally I saw a woman who could talk English standing calmly all alone near the trader's store.

"What's that man saying?" I demanded.

"He says," she answered quietly, " 'Prepare to fight! We are going to shoot into the agency!' "

I thought that such a warning to all within earshot, so carefully given by those terrified and messiah-crazed Indians, was an act greatly to their credit. I believe it has gone unrecorded until now. Of course, as soon as the crier had ridden back toward the northern hills, the Sioux began to fire upon the agency.

"So they mean to attack us now," I thought, "while defenders are few."

I knew that the 9th Cavalry, colored, was off on a raid in the north. In fact the only army troops here were the remnant of Captain Illsley's battery and some of the 2nd Infantry, who, sure that all trouble was over, had been breaking camp and packing their wagon train, ready to start back eastward.

I hunted anxiously for Bright Eyes. Our own lodging place was deserted and locked. I hurried to the big group of women and children, and there in the center I found my wife, standing on a box and calling out:

"Why do you come here? These thin board buildings can't protect you from bullets. They'd go right through them. Go back to the log houses."

Just then Major Butler, cantering up, called to me:

"Please give Bright Eyes my compliments and tell her the order is for women and children to retire to the log houses for safety and that she's requested to force them to do so."

He galloped off, but wheeled back to add:

"Please tell her that she herself must stay in a log house. Stray bullets are flying all around here."

Bright Eyes soon herded the others safely into the log houses, but she refused to stay there. Soon afterward the major found her standing on a well curb on the firing line, for a better view of the whole field of operations.

Those bullets came from a deep gulch on the north, where several of Crow Dog's bad men were lurking in order to fire into the agency. The northern hills, too, now were covered with Sioux on horseback; we could see the sunlight flash on the barrels of their Winchester rifles. These braves—fully two thousand in all—could have captured Pine Ridge in twenty minutes if they had meant war; instead, they were merely gathering as a rear guard for the women and children while these fled for refuge to the Bad Lands.

I went over to where the troops stood lined up, waiting—though for the life of me I could not see how they could be of the slightest use where they were. I sat down on a cracker box to take notes; now and then the dust would fly up when a rifle ball struck the ground not far away.

A soldier with a camp stove on his back went by; suddenly his hat flew off. He set the stove down, retrieved his hat, resumed his load and walked on. An idea struck him. He took off his hat and looked at it, then he started to run. An officer shouted to him to halt, followed him, and looked at the hat. Then he brought it back and walked along the ranks, showing them a bullet hole through the crown. Then he gave it back to its owner and told him to hurry on.

The battery lieutenant came over and remarked to me:

"I've been in the Army ten years, and this is the first time I was ever under fire, if you can call this 'under fire.' We've been standing here a long time doing nothing, and I begin to feel queer. There are enough Sioux on those hills to massacre us all in no time!"

"I know exactly how you feel," I sympathized. "I've felt that way many times myself—a good many times. Do something—and in ten minutes you'll be all right."

"There's nothing to do," he protested. "I have every man in place. I've examined the ammunition; I've sighted every gun myself. There's nothing whatever to do but stand still."

He went off to his guns, but soon he came back with a smile on his face, feeling all right. Undoubtedly in a fierce fight that officer would prove the bravest of the lot.

General Wheaton came over to me next.

"Is it necessary," he asked, "for you to be so far in front? Spent balls are falling occasionally all along here. None have dropped here yet, but some might."

The firing from the gulch now became almost continuous, so one company was ordered to retire behind some ricks of cordwood north of the buildings. About a hundred yards short of there three soldiers fell; the rest went on into position as ordered. I saw a young photographer, who had been taking pictures around there, run up to the wounded men and calmly photograph them while the bullets whistled past his ears. He heard sharp orders to leave; when he did not go, he was placed under arrest.

The agency had another protective force—about eighty Indian police—but lately the new agent and a few civilian employees had kept steadily asserting that in any crisis those police would join the hostiles and murder everybody in the agency. Their troop was thrown out in a line west of headquarters, under an army officer who, in spite of General Brooke's strict orders that the gulch firing should not be returned, had been having a hard time to restrain his men. But when they saw the infantry fired on as it made for the cordwood shelter, those police could not be held back any longer.

I was just behind them when they broke away from their officer and charged the hostile gang in the gulch. I saw them go right over a high five-wire fence—how, I still don't know. Soon they had cleared out all those hostiles and were willing to let their officer call them back into line. As I walked along their ranks, one policeman pointed proudly to his cartridge belt. There were five vacant spaces in it.

We heard occasional firing until sundown, when the Sioux host on the hills began to depart northward. Such camp followers and whites as had fled south from the agency had been more than replaced by the frightened Indian women and children who kept thronging in. The agency white folk—missionaries, teachers, and employees—were barricading their doors as best they could. So far as I could learn, nothing had been done to defend the place from an attack.

With sunset the weather turned intensely cold. About seven o'clock that night the 7th Cavalry brought in from Wounded Knee a long train of dead and wounded soldiers and Indians. Forty-nine wounded Sioux women and children had been piled into a few old Indian wagons. The army wagons, including the train I had met and sent on, had been cleared of all stores and used to bring in the wounded soldiers and Sioux warriors. The former loads had been left strewn over the battlefield— large quantities of bacon, wooden cracker boxes, sacks of rice, and other supplies—abandoned there for days in a region of almost starving Indians, but not one red man would touch them.

The many wounded troopers and the five wounded Sioux warriors were all taken promptly to the soldiers' quarters for treatment, but the wounded women and children were left lying in their open wagons in the bitter cold. Major Butler, ordered to take charge of them, could not think of any available shelter for them. I suggested that the Episcopal rector, himself a full-blooded Sioux, might lend his church for them. He at once gladly turned it over to the Army. When Major Butler and I went there together that night of December 29 to plan accommodations, we found the building still adorned with its Christmas greens. Across the chancel front, above the pulpit, hung a great banner on which we read: "Peace on earth, good will to men."

Major Butler ordered the seats torn out and the floor covered a foot deep with hay. On this they laid the rows of wounded. Near the middle of the church I noticed a beautiful young Indian woman tossing off in delirium the blanket kindly hands had spread over her. She had been shot through the hips.

Nothing I have seen in my whole varied life has ever affected or depressed or haunted me like the scenes I saw that night in that church, under the festival decorations of the Prince of Peace, which hung above the rows of suffering, innocent women and children. For all their agony not one of them uttered a word of complaint. In fact the only sound in the place was the voice of a little three-year-old girl who stood near the entrance, beside the one unwounded old woman, who held a baby on her lap. Though the grandmother tried to hush her, the little child kept saying slowly over and over, "*Min-nie, min-nie, min-nie,*" which I knew was the Sioux word for water.

There was no water there yet. I went out and fetched a bucketful and a tin cup. As the child looked frightened at seeing a white man coming so near her, I handed a cup of water to the old woman, telling her to give it to the child, who grabbed it as if parched with thirst. As she swallowed it hurriedly, I saw it gush right out again, a bloodstained stream, through a hole in her neck.

Heartsick, I went to the general hospital to find the surgeon, Major Hartsuff, and beg him to tend those poor sufferers at once. To my surprise, though there were plenty of available buildings and it was a zero night, I found the busy surgeon caring for his sixty sick and wounded troopers—in tents. I told him what shape the injured women and children were in.

"Four nursing babies whose mothers were killed," I added, "must have been without food since early this morning."

"My first duty is to these wounded soldiers," he reminded me, "but as soon as I can leave them, I'll come."

Meanwhile he gave me morphine for the worst cases and told me to relieve the suffering all I could until he could get there. At the last moment he called me back to take two bottles of beef extract.

"Make hot soup with that for the nursing babies. It might harm a tiny white child, but the Indians have lived on meat for ages, and their babies will grow fat on it."

When he reached the church about two o'clock that morning, I joined him. For a moment he stood there near the door, looking over the mass of suffering and dying women and children—looking at the banner above them. The silence they kept was so complete that it was oppressive; we did not hear a sigh or a groan.

Then to my amazement I saw that surgeon, who I knew had served in the Civil War, attending the wounded in most of the battles from the Wilderness to Appomattox, begin to grow pale and waver. He sat down abruptly.

"What's the matter, Major?" I questioned anxiously.

"This is the first time I've seen a lot of women and children shot to pieces," he answered weakly. "I can't stand it."

He went outside and sat down on a log. I had just smelled hot coffee from an officer's tent near by. I went and begged for a good big cup of it, which I poured down Hartsuff. With this help he was able to put the job through, though before the end he was almost ready to fall from nervous exhaustion.

Long before this our Indian hostess and Bright Eyes had come to the church. We all helped Major Hartsuff all we could. Elaine Goodale, the poet, then the supervisor of an Indian school, and a year later the wife of a Sioux Indian, had also come to help. She and Bright Eyes stayed on duty as nurses all the rest of the night.

After the doctor had begun working, the old grandmother asked Bright Eyes and our hostess, "When will they kill us?"

"Kill you?" our hostess exclaimed, horrified. "They won't kill you at all. Their doctor is here now to help make you well. White people do not kill prisoners and women and children."

"But we saw them kill or wound all those women and children today. We know they've brought us in here to make a feast and then kill us."

Bright Eyes then talked earnestly to her and the others, assuring them that they would all be taken care of, would be doctored while they were sick, and fed when they were hungry. Up to the moment when they actually began to believe her they still kept up their unnatural silence, for they were following their religious ideals in not letting their enemies hear them complain. They must die as Indians should. But the instant they were freed from that duty, they began to moan and cry so dreadfully that we could hardly bear to hear them.

To this day I shudder whenever that scene comes back to me—even though I know that in spite of their frightful wounds most of those sufferers finally recovered.

Next morning the 9th Cavalry, colored, under Colonel Henry, got back from its northerly expedition. The colonel, hearing of the Wounded Knee affair, had promptly abandoned his wagon train and headed the soldiers for Pine Ridge, covering a hundred miles in twenty-four hours at terrible cost to their horses' strength. Near the agency a small band of Indians had attacked them. That same day the 7th Cavalry, sent northward after the fleeing Indians, got pocketed between the hills, where the Indians promptly closed in around them and might have exterminated them if Colonel Henry had not brought out his tired but brave 9th Cavalry to rescue them and clear those hills of all hostiles.

All sorts of rumors of a coming attack on the agency were afloat, but still no defensive measures had been taken. That same evening some buildings to the north of Pine Ridge were burned to the ground.

I had to send off our dispatches, but I could not hire a man for any price to carry them to the railroad, so about nine o'clock that evening I started off alone for Rushville. As soon as my telegraphing was done, I called at the headquarters of Colonel Colby, commander of the Nebraska State Militia. Soon Buffalo Bill, who had left Pine Ridge shortly after I did, came in, excitedly declaring that the Indians had broken loose and were burning buildings in all directions.

"They'll overrun all northern Nebraska," he asserted.

Colonel Colby listened quietly and then pointed to a military map which lay on the desk in front of him. He showed us where he had stationed his troops, and said that the Indians would have to do some fighting before they got into Nebraska at all.

Apparently the Rushville restaurants and saloons kept open all night. For an outrageous price I got my horse fed and had a meal myself. I reached Pine Ridge again before daylight, after a total ride of fifty miles.

Before I was awake Wednesday morning, an orderly came with the message that General Miles, who had arrived during the night back from the north, where his troop was drawn up behind the hostile Indians, wished to see Bright Eyes and me. I dressed hastily; we went to headquarters and sent in our cards. The orderly came back in a moment with word that the General was shaving, but would receive us very soon. Then General Miles talked with us for half an hour. After that he mounted his horse and with only one orderly made a circuit of the agency, riding far out on the hills.

An hour or so later, while I stood talking with General Wheaton in front of his quarters, I saw Miles and the orderly approaching. As he rode up, I decided he might have something private to say to Wheaton; so I started to walk away.

"Wait a moment!" Miles called to me. Then he remarked to General Wheaton in an ordinary conversational tone:

"Put a company out on that rising ground east of the agency and throw up some works for defense. Send the Gatling gun along with it. Put another company on the rising ground south-east of the church building. Give them a Hotchkiss. Put another company on the point behind the schoolhouse to the west. Put your strongest company there and give them two Hotchkiss guns. They had better throw up a strong work there. To the north, on that hill west of the road"—he pointed to the place—"put another company and send the three-inch gun along."

Then he handed his orderly the bridle of his horse and suggested to me, "Let's take a walk."

We walked southward for nearly a mile, turning back after we reached a long line of rifle pits, facing the wrong way, which General Brooke had had the worn-out 9th Cavalry turn out in the night to dig as a defense for a retreat in case the agency was assaulted. All the way out and back General Miles was busily discussing with me various topics of Indian life and habits. He made no allusions whatever to existing conditions at the agency, but within an hour after he had given those defense orders to General Wheaton the whole Sioux nation could not have taken Pine Ridge. The works I had heard him direct Wheaton to have thrown up would have raked every available approach with their fire.

34.

Warfare Yields to Peace

There was no more shooting after General Miles came to Pine Ridge. The agent whose poor judgment originally had caused the trouble was soon dismissed by the President's orders, and an army captain, appointed by General Miles, was given charge of the agency—a step which delighted me. In fact President Harrison, when he realized the situation, disposed of all civilian agents for that critical year, placing the agency problems everywhere in the experienced hands of army men.

Out at Wounded Knee, because a storm set in, followed by a blizzard, the bodies of the slain Indians lay untouched for three days, frozen stiff where they had fallen. Finally they were buried in a large trench dug on the battlefield itself.

On that third day Colonel Colby of the Nebraska Militia, as he crossed the ground where the dead Indians lay, saw the blanket of a corpse move without apparent cause. When he had watched it a moment, he decided to investigate the movement. Under the blanket, snuggled up to its dead mother, who perhaps with her last breath had wrapped it carefully from the cold, he found a little suckling baby girl. It was uninjured except that one side of its face was somewhat frozen. I saw Colonel Colby come riding rapidly into Pine Ridge with that baby on his saddle pommel, and I watched him handle the little Sioux child as tenderly as he would have handled one of his own flesh and blood. They gave the tiny girl some hot beef extract for her first feeding in three days—and she lived and throve. Afterward Colonel Colby took her home with him to Beatrice, Nebraska, adopted her, and educated her.

General Miles, doubtless largely to show the tribes that the government was friendly, ordered in advance that if any of the wounded Indians at Pine Ridge should die, they were to be buried with military honors. By chance the first to die was a baby; so its little body was carried in an army wagon, with an escort under command of a military captain, to the agency burial ground a mile away. There it was interred with the full military honors—taps, bugle, service, and all—except the firing of a salute. This was probably the first Indian baby who was ever honored thus by army troops. And all the other Indians who died there were buried in the same way as honorable fallen foes.

Soon under equally wise and kindly treatment in other ways at General Miles's hands, the Sioux returned to their various agencies. Peace reigned again over all the reservations.

So ended the "War of 1890," the last important shots ever exchanged between United States Army troops and the Indians. For thereafter the white men in power learned, some of them reluctantly, that they could no longer say to any thief in the land, "There is the Indian. Go and rob him. You will be safe from punishment because we have said that he shall not appeal to the courts. If he gets exasperated and turns on you to kill you, we will send the Army of this great government and will kill enough of his tribe so that the remainder will be willing to stand still and be robbed without resistance."

At last every man in this country, regardless of race or color, had become equal to every other man before the law; even the Indians now were recognized as persons. As I have said earlier, had there been time for some adaptation of the Dawes Act, which was the practical expression of that great change, to have been put into effect in the Dakotas, the pathetic massacre of Wounded Knee would not have occurred—forever to haunt the memories of those who saw its results.

Thus the passing of the Indian Ring and the legal recognition of the Indians as human beings, who possessed genuine rights of their own, at last actually and directly fulfilled the prophecies which we who fought for those ends had predicted over ten years before in starting the fight. They truly put an end to Indian wars.

A few years after the Battle of Wounded Knee I went again to visit the tribe I had known in my boyhood. Since my depressing attempt some thirty years before, I had had no heart to seek them out, but now I knew that the Dawes Act already was functioning to help them.

When I asked for Two Bears, I was directed to a good frame house. He and his wife, both truly old by now, greeted me with joy and very evident pride in their home. When they told me: "Come and eat," I was thankful to feel sure that feeding me would not mean any sacrifice on their part.

"I rent all my hundred and sixty acres to a white man," Two Bears informed me, "except a little patch here near the house."

"Which you're always too tired to work in," his wife chipped in scornfully.

"What does it matter if I don't work?" Two Bears argued. "We've plenty to eat nowadays, good clothes to wear, and nothing that has to be done. It's all the time like the old days after we'd killed a fine supply of buffalo. We're old. Why shouldn't we rest?"

This time I joyfully hunted up Dubamonie, who greeted me in his old firm, quiet, listening way. The later years had treated him kindly. He now had a well-built house, ten head of horses, and thirty-seven head of cattle. He no longer had to send his family out to beg food—and he no longer was compelled to give away broadcast every asset which his intelligence or his bravery might bring him. The rest of his former band, or their children who survived them, were becoming adjusted to the new life and were adapting themselves to the white style of living with whatever variations each man or woman individually preferred.

From this group I went on to the Omaha tribe, who, because they had started earlier along the new path, had been able to push ahead with even greater strides. Many whom I had known were dead, but Wajapa still lived—and in a style which took my breath away. For I found him in a large house which had hot and cold water, a bathroom, good furniture, fine table linen, comfortable couches, and lace window curtains. In his coach house I saw an impressive-looking carriage. Several of his children spoke faultless English; three or four were graduates of Eastern universities.

Two sisters, near relatives of Bright Eyes, told me the story of his years since our Dakota trip. These women lived on the border of the reservation; one of them, who had studied in a noted medical school for women, had graduated at the head of her class with a gold medal for excellence in scholarship and science. She had so many white patients that she often had to turn some of them over to other doctors.

Wajapa, they told me, had become an outstanding individual among the Indians. For some years after the Omaha tribe received their allotments he had taken the changed basis of life very hard because he was so determined to walk in the new path and act in every possible way like a white man. On account of his many children he had been allotted a large amount of land.

Because he refused to go to dances or to give ostentatiously he became before long the most unpopular man in his tribe. His friends dropped away, but Wajapa stuck to his chosen road. With his own hands he built a small frame house; for this he bought a stove, a table, chairs, and a bedstead. Then he invested in a cow, chickens, and some pigs. He planted corn, and was the second man in the tribe to plant any wheat. Every venture prospered. Next, he sent his children off to Eastern schools, but unfortunately just at that time of triumph his wife died, leaving him wholly alone. And to the scandal of the community Wajapa, firm to his principles even in this tragic moment—and perhaps remembering the funeral on the Dakota prairie and our comments thereon—refused to strip his household of everything it owned. In fact Wajapa set his jaw and gave away nothing at all.

He had sown the wind! When in due time he went forth to court a second wife, no Indian woman of the better class would look at him, and he would not look at any of the lower type. Instead he did what many a white widower has done, but practically never an Indian: he stayed alone on his farm, working hard, and he cooked his own meals and washed the dishes himself. Before long his eldest daughter, highly educated and accomplished, came home from the East, but she immediately was called away to teach in another tribe.

"When we used to see Wajapa coming into town to buy supplies," the woman doctor told me, "we pitied him very much and tried in every way to get him a wife. He looked so sad, but he still had the name of having been stingy and heartless at his first wife's funeral.

"By our custom no Indian widow ever remarries until her husband has been dead for four years. There was one neat, tidy, hard-working widow available and completely eligible whose husband had been dead for five years. So one day Wajapa asked my sister, who was visiting at the agency, to go to see this desirable widow and put in a good word for him. But though my sister did her best to praise his unusually fine qualities, the widow asserted firmly that she would have nothing to do with him.

"Six months later we both visited the agency and this time Wajapa asked me to try. But the instant the woman saw me, she announced:

"'You can go right away. I know what you've come for. You want to talk for Wajapa.'

"When I told poor Wajapa her answer, I had never seen any man look so sad. Yet only a week afterward he drove past me on his way out of town singing at the top of his voice. I had not heard him sing since his wife died, but I soon learned why he sang now. The very night that the widow had sent me away unheard, Wajapa had started homeward past her house—and she had spoken to him. And very soon they were married."

One day during my visit Wajapa and I stood side by side on a hill that overlooked a small valley where a few tents and some little frame houses were huddled together. We heard drumbeats rising up from one of the tents; evidently a dance was on. Wajapa scowled in open disgust. After some minutes he commented to me:

"What will become of them no one knows. Nobody can help them. They must help themselves or perish."

Many months afterward I looked down from another hill upon a great circle of tents which had risen lately in a triangular valley. On two sides of the circle ran heavily wooded streams. In the center, around a large dancing tent, strolled throngs of Indians in gay blankets, paint, and beads. Behind the tents I could see thin slices of meat hanging on poles to dry. Children with little bows and arrows ran along shooting at butterflies. On the hills which formed the third side of this camp many ponies were grazing. Had the clock been turned back forty years here on the bank of the Missouri River? Not wholly, for although in the open valley itself one could see only those primitive scenes of nomadic life, beyond in every direction stood large frame dwellings. Even in the woods which fringed the camp white house walls shone out here and there.

For old times' sake the life of the past had been rebuilt for a moment in the heart of the present. There below me lay the annual encampment of these Indians and their friends and kindred, thronged as eagerly by those who "walked in the new path" as by those who clung doggedly to all of the old ways they could manage to retain. Even Wajapa had come, and had unbent enough to say frankly that it was good, once a year, to form again the great circle and renew the old ceremonies so that the children should not forget the way their fathers had lived on this very soil for generations before the white men came.

Many of the Indians I watched sauntering there in their blankets and paint were finely educated; all the rest of the year some of them followed skilled professions in the East. A doctor with a large white practice, an artist fresh from a New York studio, a high-salaried government official from Washington, the principal of a high school for white children who had won her chance by a competitive examination—all these went strolling along, joking, carefree, like white men off on a camping trip in the woods.

For ten days these brilliant Indians and all their kin and fellow tribesmen had reproduced all the old ceremonial dances except one or two of the holy dances for which no one today remembered the proper holy words; and no one cared to tempt fate by reciting them incorrectly. Also the tribe now lacked its most holy thing, which a wandering ethnologist had bribed away from the family who were in charge of it, and had carried off triumphantly to the Smithsonian Institution. The nomads' old tokens of reverence had become treasure trove for museums.

At last the Indians reluctantly began to drift away out of the past. I watched big gaps growing in the great circle. Beside me two or three families, who also had climbed the hill for a last look, halted and contrived with their wagons and tent cloths to set up shields against the hot sun. Lying in that scanty shade were Dubamonie and old Two Bears, who of course had ridden up there in perfect comfort.

"Why did you stop here," I asked the latter, "instead of going right on home?"

His answer carried me straight back forty years.

"The hill was long and I was tired, so I stopped to rest."

Up the steep slope weary ponies tugged a dusty spring wagon with two white missionaries in front and two Indian ministers behind, all plainly homeward bound from the big annual Christian meeting which had just been held somewhere up in the north. As they halted to breathe the horses, I greeted them and asked with natural curiosity:

"Why didn't you follow the level road along by the encampment?"

A white missionary answered that one of the Indian brethren there in the back seat had objected to going through or even near that camp. I must have shown my surprise, for the Indian minister himself leaned forward to volunteer sternly:

"Those dances are the ruin of the Indian. They are a temptation which the devil always keeps before them. I have known hundreds of good men and women ruined by them. Instead of taking care of their families, they waste their time there and give away their possessions. The new ways cannot be blended with the old ways. Have you forgotten the fate of Sunshine?"

I looked still more intently at the speaker, and as if through an odd mask of nearly white hair and deeply seamed wrinkles I saw—Chazaninga.

The missionaries drove on; the families on the hill packed up their tent cloths to depart. Dubamonie of the wise, quiet smile picked up the reins of the two strong young horses he was driving for old Two Bears, who nodded a sleepy good-by. I lingered alone, looking down where the great circle of the tribe once had stood so often and lately had gleamed in the sun for ten short days. Though Chazaninga's words had waked a pathetic memory, I was sincerely glad that some small part of all which had been finest in the old life had been and would continue to be revived in the new. For if the new life were to succeed, its keynote must be, not governmental or religious repression, but inspiration; not the old restrictive bonds of tradition, superstition, or childlike fear, but a new freedom born of a whole-souled understanding of its own rights and duties and of the rights and duties of others—until every Indian man and woman should realize with Bright Eyes that "law is liberty."

And where could I find more fitting words for closing these memoirs of the plains than the thanksgiving which Standing Bear uttered, back in 1879, when the first judge ever to hear a case brought by an Indian had just set the captive red man free to follow the path of equal opportunity?

"Hitherto, when we have been wronged," the old chief said impressively to the lawyer who had defended him, "we went to war to assert our rights. . . . We had no law to punish those who did wrong to us; so we took our tomahawks and went to kill. If they had guns and could kill us first, it was the fate of war. But you have found a better way. You have gone into the court for us, and I find that our wrongs can be righted there. Now I have no more use for the tomahawk. I want to lay it down forever."

Stooping, he placed the weapon on the floor at his feet; then, standing erect with folded arms, he continued firmly:

"I lay it down. I have no more use for it. . . . I can now seek the ways of peace."

Buckskin and blanket days were done.